BY ANTONIN SCALIA

The Essential Scalia: On the Constitution,
the Courts, and the Rule of Law

On Faith: Lessons from an American Believer

Scalia Speaks: Reflections on Law, Faith, and Life Well Lived

A Matter of Interpretation: Federal Courts and the Law

Reading Law: The Interpretation of Legal Texts
(with Bryan A. Garner)

Making Your Case: The Art of Persuading Judges
(with Bryan A. Garner)

THE ESSENTIAL SCALIA

THE
ESSENTIAL
SCALIA

On the Constitution, the Courts,
and the Rule of Law

ANTONIN SCALIA

EDITED BY JEFFREY S. SUTTON
AND EDWARD WHELAN

CROWN
FORUM
NEW YORK

Published in the United States by Crown Forum, an imprint of Random House,
a division of Penguin Random House LLC, New York.

CROWN FORUM with colophon is a registered trademark of
Penguin Random House LLC.

LIBRARY OF CONGRESS CATALOGING-IN-PUBLICATION DATA
Names: Scalia, Antonin, author. | Sutton, Jeffrey S. (Jeffrey Stuart), 1960– editor. |
Whelan, Edward, 1960– editor.
Title: The essential Scalia / Antonin Scalia ; edited by Jeffrey S. Sutton and Edward Whelan.
Description: New York : Crown Forum, 2020. | Includes index. |
Identifiers: LCCN 2020007842 (print) | LCCN 2020007843 (ebook) |
ISBN 9781984824103 (hardcover) | ISBN 9781984824110 (ebook)
Subjects: LCSH: Judicial opinions—United States. | Law—United States—Cases. |
LCGFT: Court decisions and opinions.
Classification: LCC KF213.S32 S33 2020 (print) | LCC KF213.S32 (ebook) |
DDC 347.73/2634—dc23
LC record available at https://lccn.loc.gov/2020007842
LC ebook record available at https://lccn.loc.gov/2020007843

randomhousebooks.com

Printed in Canada on acid-free paper

246897531

FIRST EDITION

Book design by Victoria Wong

To Maureen Scalia

And when the last law was down—and the Devil turned round on you—where would you hide, Roper, the laws all being flat? This country's planted thick with laws from coast to coast—Man's laws, not God's—and if you cut them down . . . d'you really think you could stand upright in the winds that would blow then?

—St. Thomas More to his son-in-law William Roper, in Robert Bolt's *A Man for All Seasons*

Contents

Foreword

JUSTICE ELENA KAGAN

In the six years Nino and I served together on the Supreme Court, I held to an unwavering rule. When Nino circulated a new opinion, I would put aside whatever else I was doing to read it. Whether I expected to agree or to disagree, I wanted to know immediately—not in a day or in an hour but right now—what Nino had to say. I wanted to dive into his inimitable writing style. To marvel at the power of his mind. And most important, to take the measure of his ideas.

I envy the reader who has picked up this book, as I once picked up those opinions, not knowing what he or she will find. Don't get me wrong: Justice Scalia's writings on the law wear well. They bear re-reading and re-reading again. (As a former law professor, I read some of them a dozen times or more, and kept seeing or learning something new.) But in these last few years, I have missed the enjoyment and excitement—even the exasperation—that came from thinking about Nino's latest opinion. I doubt that anyone who turns the final page of this book will wonder why.

No one has ever written quite like Nino, and no one ever will. He was a master of the aphorism, the analogy, the metaphor, the aside. His prose was simply ingenious—clever and pungent, pithy and sharp, plainspoken yet utterly original. Judge Sutton (no mean stylist himself) gives some of the best-known examples in his introduction: the test that asked judges to figure out "whether a particular line is longer than a particular rock is heavy"; the problem with legislation creating a "sort of junior-varsity Congress"; the interpretive rule that Congress doesn't "hide elephants in mouseholes." And there are plenty more. The oft-interred doctrine that "like some ghoul in a late-night horror movie . . . repeatedly sits up in its grave and shuffles abroad." The First Amendment's prohibition of a statute that "license[d] one side of a debate to fight freestyle, while requiring the other to follow Marquis of Queensberry rules." Maybe most famous of all, the counterpoint to the kind of constitutional peril that comes "clad . . . in sheep's clothing": "But this wolf comes as a wolf." Line after line, it is captivating stuff, full of wit, dash, and verve.

But the style was not for the sake of style: it was always in the service of ideas. Nino loved ideas—thinking about them, talking about them, arguing about them, as well as writing about them. That love may explain why he found it so natural to befriend colleagues with whom he often disagreed (yes, like me). Echo chambers, I suspect, bored him; it was difference of opinion that enlivened conversation, sparked debate, and created opportunities for learning. His love of intellectual exchange similarly accounts for his preeminent role in the Court's oral arguments. When I was solicitor general, I half dreaded, half hoped for questions from Justice Scalia. They were as hard as questions come, but also direct and fair—designed not to trip me up, but simply to confront me with whatever was the principal weakness in my position. And for the most part, they really were questions: Justice Scalia let me respond in full and listened attentively to what I said. Once, when he had asked me a series of impossible questions, I asked him one back. A bad call: the Chief Justice rightly stepped in to remind me that lawyers don't get to put Supreme Court justices on the spot. But absent that intervention, I'm confident Justice Scalia would have answered the question (which was probably why I presumed to ask it)—decorum thus giving way to substantive debate. And of course, that same kind of give-and-take could occur on the page. For all Nino's stylistic flair, the real strength of his writing—especially when he concurred or dissented—lay in its passionate yet disciplined engagement with ideas. Look for it throughout this volume: in sentence after sentence, paragraph after paragraph, Nino laid out—cogently, logically, with analytic rigor and precision, and at times with the elegance of a mathematical proof—deep and provocative understandings of the way the law should work. (Read *Mistretta*; read *Morrison*; read *R.A.V.* I may or may not agree. But . . .

wow.) It's possible that Nino wrote so well *because* he thought so well. And even if not, the main thing is the thought, memorable and lasting.

I often ask myself how Nino would have reasoned through some legal problem. That exercise sometimes persuades me to come out the same way; over the years, Nino convinced me of things I didn't first think (see, for example, *Johnson*), as I also did him (not mine to reveal). But the Nino test makes my work better even when—or especially when—I wind up disagreeing. I discovered this effect early on, in my very first opinion. The Court's tradition is that a justice's maiden majority be unanimous. But Nino thought that silly: what was the point, he asked me (as he pretended to seek my permission for his solo dissent), of a convention that shied away from, rather than delighted in, the clash of ideas? So I was forced to respond to Nino's incisive views on the car-ownership deduction in bankruptcy law and, in that way, to make my own argument tighter and more convincing. From that day to this one, I have written many of my opinions while imagining a miniature Nino sitting on my right shoulder. That Nino has never gotten me to pull my punches. To the contrary, he's led me (as the real Nino would have liked) to work harder and dig deeper, to search for the arguments that can withstand his mighty ripostes, to plug every hole in my analysis that he so gleefully finds. Nino has upped my game as a judge. And I'll dare to speak for my colleagues by saying that Nino's peculiarly trenchant form of legal argument has done the same for the whole Court. Even after his death, it rings in our ears.

Most enduring of all will be Nino's views on legal method, and particularly on statutory and constitutional interpretation. To be frank, I don't buy them hook, line, and sinker. I share lots but not all of his (statutory) textualist commitments, fewer of his (constitutional) originalist ones. (I spun out some of our similarities and differences when I had the honor of giving the Scalia Lecture at Harvard Law School; Nino being Nino, he watched a livestream and sent me a long email afterwards to continue our jurisprudential conversation.) But Nino's interpretive theories, communicated in that distinctive, vivid prose, have transformed this country's legal culture, the very ground of our legal debate. They have changed the way all of us (even those who part ways with him at one point or another) think and talk about the law. In reading a statute, does anyone now decline to focus first on its text in context? When addressing constitutional meaning, does anyone now ignore Founding principles? Maybe most important, in defending *any* interpretive stance, does anyone dispute the need—which drove Nino's views—to constrain judges from acting on their personal policy preferences? The answer, I think, is no (or something exceedingly close). And for that, Justice Scalia deserves much of the credit. It is why he will go down in history as one of the most significant, and also one of the greatest, Supreme Court justices.

I'm afraid those last remarks sound notably heavy. Rest assured, the writings in this book are anything but. Nino couldn't write a heavy sentence if he tried. So, for sure, learn from the contents of this book. And equally, challenge the contents of this book. (Nino would have wanted you to.) But above all else, enjoy them.

Introduction

JUDGE JEFFREY SUTTON

Long before I became a federal judge, I had the good fortune of clerking for Justice Scalia. How life-changing—how much fun—to come across someone early in my legal career with such a rigorous intellect, spirit of curiosity, and fearless character. Once you had a drink at that well, there was no turning back. If anyone knew how to inspire a young person to turn law into a calling, it was Justice Scalia.

Most memorable was his passion for *every* case. During his thirty years on the Supreme Court, Justice Scalia wrote 870 opinions: 281 majority opinions, 315 concurrences, and 274 dissents. He seemed to enjoy every one of them, penning engaging opinions in landmark and humdrum cases alike. No matter the stakes, he prized coherence—always—and his mind didn't come to rest until each string of thought had come into tune. He showed that all cases, great and small, deserve the same rigor and care.

All of this seemed to come easily to him because competitions of the mind came naturally to him. If there is one aspect of Justice Scalia seared into my mind, it's the value he placed on ideas. Few things made him happier than a vigorous debate over the right way to think about a problem. I thought of him as the chess master who comes to the park on a Saturday morning and is disappointed to see just ten other chess players willing to take him on. Even his first book, *A Matter of Interpretation*, excerpted in several places here, is written, revealingly, in a debate format. He presented a theory of judging, then asked several prominent professors to challenge him, signaling confidence, humility, and transparency all at once.

As much as Justice Scalia relished the give-and-take of debate, he did not let it interfere with relationships. Some of his closest friends on the Court were colleagues with whom he vigorously disagreed at times. It makes me smile to know that many Americans, and nearly all American judges, know that Justice Scalia attended one opera after another with Justice Ginsburg and taught Justice Kagan how to hunt. Who can say what showed more collegiality: enduring thirty-five years of long, difficult-to-follow operas, or teaching a potential adversary how to use a gun?

During one of my last visits with Justice Scalia, I saw striking evidence of the Scalia-Ginsburg relationship. As I got up to leave his chambers, he pointed to two dozen roses on his table and noted that he needed to take them down to "Ruth" for her birthday. "Wow," I said, "I doubt I have given a total of twenty-four roses to my wife in almost thirty years of marriage." "You ought to try it sometime," he retorted. Unwilling to give him the last word, I pushed back: "So what good have all these roses done for you? Name one five-four case of any significance where you got Justice Ginsburg's vote." "Some things," he answered, "are more important than votes."

I let him have the last word.

A high point of my clerkship year was listening to him give a dramatic reading of one of his dissents to the "clerkerati," as he affectionately called us. You might have thought he was delivering a soliloquy from *Macbeth*. A suffering acknowledgment here, a dramatic waving of the hand there, and a twinkle in his eye throughout left one wondering whether this writing concerned a legal dispute after all. Justice Scalia took joy in writing well.

The clerkship also came with humbling moments, some self-inflicted. I wrote a draft dissent for the justice that at one point drew a comparison with the Know-Nothing Party of the nineteenth century. Crestfallen when the justice removed the line from the draft opinion, I had the audacity to ask him why he had taken it out. "Well, Jeff," he explained, "the first reason is that you spelled it 'No-nothingism.'" I couldn't bring myself to ask him for the second reason. Know nothing indeed.

For those who never had a chance to work with Justice Scalia, there's another way to know him: read his opinions and articles and speeches. Each time he wrote, his audience was anyone with an interest in the American legal system, whether a first-year law student or an engaged citizen. As a former law professor, he knew how to weave a narrative with amusing asides and clever analogies to present his arguments in the most accessible terms. Once on the Court, he never stopped teaching; his classroom just got bigger.

What you read is what you get with Justice Scalia. He took great care with the written word and meant every word he wrote. All of his colors come through in his writings, as he was not the kind of judge to mask his true views about the right answer to a legal problem. That's especially so with his dissents and concurrences, when he did not have to write for the Court or account for a colleague's take on the case.

Witness this excerpt from one of his dissents, which arose in a criminal case and concerned a question that judges see all the time—whether eyewitnesses to a crime had accurately identified the defendant as the culprit. Justice Scalia objected to the majority's position that new evidence could have changed the verdict, making the point in a memorable and convincing manner. The Court's objection, he pointed out, was that the four eyewitnesses could identify the defendant as the assailant "not by his height and build, but *only by his face*." But that ought to be enough, he insisted:

> Facial features are *the primary means* by which human beings recognize one another. That is why police departments distribute "mug" shots of wanted felons, rather than Ivy-League-type posture pictures; it is why bank robbers wear stockings over their faces instead of floor-length capes over their shoulders; it is why the Lone Ranger wears a mask instead of a poncho; and it is why a criminal defense lawyer who seeks to destroy an identifying witness by asking "You admit that you saw only the killer's face?" will be laughed out of the courtroom.[1]

Or take this opening from a technical case about administrative law from his early years as a judge: "This case, involving legal requirements for the content and labeling of meat products such as frankfurters, affords a rare opportunity to explore simultaneously both parts of Bismarck's aphorism that 'No man should see how laws or sausages are made.'"[2]

Justice Scalia's opinions stand out for their lucidity and rigorous analysis—and off-the-beaten-path imagery that captured the problem at hand. Surely there was a separation-of-powers problem with the creation of "a sort of junior-varsity Congress,"[3] or a flaw in a dormant Commerce Clause test that asked judges to divine "whether a particular line is longer than a particular rock is heavy."[4] By the same token, who could argue with his observation that Congress "does not . . . hide elephants in mouseholes"?[5] The justice could cut to the heart of a matter and signal that a colorful opinion was coming just by re-framing the question presented: "It ha[s] been rendered the solemn duty of the Supreme Court of the United States . . . to decide What Is Golf."[6] Say what you will about Justice Scalia, his opinions never put anyone to sleep.

If Justice Scalia inspired his clerks and law students with writing that leaped off the page, he inspired advocates in other ways. Long before he unsheathed his pen, advocates confronted his tenacity in the courtroom, something I experienced firsthand during my dozen oral arguments at the Court. His deep convictions about the proper role of the federal courts, his capacity to identify the soft tissue in any argument, and his flinty-minded, sometimes sidesplitting wit commanded every lawyer's attention. One wonders if any justice before or since has caused advocates to lose more sleep in the days and weeks before an oral argument as they tried to anticipate what he might ask and how they might answer it.

Every advocate had to come to grips with Justice Scalia's track record on the issue at stake and his clear-eyed philosophy about the proper way to interpret laws. He tested every advocate with signature questions that went to the core of the case. If you were looking for a tepid or coy justice, he was not your man. The other side of it was that he let you know during the argument just where you stood while there was still time to do something about it, whether by correcting a mis-impression or tacking to a different point. Advocates came to appreciate his candor (most of the time). The North Star to

Justice Scalia was getting the reasoning right—an admonition he never ceased to urge on others and never desisted to accept for himself.

You cannot be a lawyer today, a good lawyer anyway, without understanding Justice Scalia's methods of interpretation. Originalism, his way of interpreting the Constitution, and textualism, his way of interpreting statutes, are now forever linked to him. Both methods turn on the same essential insights: language has meaning (that's why we use words rather than musical notes or colors to make a law), and that meaning is fixed and does not evolve (that's why we write the words down in the first place).

Today's lawyers live in a world in which many Supreme Court precedents turn on these methods of interpretation. And today's lawyers regularly will argue cases in the federal and state courts before judges who respect originalism and textualism thanks to Justice Scalia's influence. Good luck to the lawyer who has not become familiar with these terms of debate and interpretation. Agree or disagree with Justice Scalia, you had better be able to speak his language, no less today than when he walked the halls of the Court.

Justice Scalia, by the way, would resist the notion that he had anything to do with *creating* originalism or textualism. Any such thought missed his central point—that the courts had lost their way by neglecting to use these tried-and-true ways of interpreting law, each essential to preserving judges' proper role in our democratic system. Day and night, he steadfastly pointed out, these were the only legitimate ways for judges to fulfill their responsibilities without exceeding their duties, the only ways judges traditionally had understood their functions through most of the first 150 years of our history, and the only ways the Founders would have thought it appropriate for judges to do their jobs.

It's a good idea not to lose track of another aspect of Justice Scalia. He was first, last, always a proud American who cared deeply about this country. The son of an immigrant, he did not take citizenship for granted. His views about the Constitution, the role of the courts, and the rule of law sprang from his deep loyalty to our shared country and, what mattered greatly to him, our shared future. Some of his most impassioned dissents arose from cases in which he thought the Court was losing track of the finer points of our heritage and what it means to be an American and how the Constitution permits us to be governed.

Besides the danger of politicizing the courts if judges did not ground their decisions in the original meaning of the Constitution, Justice Scalia worried that the failure to honor the language of the Constitution would lead to backsliding. If we permit life-tenured federal judges to *add* rights not in the Constitution to account for new social and political pressures, he worried, we will also permit them to *subtract* rights that actually are in the Constitution for similar reasons. Think of the many protections in the Bill of Rights for individuals charged with crimes. Federal judges who pay too much attention to shifting social and political winds are as apt to over-protect as to under-protect constitutional guarantees—and are especially at risk of diminishing the rights of those with the least political influence: individuals charged with crimes. Just as he protested decisions of the Court that he thought placed new restrictions on criminal sentences that had no basis in the Constitution, so he forcefully resisted efforts, in cases like *Craig* and *Crawford*, to narrow defendants' constitutional right to "confront" the witnesses against them. What can go up in inventing new rights can come down in diluting rights actually in the Constitution.

Some people wonder if it's fair to treat the Constitution's meaning as fixed in view of the narrow segment of the population represented at the Constitutional Convention in Philadelphia in 1787. Fair question. No women or people of color participated in the Constitution's creation, and of course the original Constitution contained the original sin of permitting slavery. The bargains made in Philadelphia, true enough, were more aspirational than perfect. But this was not lost on Justice Scalia. Read the list of attendees at the convention at Philadelphia in 1787, and ask yourself how many of them were Italian American. Or how many were Catholic? As the first Italian American justice on the Supreme Court, he was hardly unaware of the risks of ethnic bigotry, exclusion, and faith-based discrimination in this country. But to all of this he would have given the same response, the very response he offered in *United States v. Virginia*: the Framers "left us free to change"—free to change, that is, in the ways permitted by the Constitution. Empowering five members of a nine-member Supreme Court to be the authors of those changes, however, was not one of those ways. And it assuredly is not a way that is *more representative* of the many citizens of our diverse country.

Justice Scalia's concerns about the role of the courts in American government remain front and center today. The most recent presidential election, by many accounts, turned on a significant number of Americans treating their vote for the president of the United States as a proxy to fill one seat on a nine-member Court—the vacancy left by Justice Scalia's untimely death. Talk about foreshadowing. In many of his most vigorous dissents, Justice Scalia warned about the danger of politicizing the Court by allowing life-tenured federal judges to expand or contract constitutional protections in accordance with perceived changes in our political or social values.

In thinking about a path forward, Justice Scalia's writings are a good place to start. He devoted a career to addressing one of the key dilemmas in American government—that we aspire to be "a government of laws and not of men" and yet permit a small group of men and women, our nine Supreme Court justices, to have the final say over the meaning of the Constitution. The longer I have been a judge, the more I have come to admire his efforts to address the bookend risks of a Court that does too much or does too little in resolving cases and controversies about the meaning of our Constitution.

Justice Scalia's writings, best of all, let the world know how *he* should be judged. With his clarity of thought and facility with language came a transparency of method about how to answer these vexing questions. The justice left little doubt about how the Scalia scorecard worked—what the benchmarks were for a fair decision in the case at hand and for equal treatment between that case and the next one down the road. It's one thing to say that justice is blind. It's quite another to prove it by treating seen and unseen cases alike.

Many of these considerations led the justice to write "A Rule of Law as a Law of Rules" in 1989—the first article featured in this collection. At that point, he had been a judge for almost seven years, four on the D.C. Circuit and nearly three on the Supreme Court. Like any judge with a conscience and scores of rulings behind him, he could see which ideas had produced principled distinctions and which ideas had not. The article reveals a judge wrestling with how to decide cases and write opinions in ways that bound him to consistency in the future—and ensured that each of his decisions fairly reflected the meaning of the Constitution or a federal law, not the preferences of citizen Antonin Scalia.

Let the reader be the judge of how he did. He would not have minded. Much to the contrary. He would have taken it for the compliment that it is—that he left us with a theory of judging to measure his rulings against. As Justice Scalia correctly understood, and as I can attest, the greatest challenge of judging is to adopt a theory of interpretation that is resilient, one that forces the judge to follow the law where it leads. A theory of judging that does not hurt from time to time, that instead merely mirrors the judge's policy preferences, is not much of a theory.

All in all, Justice Scalia had many talents: he wrote like Justice Jackson and Justice Holmes, thought like Justice Frankfurter and Justice Story, and saw the long-term stakes like Chief Justice Marshall. But all of these talents would have been worthless—truth be told, potentially dangerous—if that's all there was to the justice. The indispensable thing to say about Justice Scalia is that he passed the bedrock test of judicial character: he respected the line between law and personal opinion. That was never going to be an easy road to travel, and not only because the justice had a few ideas about how the world should work. Any judge who takes that path will inevitably face a double dose of misapprehension from the public: praise he does not want from some quarters (for outcomes they like) and criticism he does not deserve from others (for outcomes they don't like).

Don't make that mistake in reading this book. In each case, sure enough, Justice Scalia provides an answer to the question asked. That's what judges do. But don't get distracted by these results, whether this side or that side won. Over the long term, questions tend to be more important than answers—and the questions Justice Scalia relentlessly posed will be with us for a long time. The two most important questions, framed by a confident man, amount to the most humble a judge can ask: Did the People empower us to resolve this dispute? If so, on what grounds is it permissible to do so? In one way or another, every item in this collection tries to come to grips with the nature of these questions and how to answer them fairly from one case to the next.

Editors' Note

This volume presents abridged versions of Justice Scalia's opinions, articles, speeches, and testimony. For ease of reading, we have generally not used ellipses or brackets to mark deleted passages or conforming changes (such as capitalization) in the remaining text, and we have eliminated insignificant quotation marks. We have omitted many citations and have simplified others. We have edited oral testimony, and we have in a few instances altered spelling.

We have used same-page footnotes for information that we think might be of immediate interest, and we have relegated to back-of-the-book endnotes other material, including citations to, or in some instances very general descriptions of, the sources of many quoted passages.

Readers who intend to quote Justice Scalia's writings in legal briefs or scholarly work are strongly encouraged to consult the unabridged versions.

1

General Principles of Interpretation

This chapter introduces the reader to Justice Scalia's philosophy of judging. His signature article "A Rule of Law as a Law of Rules" confronts a challenge faced by all judges who try to identify a basis for deciding the case at hand that can be consistently applied in future cases. Next is a piece on originalism, which introduces the reader to Justice Scalia's views about how to interpret the Constitution. Here he criticizes the "living Constitution" approach, which invites judges to alter the meaning of constitutional provisions to meet what they perceive to be the needs of a changing society. That approach, as he saw it, aggrandizes judicial power in service of the elite policy preferences that many judges hold, sometimes to usurp the realm of representative government, other times to dilute or ignore disfavored rights. Rounding out the section is an excerpt from his book *A Matter of Interpretation*, which explains the key principles underlying Justice Scalia's text-based method for interpreting statutes. In vivid prose informed by his decades of practical experience in government, Justice Scalia explains that judges must discern the meaning of statutes from their text, not from the actual or supposed intentions of those who wrote them.

The Rule of Law

In February 1989, in the middle of his third year on the Supreme Court, Justice Scalia delivered the Oliver Wendell Holmes, Jr. Lecture at Harvard Law School.[1] The title of his lecture—"The Rule of Law as a Law of Rules"— reflected his emerging conviction that judges have a duty to anchor their decisions in clear rules that can be applied broadly. Among its many virtues, a rules-based approach fosters predictability and constrains judges.

Louis IX of France, Saint Louis, was renowned for the fair and evenhanded manner in which he dispensed justice. We have the following account from *The Life of Saint Louis* written by John of Joinville, a nobleman from Champagne and a close friend of the king:

> In summer, after hearing mass, the king often went to the wood of Vincennes, where he would sit down with his back against an oak, and make us all sit round him. Those who had any suit to present could come to speak to him without hindrance from an usher or any other person. The king would address them directly, and ask: "Is there anyone here who has a case to be settled?" Those who had one would stand up. Then he would say: "Keep silent all of you, and you shall be heard in turn, one after the other."

The judgments there pronounced, under the oak tree, were regarded as eminently just and good—though, as far as I know, Louis IX had no particular training in the customary law of any of the counties of France, or any other legal training. King Solomon is also supposed to have done a pretty good job, without benefit of a law degree, dispensing justice case by case.

That is one image of how justice is done—one case at a time, taking into account all the circumstances, and identifying within that context the "fair" result.

And yet what would Tom Paine have thought of this, who said:

> Let a day be solemnly set apart for proclaiming the charter; let it be brought forth so the world may know, that so far we approve of monarchy, that in America *the law is king*. For as in absolute governments the king is law, so in free countries the law *ought* to be king; and there ought to be no other.

As usual, of course, the Greeks had the same thought—and put it somewhat more dispassionately. In his *Politics*, Aristotle states:

> Rightly constituted laws should be the final sovereign; and personal rule, whether it be exercised by a single person or a body of persons, should be sovereign only in those matters on which law is unable, owing to the difficulty of framing general rules for all contingencies, to make an exact pronouncement.

It is this dichotomy between "general rule of law" and "personal discretion to do justice" that I wish to explore.

In a democratic system, of course, the general rule of law has special claim to preference, since it is the normal product of that branch of government most responsive to the people. Executives and judges handle individual cases; the legislature generalizes. Statutes that are seen as establishing rules of inadequate clarity or precision are criticized, on that account, as undemocratic—and, in the extreme, unconstitutional—because they leave too much to be decided by persons other than the people's representatives.

But in the context of this discussion, that particular value of having a general rule of law is beside the point. For I want to explore the dichotomy between general rules and personal discretion within the narrow context of *law that is made by the courts*. In a judicial system such as ours, in which judges are bound, not only by the text of code or Constitution, but also by the prior decisions of superior courts, and even by the prior decisions of their own court, courts have the capacity to "make" law. Let us not quibble about the theoretical scope of a "holding"; the modern reality, at least, is that when the Supreme Court of the federal system, or of one of the state systems, decides a case, not merely the *outcome* of that decision, but the *mode of analysis* that it applies will thereafter be followed by the lower courts within that system, and even by that supreme court itself. And by making the mode of analysis relatively principled or relatively fact-specific, the courts can either establish general rules or leave ample discretion for the future.

The advantages of the discretion-conferring approach are obvious. All generalizations (including, I know, the present one) are to some degree invalid, and hence every rule of law has a few corners that do not quite fit. It follows that perfect justice can only be achieved if courts are unconstrained by such imperfect generalizations. Saint Louis would not have done as well if he were hampered by a code or a judicially pronounced five-part test.

Of course, in a system in which prior decisions are authoritative, no opinion can leave *total* discretion to later judges. It is all a matter of degree. At least the very facts of the particular case are covered for the future. But sticking close to those facts, not relying upon over-arching generalizations, and thereby leaving considerable room for future judges is thought to be the genius of the common-law system. The law grows and develops, the theory goes, not through the pronouncement of general principles, but case by case, deliberately, incrementally, one step at a time. Today we decide that these nine facts sustain recovery. Whether only eight of them will do so—or whether the addition of a tenth will change the outcome—are questions for another day.

When I was in law school, I was a great enthusiast for this approach—an advocate of both writing and reading the "holding" of a decision narrowly, thereby leaving greater discretion to future courts. Over the years, however—and not merely the years since I have been a judge—I have found myself drawn more and more to the opposite view. There are a number of reasons, some theoretical and some very practical indeed.

To begin with, the value of perfection in judicial decisions should not be overrated. To achieve what is, from the standpoint of the substantive policies involved, the "perfect" answer is nice—but it is just one of a number of competing values. And one of the most substantial of those competing values, which often contradicts the search for perfection, is the appearance of equal treatment. As a motivating force of the human spirit, that value cannot be over-estimated. Parents know that children will accept quite readily all sorts of arbitrary substantive dispositions—no television in the afternoon, or no television in the evening, or even no television at all. But try to let one brother or sister watch television when the others do not, and you will feel the fury of the fundamental sense of justice unleashed. The Equal Protection Clause epitomizes justice more than any other provision of the Constitution. And the trouble with the discretion-conferring approach to judicial law making is that it does not satisfy this sense of justice very well. When a case is accorded a different disposition from an earlier one, it is important, if the system of justice is to be respected, not only that the later case *be* different, but that it *be seen to be so*. When one is dealing, as my Court often is, with issues so heartfelt that they are believed by one side or the other to be resolved by the Constitution itself, it does not greatly appeal to one's sense of justice to say: "Well, that earlier case had nine factors, this one has nine plus one." Much better, even at the expense of the mild substantive distortion that any generalization introduces, to have a clear, previously enunciated rule that one can point to in explanation of the decision.

The common-law, discretion-conferring approach is ill suited, moreover, to a legal system in which the Supreme Court can review only an insignificant proportion of the decided cases. The idyllic notion of "the court" gradually closing in on a fully articulated rule of law by deciding one discrete fact situation after another until (by process of elimination, as it were) the truly *operative* facts become apparent—that notion simply cannot be applied to a court that will revisit the area in question with great infrequency. Two terms ago, the number of federal cases heard by my Court represented just about one-twentieth of one percent of all the cases decided by federal district courts, and less than one-half of one percent of all cases decided by federal courts of appeals. The fact is that when we decide a case on the basis of what we have come to call the "totality of the circumstances" test, it is not *we* who will be "closing in on the law" in the foreseeable future, but rather thirteen different courts of appeals—or, if it is a federal issue that can arise in state court litigation as well, thirteen different courts of appeals and fifty state supreme courts. To adopt such an approach, in other words, is effectively to conclude that uniformity is not a particularly important objective with respect to the legal question at issue.

This last point suggests another obvious advantage of establishing as soon as possible a clear, general principle of decision: predictability. Even in simpler times uncertainty has been regarded as incompatible with the rule of law. Rudimentary justice requires that those subject to the law must have the means of knowing what it prescribes. It is said that one of Emperor Caligula's nasty practices was to post his edicts high on the columns so that they would be harder to read and easier to transgress. As laws have become more numerous, and as people have become increasingly ready to punish their adversaries in the courts, we can less and less afford protracted uncertainty regarding what the law may mean. Predictability, or as Llewellyn put it, "reckonability," is a needful characteristic of any law worthy of the name. There are times when even a bad rule is better than no rule at all.

I had always thought that the common-law approach had at least one thing to be said for it: it was the course of judicial restraint, "making" as little law as possible in order to decide the case at hand. I have come to doubt whether that is true. For when, in writing for the majority of the Court, I adopt a general rule, and say, "This is the basis of our decision," I not only constrain lower courts, I constrain myself as well. If the next case should have such different facts that my political or policy preferences regarding the outcome are quite the opposite, I will be unable to indulge those preferences; I have committed myself to the governing principle. In the real world of appellate judging, it displays more judicial restraint to adopt such a course than to announce that, "on balance," we think the law was violated here—leaving ourselves free to say in the next case that, "on balance," it was not. It is a commonplace that the one effective check upon arbitrary judges is criticism by the bar and the academy. But it is no more possible to demonstrate the inconsistency of two opinions based upon a "totality of the circumstances" test than it is to demonstrate the inconsistency of two jury verdicts. Only by announcing rules do we hedge ourselves in.

While announcing a firm rule of decision can thus inhibit courts, strangely enough it can embolden them as well. Judges are sometimes called upon to be courageous, because they must sometimes stand up to what is generally supreme in a democracy: the popular will. Their most significant roles, in our system, are to protect the individual criminal defendant against the occasional excesses of that popular will, and to preserve the checks and balances within our constitutional system that are precisely designed to inhibit swift and complete accomplishment of that popular will. Those are tasks which, properly performed, may earn widespread respect and admiration in the long run, but—almost by definition—never in the particular case. The chances that frail men and women will stand up to their unpleasant duty are greatly increased if they can stand behind the solid shield of a firm, clear principle enunciated in earlier cases. It is very difficult to say that a particular convicted felon who is the object of widespread hatred must go free because, on balance, we think that excluding the defense attorney from the line-up process in this case may have prevented a fair trial. It is easier to say that our cases plainly hold that, absent exigent circumstances, such exclusion is a *per se* denial of due process. Or to take an example involving the other principal judicial role: When the people are greatly exercised about "over-regulation" by the "nameless, faceless bureaucracy" in a particular agency, and Congress responds to this concern by enacting a popular scheme for legislative veto of that agency's regulations— warmly endorsed by all the best newspapers—it is very difficult to say that, on balance, this takes away too much power from the executive. It is easier to say that our cases plainly hold that Congress can formally control executive action only by law.

We should recognize that, at the point where an appellate judge says that the remaining issue must be decided on the basis of the totality of the circumstances, or by a balancing of all the factors involved, he begins to resemble a finder of fact more than a determiner of law. To reach such a stage is, in a way, a regrettable concession of defeat—an acknowledgment that we have passed the point where "law," properly speaking, has any further application. And to reiterate the unfortunate practical consequences of reaching such a pass when there still remains a good deal of judgment to be applied: equality of treatment is difficult to demonstrate and, in a multi-tiered judicial system, impossible to achieve; predictability is destroyed; judicial arbitrariness is facilitated; judicial courage is impaired.

I stand with Aristotle, then—which is a pretty good place to stand—in the view that "personal rule, whether it be exercised by a single person or a body of persons, should be sovereign only in those matters on which law is unable, owing to the difficulty of framing general rules for all contingencies, to make an exact pronouncement."[2] In the case of court-made law, the "difficulty of framing general rules" arises not merely from the inherent nature of the subject at issue, but from the imperfect scope of the materials that judges are permitted to consult. Even where a particular area is quite susceptible of clear and definite rules, we judges cannot create them out of whole cloth, but must find some basis for them in the text that Congress or the Constitution has provided. It is rare, however, that even the most vague and general text cannot be given some precise, principled content—and that is indeed the essence of the judicial craft. One can hardly imagine a prescription more vague than the Sherman Act's prohibition of contracts, combinations, or conspiracies in restraint of trade, but we have not interpreted it to require a totality-of-the-circumstances approach in every case. The trick is to carry general principle as far as it can go in substantial furtherance of the precise statutory or constitutional prescription.

Of course, the extent to which one can elaborate general rules from a statutory or constitutional command depends considerably upon how clear and categorical one understands the command to be, which in turn depends considerably upon one's method of textual exegesis. For example, it is perhaps easier for me than it is for some judges to develop general rules, because I am more inclined to adhere closely to the plain meaning of a text.

Just as that manner of textual exegesis facilitates the formulation of general rules, so does, in the constitutional field, adherence to a more or less originalist theory of construction. The raw material for the general rule is readily apparent. If a barn was not considered the curtilage of a house in 1791 or 1868 and the Fourth Amendment did not cover it then, unlawful entry into a barn today may be a trespass, but not an unconstitutional search and seizure. It is more difficult, it seems to me, to derive such a categorical general rule from evolving notions of personal privacy. Similarly, even if one rejects an originalist approach, it is easier to arrive at categorical rules if one acknowledges that the content of evolving concepts is strictly limited by the actual practices of the society, as reflected in the laws enacted by its legislatures.

It is, of course, *possible* to establish general rules, no matter what theory of interpretation or construction one employs. As one cynic has said, with five votes anything is possible. But when one does not have a solid textual anchor or an established social norm from which to derive the general rule, its pronouncement appears uncomfortably like legislation. If I did not consider my judgment governed by the original meaning of constitutional text, or at least by current social practice as reflected in extant legislation, I would feel relatively comfortable deciding case by case whether, taking into account all of the circumstances, the death sentence for this particular individual was "cruel and unusual"—but I would feel quite uncomfortable announcing firm rules (legitimated by nothing but my own sense of justice) regarding the relevance of such matters as the age of the defendant, mental capacity, intent to take a life, and so forth.

Lest the observations in this essay be used against me unfairly in the future, let me call attention to what I have *not* said. I have not said that legal determinations that do not reflect a general rule can be entirely avoided. We will have totality-of-the-circumstances tests and balancing modes of analysis with us forever—and for my sins, I will probably write some of the opinions that use them. All I urge is that those modes of analysis be avoided where possible; that the *rule* of law, the law of *rules*, be extended as far as the nature of the question allows; and that, to foster a correct attitude toward the matter, we appellate judges bear in mind that when we have finally reached the point where we can do no more than consult the totality of the circumstances, we are acting more as fact-finders than as expositors of the law.

Originalism

Justice Scalia liked to joke that people would come up to him and ask, "When did you become an originalist?" in the same tone of wonder that they might use in asking, "When did you start eating human flesh?" Over the course of his judicial career, he delivered countless speeches throughout the country and around the world explaining what originalism is. This version weaves together parts of two speeches from 1994 and 2012.[1]

I am one of a small but hardy group of judges and academics in the United States who subscribe to the principle of constitutional interpretation known as originalism. Originalists believe that the provisions of the Constitution have a fixed meaning, which does not change (except by constitutional amendment): they mean today what they meant when they were adopted, nothing more and nothing less. This is not to say, of course, that there are not new applications of old constitutional rules. The Court must determine, for example, how the First Amendment guarantee of "the freedom of speech" applies to new technologies that did not exist when the guarantee was created—to sound trucks, for example, or to government-licensed over-the-air television. In such new fields the Court must follow the trajectory of the First Amendment, so to speak, to determine what it requires—and assuredly that enterprise is not entirely cut and dried, but requires the exercise of judgment. But acknowledging the need for projection of old constitutional principles upon new physical realities is a far cry from saying what the non-originalists say: that the Constitution *changes*; that the very act which it once prohibited it now permits, and which it once permitted it now forbids.

The notion has somehow gained currency—to some extent in the United States itself, but particularly abroad—that American courts and the American people have always regarded the Constitution as a so-called "living" document, which changes from age to age as social necessity and convenience demand. John Marshall himself is invoked as supporting this view—his famous statement in *McCulloch v. Maryland* that "we must never forget that it is a constitution we are expounding" is taken to mean that constitutions, unlike other enacted laws, must grow and change and expand. Of course the statement meant (or rather *assumed*) just the opposite. Marshall's point in *McCulloch* was that since a constitution must govern for ages to come, in circumstances and under conditions we cannot yet envision, the powers it accords to the government must be broadly construed. That is to say, since the Constitution cannot be thought to mean different things from age to age, its *permanent* meaning must be broad enough to give the government the tools it will need both now and in the future.

Originalism was constitutional orthodoxy in the United States until, in historical terms, very recent times—the post–World War II era of the Warren Court. I do not mean to suggest that prior to then the Supreme Court was always faithful to the original meaning, and never departed from it in order to produce what it considered a more desirable result. Assuredly it did so. Willful judges who bend a text to their wishes have always been with us, and always will be. But in earlier times they at least had the decency to lie about it, to pretend that they were saying what the unchanging Constitution required. That is no longer necessary. Under the "living Constitution" philosophy that now dominates American jurisprudence, it no longer matters what the Constitution meant. The only relevant question is "What ought it to mean today?"

Examples abound of the changes that have been forced upon American society by this philosophy—not state by state, but instantaneously, on a national basis, from New York City to the smallest hamlet, from Maine to the Rio Grande and from New Jersey to Oregon. So that you may appreciate the vast extent of the phenomenon, I will give you a few examples:

The First Amendment to our Constitution provides that "Congress shall make no law . . . abridging the freedom of speech, or of the press." It had never been thought that "the freedom of speech" included the freedom to libel. But in 1964 the Supreme Court held, without benefit of any historical precedent, that neither federal law nor state law could permit a public figure to recover damages for libel, so long as the libel was not (in effect) intentional. Arguably a good rule that the states and the federal government should democratically adopt by legislation; but assuredly *not* what the People adopted when they ratified the First Amendment.

Also in the realm of freedom of speech, the Supreme Court held, in 1957, that pornography could not be prohibited. Only *obscenity* can be prohibited, which we have later described as consisting not of pandering to an interest in sex, but of pandering to something other than a good, healthy interest in sex, whatever that means. There was no historical precedent for this restriction upon a democratic society's ability to use its police powers to regulate matters of sexual morality. The First Amendment had never meant that the sexual permissiveness of Akron, Ohio, had to match that of Reno, Nevada. Once again, that is arguably a good idea, which the voters of Akron or of Ohio might wish to embrace (if you will forgive the pun). But it is assuredly *not* an idea that the People of the United States gave the Supreme Court the power to impose when they adopted the First Amendment.

The First Amendment to our Constitution also provides that "Congress shall make no law respecting an establishment of religion." It had never been thought that this prohibited, not merely the official favoring of one religious sect over another, but even a government policy of favoritism toward religious practice in general. Many presidents since George Washington had issued Thanksgiving proclamations, proclaiming a national holiday in gratitude to God for his blessings upon our nation. All the states had exempted property used for religious services from real-estate taxes. The military had always provided chaplains at government expense, even in an all-volunteer army. The Senate and House had had their own publicly paid chaplains. The Supreme Court itself had opened each of its sittings (and still does) with the invocation "God save the United States and this Honorable Court." Nonetheless, the Supreme Court proclaimed, in contradiction of our entire national history and several prior Supreme Court cases, that the government could not show favoritism toward religion. This is called the "principle of neutrality." In one manifestation of this doctrine, the Court held that it was unconstitutional for a public high school to begin its graduation ceremonies with a nondenominational benediction read by a rabbi.

The Fourth Amendment to our Constitution prohibits unreasonable searches and seizures. The court held in 1961—without any basis in national tradition, and indeed contrary to a prior Supreme Court case—that when an unreasonable search or seizure *does* occur, the sanction must be exclusion of the evidence from the criminal trial. The policeman will be punished by setting the criminal free. Arguably a good rule to deter unlawful police conduct. But not one that had ever been democratically prescribed in the Fourth Amendment.

The Fifth Amendment provides that no person shall be compelled in any criminal case to be a witness against himself. The Supreme Court held in 1966—with no basis in historical practice—that this requires the exclusion of seemingly voluntary confessions if they have been given by a prisoner in custody, *unless* the prisoner has formally been advised of his right to remain silent and to have an attorney—the so-called *Miranda* warning that you hear read on all the American cop shows.

The Fourteenth Amendment assures all citizens the equal protection of the laws. The Supreme Court has held that this means what it never before meant: that parties in civil and even criminal cases cannot exercise peremptory challenges on the basis of race or sex. A black defendant accused of raping a white woman cannot, for example, peremptorily strike whites or women from the jury.

But perhaps the area of our jurisprudence that most clearly reflects the "living Constitution" philosophy is that which pertains to the Eighth Amendment, the provision of our Bill of Rights that proscribes "cruel and unusual punishments." Our court has used that provision in recent years to place restrictions upon both the substance and procedure of capital punishment that never existed before and were not conceivably embodied in the amendment as originally enacted. We have prohibited, for example, the imposition of that penalty for any crime except murder—though the death penalty was until recently sometimes imposed for rape, and at the time the Eighth Amendment was adopted was even imposed for horse-thieving. We have also held that the death penalty cannot be automatic (if you are convicted of first-degree murder, you die); the sentencer must always be required to consider all mitigating circumstances and must be given the option of imposing a lesser sentence. Once again, all this may be very sensible; but it was never in the Eighth Amendment. Our cases acknowledge that, but they say that the content of the Eighth Amendment changes from age to age, to reflect "the evolving standards of decency that mark the progress of a maturing society." You will note the wide-eyed, youthful meliorism in this sentiment: every day, in every way, we get better and better. Societies always *mature*; they never *rot*. This despite the twentieth century's evidence of concentration camps and gas ovens in one of the most advanced and civilized nations of the world. Of course the whole *premise* of a constitution in general, and of a bill of rights in particular, is the very opposite of this. Certain rights are sought to be "locked in"—placed beyond the normal legislative process—out of fear that they will be disregarded by a *less enlightened* or *less virtuous* future generation.

The proponents of the living Constitution indulge the optimistic assumption that whatever changes are made in original meaning will always be in the direction of according greater individual freedom—which to their way of thinking is always *good*. Only the anarchist, of course, would agree that it is always good. Any system of government involves a balancing of individual freedom of action against community needs, and it seems to me quite foolish to assume that every further tilt in the direction of greater freedom of action is necessarily good. But assuming that to be true, I cannot for the life of me understand why the proponents of a living Constitution expect it to be a one-way street.

The "evolving standards" approach can take away old rights as well as create new ones. That has happened during my time on the court. Our Sixth Amendment provides that "[i]n all criminal prosecutions, the accused shall enjoy the right . . . to be confronted with the witnesses against him." We nonetheless held, in 1990, that in a prosecution for sexual abuse of a young child, the child could be permitted to testify out of the presence of the defendant, with the defendant observing the proceedings over closed-circuit television from another room. This procedure is acceptable, we said, where the child would be too nervous or frightened to testify in the defendant's presence.

Well, that may be a very reasonable disposition—but it is certainly not the disposition established by the Sixth Amendment. There is no doubt about what it means "to be confronted with the witnesses against" you. It means (at a minimum) that they give their damning testimony *in your presence*. The reason for that disposition is that there is something in the human psyche which makes it difficult to tell a lie in the very presence of the person being condemned. Difficult for adults, and difficult for little children too. Now perhaps, in the case of little children, the truth-finding benefit of this protection is outweighed by the truth-finding detriment of childish fear. That is, I suspect, how modern America, which is much more sensitive to "psychic trauma" than our hardy forebears, would evaluate it. But it is certainly not how the Sixth Amendment evaluated it. They had sexual abuse then; they had child witnesses then; they did not, to be sure, have closed-circuit television but they had other devices that would have achieved the same end of permitting the defendant to see the witness but preventing the witness from seeing the defendant—for example, a simple screen placed in front of the defense table. They did not permit these evasions in the case of children, but required, *in all criminal prosecutions*, the right to be confronted. In other words, our 1990 decision eliminated a right that used to exist. Perhaps it is, as I have suggested, a right that (at least in the case of child witnesses) the majority no longer cares for. But a right consists precisely of entitlement *against the wishes of the majority*. There is no blinking the fact that we have eliminated a freedom that used to exist—that the "evolving Constitution" can evolve toward less freedom as well as toward more.

One criticism lodged against originalism is that it is just camouflage for the imposition of conservative views. That is patently false.

One proof I can give is *Texas v. Johnson* (1989). There the Supreme Court held that it was a violation of the First Amendment to make unlawful the burning of an American flag. I consider that action a form of speech—which shows, by the way, that I am not a "strict constructionist." Texts should be construed neither strictly nor sloppily, but reasonably. And if you think the First Amendment covers only "speech" and "press" in the *literal* sense (which is what Justice Black said he believed), you must believe that Congress can censor handwritten mail. Of course "speech" and "press" are stand-ins for *the expression of ideas*—and that expression can be made through symbols and symbolic acts as well as through words. Semaphore and Morse code are covered, and so is the burning of a flag, a classic expression of disapproval or contempt for the government that it represents. The court held in *Johnson* that it was unconstitutional to ban the burning of a flag. It was a 5–4 decision, and I made the fifth vote. You should be in no doubt that, patriotic conservative that I am, I detest the burning of the nation's flag—and if I were king I would make it a crime. But as I understand the First Amendment, it guarantees the right to express contempt for the government, the Congress, the Supreme Court, even the nation and the nation's flag. And I could give you many other examples of opinions that I have joined and written that reach decidedly unconservative results. In the criminal-law field in particular I have insisted upon protections for the accused that a law-and-order conservative ought not to like. Far from facilitating conservative opinions, originalism prevents judges, conservatives and liberals alike, from judging according to their desires.

The most frequently pressed argument of the "living constitutionalists" is that their philosophy is absolutely essential in order to provide the necessary "flexibility" that a changing society requires. They would have you believe that the American Constitution would have snapped if it had not been permitted to bend and grow. This would be a persuasive argument if most of the "growing" that the living constitutionalists have brought upon us in the past, and are determined to bring upon us in the future, were the *elimination* of restrictions upon the governmental process. But just the opposite is true. Most living constitutionalists want to create *new* restrictions upon the legislative process, not to *eliminate* old ones. They favor, in other words, *less* flexibility in government, not *more*. As things now stand, the state and federal governments in the United States may either apply capital punishment or eliminate it, permit suicide or forbid it, permit homosexual conduct or forbid it*—all as the changing times and the changing sentiments of society may demand. But when capital punishment is held to violate the Eighth Amendment, and when suicide and homosexual conduct are held to be protected by the Fourteenth Amendment, all flexibility is gone.

That is what has happened, of course, with abortion. The Constitution says nothing about the subject. It neither forbids (as the pro-choice people claim) nor requires (as the pro-life people claim) restrictions upon it. For two centuries, laws in every state prohibited it, but now, under a living-Constitution theory, it cannot be prohibited. No use trying to persuade your fellow citizens one way or the other about the subject. It has been taken off the democratic stage. And that is, of course, precisely what those who argued for *Roe v. Wade* desired to achieve.

So don't love the living Constitution because it will bring you flexibility and choice; it will bring you rigidity, which is precisely what it is designed for. The reality of the matter is that living constitutionalists are seeking not to facilitate social change but to *prevent* it, by enshrining their views of morality or of natural law in the Constitution.

Besides supposed inflexibility, the other principal defect attributed to originalism is the difficulty of figuring out, at a distance of two hundred years, what the original understanding of a particular provision was. Modern deconstructionists, who abound in law as in literature, insist that words *have* no *inherent* meaning, and it is folly to pretend otherwise. Well, of course they have enough inherent meaning for all practical purposes, which is why these deconstructionists tend to make their arguments in learned articles composed of words, rather than in music or dance. It is true, however, that what the meaning was two hundred years ago is often difficult to discern, and

---

* No longer true after the Court's ruling in *Lawrence v. Texas* (2003).

originalists will sometimes disagree among themselves as to what it was.

A related criticism of originalism is that judges are incompetent historians. History, after all, is a science unto itself, and a science different from the science of law. Judges are trained as lawyers. What possible reason is there to believe that they can function effectively as historians? To begin with, I deny the premise that law has nothing to do with historical inquiry. Utterly central to the law is the meaning of words, and the meaning of a word often changes over time, as any reputable dictionary will show by its use of a parenthetical description such as "obs." (obsolete). Thus, the assertion that inquiry into the past has nothing to do with the law begs the question: historical inquiry has nothing to do with the law only if original meaning is irrelevant—only if the law means not what it meant when adopted, but what it ought to mean today. To tell the truth, even the most thoroughgoing non-originalist will often have to resort to historical inquiry. Otherwise, what possible meaning could he assign to such phrases in the Constitution as the "Privilege of the Writ of Habeas Corpus," "Bill of Attainder," "Letters of Marque and Reprisal," "Cases of admiralty and maritime Jurisdiction," "Corruption of Blood"?

It would not be accurate, however, to suggest that the only historical inquiry demanded of originalists is a sort of lexicographer's investigation into the verbal usage of an earlier time. That is part of the enterprise, to be sure. Let me use *District of Columbia v. Heller* (2008) as an example. There the petitioners contended that the term "bear arms" in the Second Amendment had an exclusively military connotation. It was necessary—and easy enough—for my originalist opinion for the Court to show that this was not so, by citing many examples of usage prior to and contemporaneous with adoption of the Second Amendment. This is, as I say, almost lexicographer's work. But other historical inquiry was demanded as well. One of the significant aspects of the Second Amendment was that it did not purport to *confer* a right to keep and bear arms. It did not say that "the people shall have the right to keep and bear arms," or even that "the government shall not prevent the people from keeping and bearing arms," but rather that "the right of the people to keep and bear arms" (as though it were a pre-existing right) "shall not be infringed." (The First Amendment is not so different in prescribing that Congress shall make no law abridging the freedom of speech.) In *Heller*, this reference to a pre-existing right engendered historical inquiry which showed that, indeed, the right to have arms for personal use (including self-defense) was regarded at the time of the Framing as one of the fundamental rights of Englishmen, described as such by Blackstone, and found in the explicit guarantee of the English Bill of Rights of 1689. Once that historical pedigree was understood, it was difficult to regard the guarantee of the Second Amendment as no more than a guarantee of the right to join a militia. Moreover, the prologue of the Second Amendment ("A well regulated militia being necessary for the defense of a free state") could not be logically connected with a personal right to keep and bear arms without the historical knowledge (possessed by the Framing generation) that the Stuart kings had destroyed the people's militia, not by disbanding it, but by disarming those of its members whom they disfavored. Here the opinion was surely dealing with history in a broader sense than mere lexicography.

I must concede that in some cases historical inquiry into the original meaning may be difficult. An example from the free-speech field is the 1995 case of *McIntyre v. Ohio Elections Commission*, which involved a First Amendment challenge to state requirements that all election campaign literature must identify the person or organization promulgating it. ("Printed by Citizens for Schwartz.") All the states had had such requirements and had had them for over a century. The plaintiff in the suit claimed that they were unconstitutional, since she had a right to anonymous political speech. It was quite difficult to determine what the people who ratified the First Amendment would have thought of such a claim, since the election process was so radically different before we adopted, toward the end of the nineteenth century, the Australian ballot—that is, the secret ballot. When I cannot determine what the Framers thought, I am disinclined to think that, for over a century, all the states—with no registered protest—misunderstood the First Amendment. And so I rejected the challenge. Justice Thomas, another originalist, accepted it, and wrote the opinion for the court holding such identification requirements unconstitutional. He relied for that conclusion upon the fact that the *Federalist Papers*—the most famous political tracts of the time—were published anonymously, under the name of Publius. Pseudonymous political speech was common at the time and, Justice Thomas concluded, must have been valued by the Framing generation. A not unreasonable conclusion—as, I also think, was mine.

So the originalist methodology does not always yield a clear and easy answer. But the question before the house is not whether originalism is perfect. I will stipulate that it is not. The question is whether it is better than anything else. My burden is not to show that originalism is perfect, but merely to show that it beats the other available alternatives. And that is not difficult. In the vast majority of cases—and especially the most controversial ones—the historical inquiry will be easy. Is libel of public figures prohibited by the First Amendment? Is the death penalty prohibited? Are laws against abortion, homosexual sodomy, and assisted suicide prohibited? It is a piece of cake to determine that no one in the Founding generation thought so. And for the more difficult questions, judges have the assistance of a growing number of legal historians—on law faculties and history faculties—to provide expert assistance on historical questions, just as engineers provide expert assistance on patent questions, and economists on antitrust questions.

By contrast, how are the living constitutionalists going to arrive at their decisions? To tell the truth, I don't know—and neither do they. How are they to decide what are "the evolving standards of decency that mark the progress of a maturing society"—the criterion of constitutional evolution that our Eighth Amendment opinions set forth? What would an elite group of the country's best lawyers, isolated in a marble palace, know about that? Earlier Supreme Court cases looked to the consensus of state laws. That is a dubious criterion of "evolving standards" to begin with. If it were true (which it is not) that a majority of the states have abolished the death penalty, that would not show that the people of those states consider that penalty unconstitutional, rather than just a bad idea—

any more than the fact that a majority of states forbid the union shop would show that they consider the union shop unconstitutional. In any case, the Supreme Court has abandoned this approach, and has explicitly said that what the living Constitution prescribes does not depend on any consensus of state laws, but on the judgment of the justices. Do you think that judges (that is to say, lawyers) are better at the science of What Ought To Be than at the science of history?

One of the interesting features of the massive modern attack upon originalism is that, while its many opponents are unified in the view that that mode of interpretation is wrong, they display no agreement whatever upon what is right—that is to say, no agreement upon what criterion of constitutional meaning should replace it. For of course "non-originalism" or "evolutionism" is not itself a theory of constitutional construction. It is simply an *anti*-theory—opposition to an original, fixed meaning. There is a saying in American electoral politics (invoked when an incumbent's popularity polls are very low, but the other party has no credible candidate to oppose him): "You can't beat somebody with nobody." The same is true in constitutional theory. If originalism is to be supplanted, it must be supplanted with *something*. If the judge is not to look to the original understanding of the text, what is he to look to? Here, of course, the academics explode into a hundred different groups, or indeed into as many groups as there are academics. Some would use the philosophy of John Locke; others, the philosophy of John Rawls; others, simply the "natural law," as though that defines an identifiable body of knowledge. The fact is that *no* principle of interpretation other than originalism has even the shadow of a chance of attracting general adherence. As a practical matter, there is no alternative to originalism but standardless judicial constitution-making.

And that, of course, is the very *appeal* of non-originalism for the judges: once they are liberated from the original meaning, they are liberated from any other governing principle as well. Nothing constrains their action except perhaps their estimation of how much judicial social engineering the society will tolerate. Consider, for example, how the learned legal discussion must proceed in a conference that is to determine whether there is a constitutional right to die. Well, of course the text of the Constitution says absolutely nothing about such a right. And our states have always had laws against suicide. Yes, yes, yes. But all of that is lawyerly analysis about the past, which is quite irrelevant. The question is not whether the Constitution *originally* established a right to die, but whether there is a right to die *today*. Do you think there is a right to die, Justice X? I don't. What about you, Justice Y? Let's have a show of hands. Well, that's five in favor of a right to die. Now on to the next case.

The reality is that originalism is the only game in town—the only real, verifiable criterion that can prevent judges from making the Constitution say whatever they think it should say. Show Scalia the original meaning, and he is prevented from imposing his nasty, conservative views upon the people. He is handcuffed. And if he tries to dissemble, he will be caught out. The source material is accessible to all; convenient omissions of inconvenient evidence can easily be identified; suspect conclusions can be effectively challenged. But if original meaning is not the criterion, what other criterion can there be that prevents judges from imposing their ideological preferences on society? Think about it. There is none. The living constitutionalist is a happy fella, because it turns out that the Constitution always means precisely what he thinks it ought to mean. That is indeed much of the attraction of the living Constitution. And it is an attraction not just to judges, but to the people at large. How wonderful to think that whatever you care passionately about—from abortion to the death penalty—is resolved precisely the way you think it should be *by the Constitution*. Never mind whether the people ever voted to put that in the Constitution and thus to remove it from the realm of democratic choice—only originalists care about that. It is there if it *ought* to be there. I urge you not to yield to that seductive and extremely undemocratic falsehood.

Textualism

Originalism *and* textualism, *as Justice Scalia explained, are different names for the same principles of interpretation applied in distinct contexts—originalism in constitutional interpretation, textualism in statutory interpretation. In both contexts, the principles aim to discern the meaning that a legal provision had at the time it was adopted. In this excerpt from his 1997 book,* A Matter of Interpretation,[1] *Scalia discusses how to interpret statutes and explains the benefits of textualism.*

Statutory interpretation is such a broad subject that the substance of it cannot be discussed comprehensively here. It is worth examining a few aspects, however, if only to demonstrate the great degree of confusion that prevails. We can begin at the most fundamental possible level. So utterly unformed is the American law of statutory interpretation that not only is its methodology unclear, but even its very *objective* is. Consider the basic question: what are we looking for when we construe a statute?

You will find it frequently said in judicial opinions of my court and others that the judge's objective in interpreting a statute is to give effect to the "intent of the legislature." This principle, in one form or another, goes back at least as far as Blackstone. Unfortunately, it does not square with some of the (few) generally accepted concrete rules of statutory construction. One is the rule that when the text of a statute is clear, that is the end of the matter. Why should that be so, if what the legislature *intended*, rather than what it *said*, is the object of our inquiry? In selecting the words of the statute, the legislature might have misspoken. Why not permit that to be demonstrated from the floor debates? Or indeed, why not accept, as proper material for the court to consider, later explanations by the legislators—a sworn affidavit signed by the majority of each house, for example, as to what they *really* meant?

Another accepted rule of construction is that ambiguities in a newly enacted statute are to be resolved in such fashion as to make the statute, not only internally consistent, but also compatible with previously enacted laws. We simply assume, for purposes of our search for "intent," that the enacting legislature was aware of all those other laws. Well of course that is a fiction, and if we were really looking for the subjective intent of the enacting legislature we would more likely find it by paying attention to the text (and legislative history) of the new statute in isolation.

The evidence suggests that, despite frequent statements to the contrary, we do not really look for subjective legislative intent. We look for a sort of "objectified" intent—the intent that a reasonable person would gather from the text of the law, placed alongside the remainder of the *corpus juris*. As Bishop's old treatise nicely put it, elaborating upon the usual formulation: "The primary object of all rules for interpreting statutes is to ascertain the legislative intent; *or, exactly, the meaning which the subject is authorized to understand the legislature intended*." And the reason we adopt this objectified version is, I think, that it is simply incompatible with democratic government, or indeed, even with fair government, to have the meaning of a law determined by what the lawgiver meant, rather than by what the lawgiver promulgated. That seems to me one step worse than the trick the emperor Caligula was said to engage in: posting edicts high up on the pillars, so that they could not easily be read. Government by unexpressed intent is similarly tyrannical. It is the *law* that governs, not the intent of the lawgiver. That seems to me the essence of the famous American ideal set forth in the Massachusetts constitution: a government of laws, not of men. Men may intend what they will; but it is only the laws that they enact which bind us.

In reality, however, if one accepts the principle that the object of judicial interpretation is to determine the intent of the legislature, being bound by genuine but unexpressed legislative intent rather than the law is only the *theoretical* threat. The *practical* threat is that, under the guise or even the self-delusion of pursuing unexpressed legislative intents, common-law judges will in fact pursue their own objectives and desires, extending their lawmaking proclivities from the common law to the statutory field. When you are told to decide, not on the basis of what the legislature said, but on the basis of what it *meant*, and are assured that there is no necessary connection between the two, your best shot at figuring out what the legislature meant is to ask yourself what a wise and intelligent person *should* have meant; and that will surely bring you to the conclusion that the law means what you think it *ought* to mean—which is precisely how judges decide things under the common law.

To give some concrete form to the danger I warn against, let me describe what I consider to be the prototypical case involving the triumph of supposed "legislative intent" (a handy cover for judicial intent) over the text of the law. It is called *Church of the Holy Trinity v. United States* and was decided by the Supreme Court of the United States in 1892. The Church of the Holy Trinity, located in New York City, contracted with an Englishman to come over to be its rector and pastor. The United States claimed that this agreement violated a federal statute that made it unlawful for any person to "in any way assist or encourage the importation or migration, of any alien . . . into the United States . . . under contract or agreement . . . made previous to the importation or migration of such alien . . . , to perform labor or service of any kind in the United States." The Circuit Court for the Southern District of New York held the church liable for the fine that the statute provided. The Supreme Court reversed. The central portion of its reasoning was as follows:

> It must be conceded that the act of the [church] is within the letter of this section, for the relation of rector to his church is one of service, and implies labor on the one side with compensation on the other. Not only are the general words labor and service both used [in the statute], but also, as it were to guard against any narrow interpretation and emphasize a breadth of meaning, to them is added "of any kind"; and, further, . . . the fifth section

[of the statute], which makes specific exceptions, among them professional actors, artists, lecturers, singers and domestic servants, strengthens the idea that every other kind of labor and service was intended to be reached by the first section. While there is great force to this reasoning, we cannot think Congress intended to denounce with penalties a transaction like that in the present case. It is a familiar rule, that a thing may be within the letter of the statute and yet not within the statute, because not within its spirit, nor within the intention of its makers.

The Court proceeds to conclude from various extratextual indications, including even a snippet of legislative history (highly unusual in those days), that the statute was intended to apply only to *manual* labor—which renders the exceptions for actors, artists, lecturers, and singers utterly inexplicable. The Court then shifts gears, and devotes the last seven pages of its opinion to a lengthy description of how and why we are a religious nation. That being so, it says "the construction invoked cannot be accepted as correct." It concludes:

It is a case where there was presented a definite evil, in view of which the legislature used general terms with the purpose of reaching all phases of that evil, and thereafter, unexpectedly, it is developed that the general language thus employed is broad enough to reach cases and acts which the whole history and life of the country affirm could not have been intentionally legislated against. It is the duty of the courts, under those circumstances, to say that, however broad the language of the statute may be, the act, although within the letter, is not within the intention of the legislature, and therefore cannot be within the statute.

Well of course I think that the act was within the letter of the statute, and was therefore within the statute: end of case. Congress can enact foolish statutes as well as wise ones, and it is not for the courts to decide which is which and re-write the former. I acknowledge an interpretative doctrine of what the old writers call *lapsus linguae* (slip of the tongue), and what our modern cases call "scrivener's error," where on the very face of the statute it is clear to the reader that a mistake of expression (rather than of legislative wisdom) has been made. For example, a statute may say "defendant" when only "criminal defendant" (i.e., not "civil defendant") makes sense. The objective import of such a statute is clear enough, and I think it is not contrary to sound principles of interpretation, in such extreme cases, to give the totality of context precedence over a single word. But to say that the legislature obviously misspoke is worlds away from saying that the legislature obviously over-legislated. *Church of the Holy Trinity* is cited to us whenever counsel wants us to ignore the narrow, deadening text of the statute, and pay attention to the life-giving legislative intent. It is nothing but an invitation to judicial lawmaking.

What I think is needed is not rationalization of this process but abandonment of it. It is simply not compatible with democratic theory that laws mean whatever they ought to mean, and that unelected judges decide what that is.

It may well be that the statutory interpretation adopted by the Court in *Church of the Holy Trinity* produced a desirable result; and it may even be (though I doubt it) that it produced the unexpressed result actually intended by Congress, rather than merely the one desired by the Court. Regardless, the decision was wrong because it failed to follow the text. The text is the law, and it is the text that must be observed. I agree with Justice Holmes's remark, quoted approvingly by Justice Frankfurter in his article on the construction of statutes: "Only a day or two ago—when counsel talked of the intention of a legislature, I was indiscreet enough to say I don't care what their intention was. I only want to know what the words mean." And I agree with Holmes's other remark, quoted approvingly by Justice Jackson: "We do not inquire what the legislature meant; we ask only what the statute means."

The philosophy of interpretation I have described above is known as textualism. In some sophisticated circles, it is considered simpleminded—wooden, unimaginative, pedestrian. It is none of that. To be a textualist in good standing, one need not be too dull to perceive the broader social purposes that a statute is designed, or could be designed, to serve; or too hidebound to realize that new times require new laws. One need only hold the belief that judges have no authority to pursue those broader purposes or write those new laws.

Textualism should not be confused with so-called strict constructionism, a degraded form of textualism that brings the whole philosophy into disrepute. I am not a strict constructionist, and no one ought to be—though better that, I suppose, than a non-textualist. A text should not be construed strictly, and it should not be construed leniently; it should be construed reasonably, to contain all that it fairly means.

But while the good textualist is not a literalist, neither is he a nihilist. Words do have a limited range of meaning, and no interpretation that goes beyond that range is permissible.

Of all the criticisms leveled against textualism, the most mindless is that it is "formalistic." The answer to that is, *of course it's formalistic!* The rule of law is *about* form. If, for example, a citizen performs an act—let us say the sale of certain technology to a foreign country— which is prohibited by a widely publicized bill proposed by the administration and passed by both houses of Congress, *but not yet signed by the president*, that sale is lawful. It is of no consequence that everyone knows both houses of Congress and the president wish to prevent that sale. Before the wish becomes a binding law, it must be embodied in a bill that passes both houses and is signed by the president. Is that not formalism? A murderer has been caught with blood on his hands, bending over the body of his victim; a neighbor with a video camera has filmed the crime; and the murderer has confessed in writing and on videotape. We nonetheless insist that before the state can punish this miscreant, it must conduct a full-dress criminal trial that results in a verdict of guilty. Is that not formalism? Long live formalism. It is what makes a government a government of laws and not of men.

2

Constitutional Interpretation

This chapter takes us from the abstract to the concrete, from theory to cases. It addresses constitutional interpretation in the context of a range of disputes. The scope of the topic warrants three sections: constitutional structure, civil liberties, and criminal protections. When people think of Justice Scalia, many of the landmark opinions contained in this chapter come to mind.

Constitutional Structure

Throughout his tenure, Justice Scalia sought to honor and protect the Constitution's structure—its distinct horizontal and vertical lines of power—as an essential guarantor of individual liberty. Like James Madison, he recognized that men and women were not "angels" and that electing or appointing them to government posts could result in abuses of power. By assigning three distinct kinds of governmental power (legislative, executive, and judicial) to three distinct branches of the federal government and by allocating distinct powers to the federal and state governments, the Constitution prevented the concentration of governmental power in the same hands—considered by the Founders to be the epitome of tyranny.

At his confirmation hearing in 1986, Scalia was asked to explain the success of the Constitution. His answer focused on structure over individual rights. While the Bill of Rights is "very important," he said, its provisions standing alone "do not do anything." Other countries, even those with authoritarian regimes, have "at least as good guarantees of personal freedom." Instead, Scalia explained, "what makes it work, what assures that those words are not just hollow promises, is the structure of government that the original Constitution established, the checks and balances among the three branches."

In his iconic dissent in Morrison v. Olson, *written early in his tenure, Justice Scalia put these principles to work. He objected that Congress's attempt to restrict the president's ability to remove an independent counsel—an officer who exercised executive power—violated Article II, which vests the executive power in the president and obligates him to take care that the laws be faithfully executed. As he saw it, the Constitution vests all, not some, of the executive power in the president. For Justice Scalia, this made* Morrison *an easy case: "Frequently an issue of this sort will come before the Court clad, so to speak, in sheep's clothing: the potential of the asserted principle to effect important change in the equilibrium of power is not immediately evident, and must be discerned by a careful and perceptive analysis. But this wolf comes as a wolf."* As Morrison *and the other decisions and speeches collected in this section confirm, Justice Scalia wrote with deep conviction about the Constitution's structural guarantees of liberty.*

THE IMPORTANCE OF STRUCTURE

In Praise of the Humdrum

This excerpt is from a lecture by Justice Scalia at Brown University in 1991.[1]

A bill of rights has value only if the other part of the constitution—the part that really "constitutes" the organs of government—establishes a structure that is likely to preserve, against the ineradicable human lust for power, the liberties that the bill of rights expresses. If the people value those liberties, the proper constitutional structure will likely result in their preservation even in the absence of a bill of rights; and where that structure does not exist, the mere recitation of the liberties will certainly not preserve them. So while it is entirely appropriate for us Americans to celebrate and decorate our wonderful Bill of Rights, we realize (or should realize) that it represents the fruit and not the roots of our constitutional tree. The rights it expresses are the *reasons* that the other provisions exist. But it is those other humdrum provisions—the structural, mechanistic portions of the Constitution that pit, in James Madison's words, "ambition against ambition," and make it impossible for any element of government to obtain unchecked power—that convert the Bill of Rights from a paper assurance to a living guarantee. A crowd is much more likely to form behind a banner that reads "Freedom of Speech or Death" than behind one that says "Bicameralism or Fight"; but the latter in fact goes much more to the root of the matter.

Structure Is Everything

In October 2007, Justice Scalia delivered the opening remarks at a symposium on "Separation of Powers as a Safeguard of Federalism" at Notre Dame Law School.

In the days when I taught constitutional law, the University of Chicago Law School had two constitutional courses. One was entitled "Individual Rights and Liberties," and focused primarily upon the guarantees of the Bill of Rights. The other focused upon the structural provisions of the Constitution, principally the separation of powers and federalism. That was the course I taught—and I used to refer to it as *real* constitutional law. The distinctive function of a constitution, after all, is to constitute the political organs, the governing structure, of a state. Many of the personal protections against the state taught in constitutional law courses here—restrictions upon unlawful searches and seizures, for example—used to be taught in Europe as part of administrative law. They were, to be sure, made part of our Constitution (though most of them as an appendage to the original document). And that was no doubt desirable. But it is a mistake to think that the Bill of Rights is the defining, or even the most important, feature of American democracy. Virtually all the countries of the world today have bills of rights. You would not feel your freedom secure in most of them—though you likely would in England or Australia, which are two of the very few countries that do not have bills of rights.

Consider, for example, the following sterling provisions of a modern bill of rights:

Every citizen has the right to submit proposals to state bodies and public organizations for improving their activity, and to criticize shortcomings in their work. Persecution for criticism is prohibited. Persons guilty of such persecution shall be called to account.

Citizens are guaranteed freedom of speech, of the press, and of assembly, meetings, street processions and demonstrations. Exercise of these political freedoms is ensured by putting public buildings, streets, and squares at the disposal of the people and their organizations, by broad dissemination of information, and by the opportunity to use the press, television, and radio.

Citizens are guaranteed freedom of conscience, that is, the right to profess or not to profess any religion, and to conduct religious worship, or atheistic propaganda. Incitement of hostility or hatred on religious grounds is prohibited.

Wonderful stuff. These were provisions of the 1977 constitution of the Union of Soviet Socialist Republics. They were not worth the paper they were printed on, nor are the human rights guarantees of a large number of still-extant countries governed by presidents-for-life. They are what the Framers of our Constitution called "parchment guarantees," because the *real* constitutions of those countries—the provisions that establish the institutions of government—do not prevent the centralization of power in one man or one party, thus enabling the guarantees to be ignored. Structure is everything. The constitutional structure of the United States has two main features: (1) separation and equilibration of powers and (2) federalism. Each functions to safeguard individual liberty in isolation, but they provide even greater protection working together. James Madison captured this idea when he explained (in The Federalist No. 51) that this constitutional structure provides "a double security" to the rights of the people. Discussing "considerations particularly applicable to the federal system of America," he wrote:

In a single republic, all the power surrendered by the people is submitted to the administration of a single government; and the usurpations are guarded against by a division of the government into distinct and separate departments. In the compound republic of America, the power surrendered by the people is first divided between two distinct governments, and then the portion allotted to each subdivided among distinct and separate departments. Hence a double security arises to the rights of the people. The different governments will control each other, at the same time that each will be controlled by itself.

Those who seek to protect individual liberty ignore threats to this constitutional structure at their peril. Two examples illustrate the point. In *Morrison v. Olson*, the Supreme Court upheld the independent counsel provisions of the Ethics in Government Act of 1978, a frank and undisguised attempt by Congress to assign elsewhere the president's authority to prosecute—and to decline to prosecute—violations of the law. The accomplishment of this feat required several compromises of constitutional structure, including provision for the appointment of principal executive officers by federal judges at (in effect) the insistence of members of Congress, and restriction of the president's power to supervise and remove officers performing core executive functions. The consequences of the Act, which ultimately led to its demise, were predictable. Prosecutors with no executive supervision and essentially unlimited budgets were investigating alleged criminal wrongdoing by the president or his close associates during every administration while the Act was in effect. Some investigations lasted longer than the tenure of the attorneys general who were required to trigger the judicial appointment. The harvest of criminal convictions was sparse, but the diminution of presidential prestige, and hence of presidential power, was substantial. So was the injustice done to many "targets," who were treated to the luxury of their own personal, publicly announced, highly publicized, full-time criminal investigator (with a large full-time staff) for years on end.

In *Printz v. United States*, the Court invalidated provisions of the Brady Handgun Violence Prevention Act requiring state and local law enforcement officers to perform background checks on prospective handgun purchasers. Since the statute dealt with commerce,

Congress was free to regulate handgun purchases directly. The question in *Printz* was whether Congress could require the states to regulate such purchases on behalf of the federal government. We held that it could not for reasons of both federalism and separation of powers. As a matter of federalism, the Constitution does not authorize Congress to commandeer state officers for the enforcement of the laws that it enacts. That would vastly increase the number of federal agents, and hence the power of the federal government. And it would allow Congress and the president to evade apparent responsibility for (not to mention the cost of) enforcing unpopular federal mandates. As a matter of separation of powers, commandeering state law enforcement officers would enable Congress to avoid the essential check that the laws it enacts depend for their execution upon the competing political branch of the presidency. The Act thus undermined both pillars of the "double security . . . to the rights of the people" that Madison described.

SEPARATION OF POWERS

Learn to Love Gridlock

In October 2011, Justice Scalia and Justice Breyer presented testimony at a Senate Judiciary Committee hearing titled "Considering the Role of Judges Under the Constitution of the United States." This is from Justice Scalia's opening statement.

I am happy to be back in front of the Judiciary Committee, where I started this pilgrimage.

I speak to students quite frequently about the Constitution because I fear that we are not teaching it very well. I speak to law students from the best law schools, people presumably especially interested in the law, and I ask them: "How many of you have read the *Federalist Papers*?" Well, a lot of hands will go up. But then I say, "No, not just No. 48 and the big ones. How many of you have read the *Federalist Papers* cover to cover?" Never more than about 5 percent. And that is very sad, especially if you are interested in the Constitution.

Here is a document that says what the Framers of the Constitution thought they were doing. It is such a profound exposition of political science that it is studied in political science courses in Europe. And yet we have raised a generation of Americans who are not familiar with it.

So when I speak to these groups, I ask them: "What do you think is the reason that America is such a free country? What is it in our Constitution that makes us what we are?" And the response I get—and you will get this from almost any American—is freedom of speech, freedom of the press, no unreasonable searches and seizures, no quartering of troops in homes, etc.—the marvelous provisions of the Bill of Rights.

But then I tell them, "If you think that the Bill of Rights is what sets us apart, you are crazy." Every banana republic has a bill of rights. Every president-for-life has a bill of rights. The bill of rights of the former "evil empire," the Union of Soviet Socialist Republics, was much better than ours. We guarantee freedom of speech and of the press. Big deal. They guaranteed freedom of speech, of the press, of street demonstrations and protests, and anyone who is caught trying to suppress criticism of the government will be called to account. Whoa, that is wonderful stuff.

Of course, they were just words on paper, what our Framers would have called a "parchment guarantee." And the reason is that the real constitution of the Soviet Union—its structure—was totalitarian. Think of the word *constitution*. It does not mean a bill of rights. It means structure. When you say a person has a sound constitution, you mean he has a sound structure. Structure is what our Framers debated that whole summer in Philadelphia, in 1787. They did not talk about a Bill of Rights; that was an afterthought, wasn't it? The real constitution of the Soviet Union did not prevent the centralization of power in one person or in one party. And when that happens, the game is over.

So the real key to the distinctiveness of America is the structure of our government. One part of that, of course, is the independence of the judiciary, but there is a lot more. There are very few countries in the world, for example, that have a bicameral legislature. England has a House of Lords for the time being, but the House of Lords has no substantial power. It can just make the Commons pass a bill a second time. France has a senate; it is honorific. Italy has a senate; it is honorific too. Very few countries have two separate bodies in the legislature equally powerful. It is a lot of trouble, as you gentlemen doubtless know, to get the same language through two different bodies elected in a different fashion.

Very few countries in the world have a separately elected chief executive. Sometimes I go to Europe to speak in a seminar on separation of powers, and when I get there, I find that all we are talking about is independence of the judiciary. Because the Europeans do not even try to divide the two political powers, the two political branches—the legislature and the chief executive. In all of the parliamentary countries, the chief executive is the creature of the legislature. There is never any disagreement between the majority in the legislature and the prime minister, as there is sometimes between you and the president. When there is a disagreement, they just kick him out. They have a no-confidence vote, a new election, and they get a prime minister who agrees with the legislature.

The Europeans look at our system and they say, well, the bill passes one House, but it does not pass the other House (perhaps because the other House is in the control of a different party). Or it passes both Houses, and then the president vetoes it. They look at this and they say, "It is gridlock."

And I hear Americans saying this nowadays, too. They talk about a dysfunctional government because there is disagreement. Well, the Framers would have said, "Yes, that is exactly the way we set it up. We wanted this to be power counteracting power because the main ill that besets us" is, as Madison said in The Federalist No. 62 when he justified the inconvenience of a separate Senate, "an excess of lawmaking."

So Americans should understand that and learn to love the separation of powers, which means learning to love the gridlock that it sometimes produces. The Framers believed that would be the main protection of minorities—the main protection. If a bill is about to pass that really comes down hard on some minority, so that they think it terribly unfair, it does not take much to throw a monkey wrench into this complex system.

LEGISLATIVE POWER

No Junior-Varsity Congresses—
Mistretta v. United States (1989)

Dissent

The Sentencing Reform Act of 1984 created the U.S. Sentencing Commission and conferred on it the duty to establish binding guidelines to be used by federal judges in determining criminal sentences. By a vote of 8 to 1, the Court ruled that the Sentencing Commission had the constitutional authority to issue the sentencing guidelines. In his dissent, Justice Scalia objected that the Act had made "a pure delegation of legislative power" to the Sentencing Commission and had thereby created a fourth branch of the federal government, "a sort of junior varsity Congress."

While the products of the Sentencing Commission's labors have been given the modest name "Guidelines," they have the force and effect of laws, prescribing the sentences criminal defendants are to receive. A judge who disregards them will be reversed. I dissent from today's decision because I can find no place within our constitutional system for an agency created by Congress to exercise no governmental power other than the making of laws.

Petitioner's most fundamental and far-reaching challenge to the Commission is that Congress's commitment of such broad policy responsibility to any institution is an unconstitutional delegation of legislative power. It is difficult to imagine a principle more essential to democratic government than that upon which the doctrine of unconstitutional delegation is founded: Except in a few areas constitutionally committed to the Executive Branch, the basic policy decisions governing society are to be made by the Legislature.

But while the doctrine of unconstitutional delegation is unquestionably a fundamental element of our constitutional system, it is not an element readily enforceable by the courts. Once it is conceded, as it must be, that no statute can be entirely precise, and that some judgments, even some judgments involving policy considerations, must be left to the officers executing the law and to the judges applying it, the debate over unconstitutional delegation becomes a debate not over a point of principle, but over a question of degree. Since Congress is no less endowed with common sense than we are, and better equipped to inform itself of the "necessities" of government; and since the factors bearing upon those necessities are both multifarious and (in the nonpartisan sense) highly political—including, for example, whether the Nation is at war or whether for other reasons "emergency is instinct in the situation"—it is small wonder that we have almost never felt qualified to second-guess Congress regarding the permissible degree of policy judgment that can be left to those executing or applying the law. As the Court points out, we have invoked the doctrine of unconstitutional delegation to invalidate a law only twice in our history, over half a century ago. What legislated standard, one must wonder, can possibly be too vague to survive judicial scrutiny, when we have repeatedly upheld, in various contexts, a "public interest" standard?

In short, I fully agree with the Court's rejection of petitioner's contention that the doctrine of unconstitutional delegation of legislative authority has been violated because of the lack of intelligible, congressionally prescribed standards to guide the Commission.

Precisely because the scope of delegation is largely uncontrollable by the courts, we must be particularly rigorous in preserving the Constitution's structural restrictions that deter excessive delegation. The major one, it seems to me, is that the power to make law cannot be exercised by anyone other than Congress, except in conjunction with the lawful exercise of executive or judicial power.

The whole theory of *lawful* congressional "delegation" is not that Congress is sometimes too busy or too divided, and can therefore assign its responsibility of making law to someone else; but rather that a certain degree of discretion, and thus of lawmaking, *inheres* in most executive or judicial action, and it is up to Congress, by the relative specificity or generality of its statutory commands, to determine—up to a point—how small or how large that degree shall be. Thus, the courts could be given the power to say precisely what constitutes a "restraint of trade," or to adopt rules of procedure, or to prescribe by rule the manner in which their officers shall execute their judgments because that "lawmaking" was ancillary to their exercise of judicial powers. And the Executive could be given the power to adopt policies and rules specifying in detail what radio and television licenses will be in the "public interest, convenience or necessity," because that was ancillary to the exercise of its executive powers in granting and policing licenses and making a "fair and equitable allocation" of the electromagnetic spectrum. Or, to take examples closer to the case before us: Trial judges could be given the power to determine what factors justify a greater or lesser sentence within the statutorily prescribed limits, because that was ancillary to their exercise of the judicial power of pronouncing sentence upon individual defendants. And the President, through the Parole Commission subject to his appointment and removal, could be given the power to issue Guidelines specifying when parole would be available, because that was ancillary to the President's exercise of the executive power to hold and release federal prisoners.

As Justice Harlan wrote for the Court in *Field v. Clark* (1892):

> The true distinction is between the delegation of power to make the law, which necessarily involves a discretion as to what it shall be, and conferring authority or discretion *as to its execution*, to be exercised under and in pursuance of the law. The first cannot be done; to the latter, no valid objection can be made.

In the present case, however, a pure delegation of legislative power is precisely what we have before us. It is irrelevant whether the standards are adequate, because they are not standards related to the exercise of executive or judicial powers; they are, plainly and simply, standards for further legislation.

The lawmaking function of the Sentencing Commission is completely divorced from any responsibility for execution of the law or adjudication of private rights under the law. It is divorced from responsibility for execution of the law because the Commission neither exercises any executive power on its own, nor is subject to the control of the President, who does. The only functions it performs, apart from prescribing the law, conducting the investigations useful and necessary for prescribing the law, and clarifying the intended application of the law that it prescribes, are data collection and intragovernmental advice-giving and education. These latter activities—similar to functions performed by congressional agencies and even congressional staff—neither determine nor affect private rights, and do not constitute an exercise of governmental power. And the Commission's lawmaking is completely divorced from the exercise of judicial powers since, not being a court, it has no judicial powers itself, nor is it subject to the control of any other body with judicial powers. The power to make law at issue here, in other words, is not ancillary, but quite naked. The situation is no different in principle from what would exist if Congress gave the same power of writing sentencing laws to a congressional agency such as the General Accounting Office, or to members of its staff.

The delegation of lawmaking authority to the Commission is, in short, unsupported by any legitimating theory to explain why it is not a delegation of legislative power.

By reason of today's decision, I anticipate that Congress will find delegation of its lawmaking powers much more attractive in the future. If rulemaking can be entirely unrelated to the exercise of judicial or executive powers, I foresee all manner of "expert" bodies, insulated from the political process, to which Congress will delegate various portions of its lawmaking responsibility. How tempting to create an expert Medical Commission (mostly M.D.'s, with perhaps a few Ph.D.'s in moral philosophy) to dispose of such thorny, "no-win" political issues as the withholding of life-support systems in federally funded hospitals, or the use of fetal tissue for research. This is an undemocratic precedent that we set—not because of the scope of the delegated power, but because its recipient is not one of the three Branches of Government. The only governmental power the Commission possesses is the power to make law; and it is not the Congress.

Today's decision follows the regrettable tendency of our recent separation of powers jurisprudence to treat the Constitution as though it were no more than a generalized prescription that the functions of the Branches should not be commingled too much—how much is too much to be determined, case-by-case, by this Court. The Constitution is not that. Rather, as its name suggests, it is a prescribed structure, a framework, for the conduct of Government. In designing that structure, the Framers themselves considered how much commingling was, in the generality of things, acceptable, and set forth their conclusions in the document. That is the meaning of the statements concerning acceptable commingling made by Madison in defense of the proposed Constitution, and now routinely used as an excuse for disregarding it. When he said, as the Court correctly quotes, that separation of powers "d[oes] not mean that these [three] departments ought to have no *partial agency* in, or no *control* over, the acts of each other," The Federalist No. 47, his point was that the commingling specifically provided for in the structure that he and his colleagues had designed—the Presidential veto over legislation, the Senate's confirmation of executive and judicial officers, the Senate's ratification of treaties, the Congress's power to impeach and remove executive and judicial officers—did not violate a proper understanding of separation of powers. He would be aghast, I think, to hear those words used as justification for ignoring that carefully designed structure so long as, in the changing view of the Supreme Court from time to time, "too much commingling" does not occur. Consideration of the degree of commingling that a particular disposition produces may be appropriate at the margins, where the outline of the framework itself is not clear; but it seems to me far from a marginal question whether our constitutional structure allows for a body which is not the Congress, and yet exercises no governmental powers except the making of rules that have the effect of laws.

I think the Court errs, in other words, not so much because it mistakes the degree of commingling, but because it fails to recognize that this case is not about commingling, but about the creation of a new Branch altogether, a sort of junior varsity Congress. It may well be that, in some circumstances, such a Branch would be desirable;

perhaps the agency before us here will prove to be so. But there are many desirable dispositions that do not accord with the constitutional structure we live under. And, in the long run, the improvisation of a constitutional structure on the basis of currently perceived utility will be disastrous.

The Commerce Clause Is Not *Carte Blanche*— *NFIB v. Sebelius* (2012)

Dissent (jointly authored with Justices Kennedy, Thomas, and Alito)

The constitutional challenges to the health care reform act that President Obama signed into law in 2010—known as the Patient Protection and Affordable Care Act and sometimes referred to as Obamacare—generated a sharply divided ruling by the Court. In this excerpt, Justice Scalia and his fellow dissenters explain their conclusion that Congress lacked constitutional authority to mandate that individuals purchase health insurance.

Congress has set out to remedy the problem that the best health care is beyond the reach of many Americans who cannot afford it. It can assuredly do that, by exercising the powers accorded to it under the Constitution. The question in this case, however, is whether the complex structures and provisions of the Patient Protection and Affordable Care Act go beyond those powers. We conclude that they do.

This case is in one respect difficult: It presents two questions of first impression. The first of those is whether failure to engage in economic activity (the purchase of health insurance) is subject to regulation under the Commerce Clause. Failure to act does result in an effect on commerce, and hence might be said to come under this Court's "affecting commerce" criterion of Commerce Clause jurisprudence. But in none of its decisions has this Court extended the Clause that far. The second question is whether the congressional power to tax and spend permits the conditioning of a State's continued receipt of all funds under a massive state-administered federal welfare program upon its acceptance of an expansion to that program. Several of our opinions have suggested that the power to tax and spend cannot be used to coerce state administration of a federal program, but we have never found a law enacted under the spending power to be coercive. Those questions are difficult.

The case is easy and straightforward, however, in another respect. What is absolutely clear, affirmed by the text of the 1789 Constitution, by the Tenth Amendment ratified in 1791, and by innumerable cases of ours in the 220 years since, is that there are structural limits upon federal power—upon what it can prescribe with respect to private conduct, and upon what it can impose upon the sovereign States. Whatever may be the conceptual limits upon the Commerce Clause and upon the power to tax and spend, they cannot be such as will enable the Federal Government to regulate all private conduct and to compel the States to function as administrators of federal programs.

That clear principle carries the day here. The striking case of *Wickard v. Filburn* (1942), which held that the economic activity of growing wheat, even for one's own consumption, affected commerce sufficiently that it could be regulated, always has been regarded as the *ne plus ultra* of expansive Commerce Clause jurisprudence. To go beyond that, and to say the *failure* to grow wheat (which is *not* an economic activity, or any activity at all) nonetheless affects commerce and therefore can be federally regulated, is to make mere breathing in and out the basis for federal prescription and to extend federal power to virtually all human activity.

Article I, § 8, of the Constitution gives Congress the power to "regulate Commerce . . . among the several States." The Individual Mandate in the Act commands that every "applicable individual shall for each month beginning after 2013 ensure that the individual, and any dependent of the individual who is an applicable individual, is covered under minimum essential coverage." If this provision "regulates" anything, it is the failure to maintain minimum essential coverage. One might argue that it regulates that failure by requiring it to be accompanied by payment of a penalty. But that failure—that abstention from commerce—is not "Commerce." To be sure, *purchasing* insurance is "Commerce"; but one does not regulate commerce that does not exist by compelling its existence.

In *Gibbons v. Ogden* (1824), Chief Justice Marshall wrote that the power to regulate commerce is the power "to prescribe the rule by which commerce is to be governed." That understanding is consistent with the original meaning of "regulate" at the time of the Constitution's ratification, when "to regulate" meant "to adjust by rule, method or established mode," "to adjust by rule or method," "to adjust, to direct according to rule," "to put in order, set to rights, govern or keep in order."[1] It can mean to direct the manner of something but not to direct that something come into being. There is no instance in which this Court or Congress (or anyone else, to our knowledge) has used "regulate" in that peculiar fashion. If the word bore that meaning, Congress's authority "[t]o make Rules for the Government and Regulation of the land and naval Forces" would have made superfluous the later provision for authority "[t]o raise and support Armies" and "[t]o provide and maintain a Navy."

We do not doubt that the buying and selling of health insurance contracts is commerce generally subject to federal regulation. But when Congress provides that (nearly) all citizens must buy an insurance contract, it goes beyond adjusting by rule or method or directing according to rule; it directs the creation of commerce.

The Government presents the Individual Mandate as a unique feature of a complicated regulatory scheme governing many parties with countervailing incentives that must be carefully balanced. Congress has imposed an extensive set of regulations on the health insurance industry, and compliance with those regulations will likely cost the industry a great deal. If the industry does not respond by increasing premiums, it is not likely to survive. And if the industry does increase premiums, then there is a serious risk that its products—insurance plans—will become economically undesirable for many and prohibitively expensive for the rest.

Here, however, Congress has impressed into service third parties, healthy individuals who could be but are not customers of the relevant industry, to offset the undesirable consequences of the regulation. Congress's desire to force these individuals to purchase insurance is motivated by the fact that they are further removed from the market than unhealthy individuals with pre-existing conditions, because they are less likely to need extensive care in the near future. If Congress can reach out and command even those furthest removed from an interstate market to participate in the market, then the Commerce Clause becomes a font of unlimited power, or in Hamilton's words, "the hideous monster whose devouring jaws . . . spare neither sex nor age, nor high nor low, nor sacred nor profane." The Federalist No. 33.

At the outer edge of the commerce power, this Court has insisted on careful scrutiny of regulations that do not act directly on an interstate market or its participants. The lesson of our cases is that the Commerce Clause, even when supplemented by the Necessary and Proper Clause, is not *carte blanche* for doing whatever will help achieve the ends Congress seeks by the regulation of commerce.

EXECUTIVE POWER

This Wolf Comes as a Wolf—
Morrison v. Olson (1988)

Dissent

Justice Scalia's solo dissent in Morrison v. Olson, *at the end of just his second term on the Court and in the face of a majority opinion by Chief Justice William H. Rehnquist, was one of his all-time favorite opinions and provided perhaps the earliest compelling evidence that he would be an extraordinary justice.*

The Ethics in Government Act of 1978 created a special court consisting of three sitting judges designated by the chief justice. It required that the attorney general, upon investigating high-ranking executive-branch officials for violations of federal criminal laws, report to that court whether there were "reasonable grounds to believe that further investigation or prosecution is warranted." When he determined that reasonable grounds did exist, the special court would appoint an "independent counsel" to conduct that further investigation or prosecution and would define the scope of the independent counsel's prosecutorial jurisdiction. Only the attorney general could remove an independent counsel from his position, and only for "good cause."

By a vote of 7 to 1, the Court ruled that the statutory provisions governing the independent counsel did not impermissibly interfere with the president's executive powers under Article II of the Constitution.

A mere decade later, the constitutional wisdom of Scalia's dissent was widely celebrated. Congress chose not to re-authorize the statutory independent-counsel provisions when they expired in 1999. (The Department of Justice instead adopted its own "special counsel" regulations.)

It is the proud boast of our democracy that we have "a government of laws, and not of men." Many Americans are familiar with that phrase; not many know its derivation. It comes from Part the First,

Article XXX, of the Massachusetts Constitution of 1780, which reads in full as follows:

> In the government of this Commonwealth, the legislative department shall never exercise the executive and judicial powers, or either of them: The executive shall never exercise the legislative and judicial powers, or either of them: The judicial shall never exercise the legislative and executive powers, or either of them: to the end it may be a government of laws, and not of men.

The Framers of the Federal Constitution similarly viewed the principle of separation of powers as the absolutely central guarantee of a just government. In No. 47 of The Federalist, Madison wrote that "no political truth is certainly of greater intrinsic value, or is stamped with the authority of more enlightened patrons of liberty." Without a secure structure of separated powers, our Bill of Rights would be worthless, as are the bills of rights of many nations of the world that have adopted, or even improved upon, the mere words of ours.

That is what this suit is about. Power. The allocation of power among Congress, the President, and the courts in such fashion as to preserve the equilibrium the Constitution sought to establish—so that "a gradual concentration of the several powers in the same department," The Federalist No. 51, can effectively be resisted. Frequently an issue of this sort will come before the Court clad, so to speak, in sheep's clothing: the potential of the asserted principle to effect important change in the equilibrium of power is not immediately evident, and must be discerned by a careful and perceptive analysis. But this wolf comes as a wolf.

Article II, § 1, cl. 1, of the Constitution provides: "The executive Power shall be vested in a President of the United States."

This does not mean *some* of the executive power, but *all* of the executive power. It seems to me, therefore, that the decision of the Court of Appeals invalidating the present statute must be upheld on fundamental separation of powers principles if the following two questions are answered affirmatively: (1) Is the conduct of a criminal prosecution (and of an investigation to decide whether to prosecute) the exercise of purely executive power? (2) Does the statute deprive the President of the United States of exclusive control over the exercise of that power?

The independent counsel is vested with the "full power and independent authority to exercise all *investigative and prosecutorial* functions and powers of the Department of Justice [and] the Attorney General."[1] Governmental investigation and prosecution of crimes is a quintessentially executive function.

As for the second question, whether the statute before us deprives the President of exclusive control over that quintessentially executive activity: the Court does not, and could not possibly, assert that it does not. That is indeed the whole object of the statute. Instead, the Court points out that the President, through his Attorney General, has at least *some* control. "Most important" among these controls, the Court asserts, is the Attorney General's "power to remove the counsel for good cause." This is somewhat like referring to shackles as an effective means of locomotion. As we recognized in *Humphrey's Executor v. United States* (1935)—indeed, what *Humphrey's Executor* was all about—limiting removal power to "good cause" is an impediment to, not an effective grant of, Presidential control.

The checks against any branch's abuse of its exclusive powers are twofold: First, retaliation by one of the other branch's use of *its* exclusive powers: Congress, for example, can impeach the executive who willfully fails to enforce the laws; the executive can decline to prosecute under unconstitutional statutes; and the courts can dismiss malicious prosecutions. Second, and ultimately, there is the political check that the people will replace those in the political branches (the branches more "dangerous to the political rights of the Constitution," The Federalist No. 78) who are guilty of abuse. Political pressures produced special prosecutors—for Teapot Dome and for Watergate, for example—long before this statute created the independent counsel.

The Court has, nonetheless, replaced the clear constitutional prescription that the executive power belongs to the President with a "balancing test." What are the standards to determine how the balance is to be struck, that is, how much removal of Presidential power is too much? Many countries of the world get along with an executive that is much weaker than ours—in fact, entirely dependent upon the continued support of the legislature. Once we depart from the text of the Constitution, just where short of that do we stop? The most amazing feature of the Court's opinion is that it does not even purport to give an answer. It simply *announces*, with no analysis, that the ability to control the decision whether to investigate and prosecute the President's closest advisers, and indeed the President himself, is not "so central to the functioning of the Executive Branch" as to be constitutionally required to be within the President's control. Apparently that is so because we say it is so. Having abandoned as the basis for our decisionmaking the text of Article II that "the executive Power" must be vested in the President, the Court does not even attempt to craft a *substitute* criterion—a justiciable standard, however remote from the Constitution—that today governs, and in the future will govern, the decision of such questions. Evidently, the governing standard is to be what might be called the unfettered wisdom of a majority of this Court, revealed to an obedient people on a case-by-case basis. This is not only not the government of laws that the Constitution established; it is not a government of laws at all.

The purpose of the separation and equilibration of powers in general, and of the unitary Executive in particular, was not merely to assure effective government but to preserve individual freedom. Those who hold or have held offices covered by the Ethics in Government Act are entitled to that protection as much as the rest of us, and I conclude my discussion by considering the effect of the Act upon the fairness of the process they receive.

Only someone who has worked in the field of law enforcement can fully appreciate the vast power and the immense discretion that are placed in the hands of a prosecutor with respect to the objects of his investigation. Justice Robert Jackson, when he was Attorney General under President Franklin Roosevelt, described it in a memorable speech to United States Attorneys, as follows:

There is a most important reason why the prosecutor should have, as nearly as possible, a detached and impartial view of all groups in his community. Law enforcement is not automatic. It isn't blind. One of the greatest difficulties of the position of prosecutor is that he must pick his cases, because no prosecutor can even investigate all of the cases in which he receives complaints. If the Department of Justice were to make even a pretense of reaching every probable violation of federal law, ten times its present staff will be inadequate. We know that no local police force can strictly enforce the traffic laws, or it would arrest half the driving population on any given morning. What every prosecutor is practically required to do is to select the cases for prosecution and to select those in which the offense is the most flagrant, the public harm the greatest, and the proof the most certain.

If the prosecutor is obliged to choose his case, it follows that he can choose his defendants. Therein is the most dangerous power of the prosecutor: that he will pick people that he thinks he should get, rather than cases that need to be prosecuted. With the law books filled with a great assortment of crimes, a prosecutor stands a fair chance of finding at least a technical violation of some act on the part of almost anyone. In such a case, it is not a question of discovering the commission of a crime and then looking for the man who has committed it, it is a question of picking the man and then searching the law books, or putting investigators to work, to pin some offense on him. It is in this realm—in which the prosecutor picks some person whom he dislikes or desires to embarrass, or selects some group of unpopular persons and then looks for an offense, that the greatest danger of abuse of prosecuting power lies. It is here that law enforcement becomes personal, and the real crime becomes that of being unpopular with the predominant or governing group, being attached to the wrong political views, or being personally obnoxious to or in the way of the prosecutor himself.

Under our system of government, the primary check against prosecutorial abuse is a political one. The prosecutors who exercise this awesome discretion are selected, and can be removed, by a President whom the people have trusted enough to elect. Moreover, when crimes are not investigated and prosecuted fairly, nonselectively, with a reasonable sense of proportion, the President pays the cost in political damage to his administration. If federal prosecutors pick people that they think they should get, rather than cases that need to be prosecuted, if they amass many more resources against a particular prominent individual, or against a particular class of political protesters, or against members of a particular political party, than the gravity of the alleged offenses or the record of successful prosecutions seems to warrant, the unfairness will come home to roost in the Oval Office. That result, of course, was precisely what the Founders had in mind when they provided that all executive powers would be exercised by a *single* Chief Executive. As Hamilton put it, "the ingredients which constitute safety in the republican sense are a due dependence on the people, and a due responsibility." The President is directly dependent on the people, and, since there is only *one* President, *he* is responsible. The people know whom to blame, whereas "one of the weightiest objections to a plurality in the executive . . . is that it tends to conceal faults and destroy responsibility." The Federalist No. 70.

That is the system of justice the rest of us are entitled to, but what of that select class consisting of present or former high-level Executive Branch officials? If an allegation is made against them of any violation of any federal criminal law (except Class B or C misdemeanors or infractions), the Attorney General must give it his attention. That in itself is not objectionable. But if, after a 90-day investigation without the benefit of normal investigatory tools, the Attorney General is unable to say that there are "no reasonable grounds to believe" that further investigation is warranted, a process is set in motion that is *not* in the full control of persons "dependent on the people," and whose flaws cannot be blamed on the President. An independent counsel is selected, and the scope of his or her authority prescribed, by a panel of judges. What if they are politically partisan, as judges have been known to be, and select a prosecutor antagonistic to the administration, or even to the particular individual who has been selected for this special treatment? There is no remedy for that, not even a political one. Judges, after all, have life tenure, and appointing a surefire enthusiastic prosecutor could hardly be considered an impeachable offense. So if there is anything wrong with the selection, there is effectively no one to blame. The independent counsel thus selected proceeds to assemble a staff. In the nature of things, this has to be done by finding lawyers who are willing to lay aside their current careers for an indeterminate amount of time, to take on a job that has no prospect of permanence and little prospect for promotion. One thing is certain, however: it involves investigating and perhaps prosecuting a particular individual. Can one imagine a less equitable manner of fulfilling the Executive responsibility to investigate and prosecute? What would be the reaction if, in an area not covered by this statute, the Justice Department posted a public notice inviting applicants to assist in an investigation and possible prosecution of a certain prominent person? Does this not invite what Justice Jackson described as "picking the man and then searching the law books, or putting investigators to work, to pin some offense on him"? To be sure, the investigation must relate to the area of criminal offense specified by the life-tenured judges. But that has often been (and nothing prevents it from being) very broad—and should the independent counsel or his or her staff come up with something beyond that scope, nothing prevents him or her from asking the judges to expand his or her authority or, if that does not work, referring it to the Attorney General, whereupon the whole process would recommence and, if there was "reasonable basis to believe" that further investigation was warranted, that new offense would be referred to the Special Division, which would in all likelihood assign it to the same independent counsel. It seems to me not conducive to fairness. But even if it were entirely evident that unfairness was in fact the result— the judges hostile to the administration, the independent counsel an old foe of the President, the staff refugees from the recently defeated administration—*there would be no one accountable to the public to whom the blame could be assigned.*

It is true, of course, that a similar list of horribles could be attributed to an ordinary Justice Department prosecution—a vindictive prosecutor, an antagonistic staff, etc. But the difference is the difference that the Founders envisioned when they established a single Chief Executive accountable to the people: the blame can be assigned to someone who can be punished.

The notion that every violation of law should be prosecuted, including—indeed, *especially*—every violation by those in high places, is an attractive one, and it would be risky to argue in an election campaign that that is not an absolutely overriding value. *Fiat justitia, ruat coelum*. Let justice be done, though the heavens may fall. The reality is, however, that it is not an absolutely overriding value, and it was with the hope that we would be able to acknowledge and apply such realities that the Constitution spared us, by life tenure, the necessity of election campaigns. I cannot imagine that there are not many thoughtful men and women in Congress who realize that the benefits of this legislation are far outweighed by its harmful effect upon our system of government, and even upon the nature of justice received by those men and women who agree to serve in the Executive Branch. But it is difficult to vote not to enact, and even more difficult to vote to repeal, a statute called, appropriately enough, the Ethics in Government Act. If Congress is controlled by the party other than the one to which the President belongs, it has little incentive to repeal it; if it is controlled by the same party, it dare not. By its shortsighted action today, I fear the Court has permanently encumbered the Republic with an institution that will do it great harm.

Worse than what it has done, however, is the manner in which it has done it. A government of laws means a government of rules. Today's decision on the basic issue of fragmentation of executive power is ungoverned by rule, and hence ungoverned by law. It extends into the very heart of our most significant constitutional function the "totality of the circumstances" mode of analysis that this Court has in recent years become fond of. Taking all things into account, we conclude that the power taken away from the President here is not really too much. The next time executive power is assigned to someone other than the President, we may conclude, taking all things into account, that it *is* too much. That opinion, like this one, will not be confined by any rule. We will describe, as we have today (though I hope more accurately) the effects of the provision in question, and will authoritatively announce: "The President's need to control the exercise of the [subject officer's] discretion is so central to the functioning of the Executive Branch as to require complete control."

This is not analysis; it is *ad hoc* judgment. And it fails to explain why it is not true that—as the text of the Constitution seems to require, as the Founders seemed to expect, and as our past cases have uniformly assumed—all purely executive power must be under the control of the President.

JUDICIAL POWER

Against Novel Theories of Standing—
Lujan v. Defenders of Wildlife (1992)

Majority opinion (joined by Chief Justice Rehnquist and Justices White, Kennedy, Souter, and Thomas)*

The doctrine of standing governs who has a sufficient personal stake in a controversy to pursue judicial resolution of the matter. The requirement that a plaintiff in federal court satisfy the standing threshold has long been understood to inhere in the Constitution's specification that the "judicial Power shall extend to" certain types of "Cases" and "Controversies."

Justice Scalia understood the doctrine of standing to be a critical feature of the Constitution's separation of powers. Indeed, a law-review article that he wrote as a D.C. Circuit judge bears the title "The Doctrine of Standing as an Essential Element of the Separation of Powers." In that article, he observed that the federal courts' failure to enforce the traditional limits on who could sue had enmeshed the courts in policy disputes and produced "an overjudicialization of the processes of self-governance."

In this case, organizations dedicated to wildlife conservation and other environmental causes challenged a federal rule interpreting a provision of the Endangered Species Act. By a vote of 6 to 3, the Court ruled that the organizations had failed to demonstrate that the rule injured them and, therefore, the federal courts lacked the constitutional power to address their challenge.

While the Constitution of the United States divides all power conferred upon the Federal Government into "legislative Powers," "the executive Power," and "the judicial Power," it does not attempt to define those terms. To be sure, it limits the jurisdic-

---

* Justices Kennedy and Souter declined to join one sub-part of Justice Scalia's opinion, so there was not a majority for that sub-part. The excerpts here do not include that sub-part.

tion of federal courts to "Cases" and "Controversies," but an executive inquiry can bear the name "case" (the Hoffa case) and a legislative dispute can bear the name "controversy" (the Smoot-Hawley controversy). Obviously, then, the Constitution's central mechanism of separation of powers depends largely upon common understanding of what activities are appropriate to legislatures, to executives, and to courts. In The Federalist No. 48, Madison expressed the view that "it is not infrequently a question of real nicety in legislative bodies whether the operation of a particular measure will, or will not, extend beyond the legislative sphere," whereas "the executive power [is] restrained within a narrower compass and . . . more simple in its nature," and "the judiciary [is] described by landmarks still less uncertain." One of those landmarks, setting apart the "Cases" and "Controversies" that are of the justiciable sort referred to in Article III—"serving to identify those disputes which are appropriately resolved through the judicial process"[1]—is the doctrine of standing. Though some of its elements express merely prudential considerations that are part of judicial self-government, the core component of standing is an essential and unchanging part of the case-or-controversy requirement of Article III.

Over the years, our cases have established that the irreducible constitutional minimum of standing contains three elements. First, the plaintiff must have suffered an "injury in fact"—an invasion of a legally protected interest which is (a) concrete and particularized; and (b) actual or imminent, not conjectural or hypothetical. Second, there must be a causal connection between the injury and the conduct complained of—the injury has to be fairly traceable to the challenged action of the defendant, and not the result of the independent action of some third party not before the court. Third, it must be likely, as opposed to merely speculative, that the injury will be redressed by a favorable decision.

Respondents propose a series of novel standing theories. The first, inelegantly styled "ecosystem nexus," proposes that any person who uses *any part* of a "contiguous ecosystem" adversely affected by a funded activity has standing even if the activity is located a great distance away. This approach, as the Court of Appeals correctly observed, is inconsistent with our opinion in *Lujan v. National Wildlife Federation* (1990), which held that a plaintiff claiming injury from environmental damage must use the area affected by the challenged activity and not an area roughly "in the vicinity" of it.

Respondents' other theories are called, alas, the "animal nexus" approach, whereby anyone who has an interest in studying or seeing the endangered animals anywhere on the globe has standing; and the "vocational nexus" approach, under which anyone with a professional interest in such animals can sue. Under these theories, anyone who goes to see Asian elephants in the Bronx Zoo, and anyone who is a keeper of Asian elephants in the Bronx Zoo, has standing to sue because the Director of the Agency for International Development (AID) did not consult with the Secretary regarding the AID-funded project in Sri Lanka. This is beyond all reason. Standing is not "an ingenious academic exercise in the conceivable,"[2] but as we have said requires, at the summary judgment stage, a factual showing of perceptible harm. It is clear that the person who observes or works with a particular animal threatened by a federal decision is facing perceptible harm, since the very subject of his interest will no longer exist. It is even plausible—though it goes to the outermost limit of plausibility—to think that a person who observes or works with animals of a particular species in the very area of the world where that species is threatened by a federal decision is facing such harm, since some animals that might have been the subject of his interest will no longer exist. It goes beyond the limit, however, and into pure speculation and fantasy, to say that anyone who observes or works with an endangered species, anywhere in the world, is appreciably harmed by a single project affecting some portion of that species with which he has no more specific connection.

We have consistently held that a plaintiff raising only a generally available grievance about government—claiming only harm to his and every citizen's interest in proper application of the Constitution and laws, and seeking relief that no more directly and tangibly benefits him than it does the public at large—does not state an Article III case or controversy.

"The province of the court," as Chief Justice Marshall said in

Marbury v. Madison (1803), "is, solely, to decide on the rights of individuals." Vindicating the *public* interest (including the public interest in Government observance of the Constitution and laws) is the function of Congress and the Chief Executive. The question presented here is whether the public interest in proper administration of the laws (specifically, in agencies' observance of a particular, statutorily prescribed procedure) can be converted into an individual right by a statute that denominates it as such, and that permits all citizens (or, for that matter, a subclass of citizens who suffer no distinctive concrete harm) to sue. If the concrete injury requirement has the separation-of-powers significance we have always said, the answer must be obvious: To permit Congress to convert the undifferentiated public interest in executive officers' compliance with the law into an individual right vindicable in the courts is to permit Congress to transfer from the President to the courts the Chief Executive's most important constitutional duty, to "take Care that the Laws be faithfully executed," Art. II, § 3. It would enable the courts, with the permission of Congress, "to assume a position of authority over the governmental acts of another and co-equal department"[3] and to become "virtually continuing monitors of the wisdom and soundness of Executive action."[4] We have always rejected that vision of our role.

Final Judgments Are Really Final—
Plaut v. Spendthrift Farm (1995)

Majority opinion (joined by Chief Justice Rehnquist and Justices O'Connor, Kennedy, Souter, and Thomas)

Just as the Constitution's separation of powers is meant to prevent the federal courts from encroaching on the processes of self-government, so also it protects them from wrongful intrusions by the political branches.

In 1987, Ed and Nancy Plaut sued Spendthrift Farm for alleged violations of federal securities laws. In 1991, the district court, relying on a just-issued Supreme Court ruling in the case of Lampf, Pleva, Lipkind, Prupis & Petigrow v. Gilbertson, *dismissed their suit for failure to comply with the applicable statute of limitations. The Plauts did not appeal that dismissal. Shortly after the judgment against them became final, Congress enacted a law that contained a provision—section 27A(b)—that commanded district courts to reinstate cases that had been dismissed on the basis of the ruling in* Lampf. *The Plauts then sought to revive their suit.*

By a vote of 7 to 2,* the Court ruled that section 27A(b), by commanding the federal courts to reopen judgments that had become final, violated the constitutional separation of powers.

We conclude that in § 27A(b) Congress has exceeded its authority by requiring the federal courts to exercise "[t]he judicial Power of the United States" in a manner repugnant to the text, structure, and traditions of Article III.

Our decisions to date have identified two types of legislation that require federal courts to exercise the judicial power in a manner that Article III forbids. The first appears in *United States v. Klein* (1872), where we refused to give effect to a statute that was said "to prescribe

---

* Justice Breyer concurred in the judgment.

rules of decision to the Judicial Department of the government in cases pending before it." Whatever the precise scope of *Klein*, however, later decisions have made clear that its prohibition does not take hold when Congress "amends applicable law."[1] Section 27A(b) indisputably does set out substantive legal standards for the Judiciary to apply, and in that sense changes the law (even if solely retroactively). The second type of unconstitutional restriction upon the exercise of judicial power identified by past cases is exemplified by *Hayburn's Case* (1792), which stands for the principle that Congress cannot vest review of the decisions of Article III courts in officials of the Executive Branch. Yet under any application of § 27A(b) only courts are involved; no officials of other departments sit in direct review of their decisions. Section 27A(b) therefore offends neither of these previously established prohibitions.

We think, however, that § 27A(b) offends a postulate of Article III just as deeply rooted in our law as those we have mentioned. Article III establishes a "judicial department" with the "province and duty . . . to say what the law is" in particular cases and controversies. *Marbury v. Madison* (1803). The record of history shows that the Framers crafted this charter of the judicial department with an expressed understanding that it gives the Federal Judiciary the power, not merely to rule on cases, but to *decide* them, subject to review only by superior courts in the Article III hierarchy—with an understanding, in short, that "a judgment conclusively resolves the case" because "a 'judicial Power' is one to render dispositive judgments."[2] By retroactively commanding the federal courts to reopen final judgments, Congress has violated this fundamental principle.

The Framers of our Constitution lived among the ruins of a system of intermingled legislative and judicial powers, which had been prevalent in the colonies long before the Revolution, and which after the Revolution had produced factional strife and partisan oppression. In the 17th and 18th centuries colonial assemblies and legislatures functioned as courts of equity of last resort, hearing original actions or providing appellate review of judicial judgments. Often, however, they chose to correct the judicial process through special bills or other enacted legislation. It was common for such legislation not to prescribe a resolution of the dispute, but rather simply to set aside the judgment and order a new trial or appeal.

The vigorous, indeed often radical, populism of the revolutionary legislatures and assemblies increased the frequency of legislative correction of judgments. Voices from many quarters, official as well as private, decried the increasing legislative interference with the private-law judgments of the courts.

This sense of a sharp necessity to separate the legislative from the judicial power, prompted by the crescendo of legislative interference with private judgments of the courts, triumphed among the Framers of the new Federal Constitution. The Convention made the critical decision to establish a judicial department independent of the Legislative Branch by providing that "the judicial Power of the United States shall be vested in one supreme Court, and in such inferior Courts as the Congress may from time to time ordain and establish." Before and during the debates on ratification, Madison, Jefferson, and Hamilton each wrote of the factional disorders and disarray that the system of legislative equity had produced in the years before the Framing; and each thought that the separation of the legislative from the judicial power in the new Constitution would cure them.

If the need for separation of legislative from judicial power was plain, the principal effect to be accomplished by that separation was even plainer. As Hamilton wrote in his exegesis of Article III, § 1, in The Federalist No. 81:

> It is not true . . . that the parliament of Great Britain, or the legislatures of the particular states, can rectify the exceptionable decisions of their respective courts, in any other sense than might be done by a future legislature of the United States. The theory neither of the British, nor the state constitutions, authorises the revisal of a judicial sentence, by a legislative act. . . . A legislature without exceeding its province cannot reverse a determination once made, in a particular case; though it may prescribe a new rule for future cases.

The essential balance created by this allocation of authority was a simple one. The Legislature would be possessed of power to "prescrib[e] the rules by which the duties and rights of every citizen are to be regulated," but the power of "[t]he interpretation of the laws" would be "the proper and peculiar province of the courts." The Judiciary would be, "from the nature of its functions, . . . the [department] least dangerous to the political rights of the constitution," not because its acts were subject to legislative correction, but because the binding effect of its acts was limited to particular cases and controversies. Thus, "though individual oppression may now and then proceed from the courts of justice, the general liberty of the people can never be endangered from that quarter . . . so long as the judiciary remains truly distinct from both the legislative and executive." The Federalist No. 78.

Section 27A(b) effects a clear violation of the separation-of-powers principle we have just discussed. It is, of course, retroactive legislation, that is, legislation that prescribes what the law *was* at an earlier time, when the act whose effect is controlled by the legislation occurred. When retroactive legislation requires its own application in a case already finally adjudicated, it does no more and no less than "reverse a determination once made, in a particular case."

It is true that Congress can always revise the judgments of Article III courts in one sense: When a new law makes clear that it is retroactive, an appellate court must apply that law in reviewing judgments still on appeal that were rendered before the law was enacted, and must alter the outcome accordingly. But a distinction between judgments from which all appeals have been forgone or completed, and judgments that remain on appeal (or subject to being appealed), is implicit in what Article III creates: not a batch of unconnected courts, but a judicial *department* composed of "inferior Courts" and "one supreme Court." Within that hierarchy, the decision of an inferior court is not (unless the time for appeal has expired) the final word of the department as a whole. It is the obligation of the last court in the hierarchy that rules on the case to give effect to Congress's latest enactment, even when that has the effect of overturning the judgment of an inferior court, since each court, at every level, must "decide according to existing laws."[3] Having achieved finality, however, a judicial decision becomes the last word of the judicial department with regard to a particular case or controversy, and Congress may not declare by retroactive legislation that the law applicable *to that very case* was something other than what the courts said it was.

Political Gerrymandering—*Vieth v. Jubelirer* (2004)

Plurality opinion* (joined by Chief Justice Rehnquist and Justices O'Connor and Thomas)

For decades, the Supreme Court tried to determine whether the federal courts have a role to play in reviewing political gerrymandering. In Davis v. Bandemer *(1986), the Court held that claims of excessive political gerrymandering are justiciable (i.e., can be decided by the courts) under the Constitution, but the justices could not agree on a standard for adjudicating those claims. In this case eighteen years later, a plurality of the Court, led by Justice Scalia, took the view that* Bandemer *should be overruled and that political gerrymandering claims are not justiciable.*

In 2019—three years after Justice Scalia's death—a majority of the Court (in Rucho v. Common Cause*) adopted Justice Scalia's reasoning in* Vieth *and rejected the notion that the federal courts have any business deciding how much political gerrymandering is "too much."*

Political gerrymanders are not new to the American scene. One scholar traces them back to the Colony of Pennsylvania at the beginning of the 18th century, where several counties conspired to minimize the political power of the city of Philadelphia by refusing to allow it to merge or expand into surrounding jurisdictions, and denying it additional representatives. And in 1812, of course, there occurred the notoriously outrageous political districting in Massachusetts that gave the gerrymander its name—an amalgam of the names of Massachusetts Governor Elbridge Gerry and the creature ("salamander") which the outline of an election district he was credited with forming was thought to resemble. "By 1840 the gerrymander was a recognized force in party politics and was generally

---

* In a case in which no single opinion garners the support of a majority of the justices, the opinion that earns the most votes in support of the Court's bottom-line decision to affirm or reverse the lower court is denominated the plurality opinion.

attempted in all legislation enacted for the formation of election districts. It was generally conceded that each party would attempt to gain power which was not proportionate to its numerical strength."[1]

It is significant that the Framers provided a remedy for such practices in the Constitution. Article I, § 4, while leaving in state legislatures the initial power to draw districts for federal elections, permitted Congress to "make or alter" those districts if it wished.

As Chief Justice Marshall proclaimed two centuries ago, "it is emphatically the province and duty of the judicial department to say what the law is." *Marbury v. Madison* (1803). Sometimes, however, the law is that the judicial department has no business entertaining the claim of unlawfulness—because the question is entrusted to one of the political branches or involves no judicially enforceable rights. "The judicial Power" created by Article III, § 1, of the Constitution is not *whatever* judges choose to do. It is the power to act in the manner traditional for English and American courts. One of the most obvious limitations imposed by that requirement is that judicial action must be governed by *standard*, by *rule*. Laws promulgated by the Legislative Branch can be inconsistent, illogical, and ad hoc; law pronounced by the courts must be principled, rational, and based upon reasoned distinctions.

Eighteen years of judicial effort with virtually nothing to show for it justify us in revisiting the question whether the standard promised by *Bandemer* exists. No judicially discernible and manageable standards for adjudicating political gerrymandering claims have emerged. Lacking them, we must conclude that political gerrymandering claims are nonjusticiable.

Appellants take a run at enunciating their own workable standard based on Article I, § 2, and the Equal Protection Clause. We consider it at length not only because it reflects the litigant's view as to the best that can be derived from 18 years of experience, but also because it shares many features with other proposed standards, so that what is said of it may be said of them as well. Appellants' proposed standard retains the two-pronged framework of the *Bandemer* plurality— intent plus effect—but modifies the type of showing sufficient to satisfy each.

To satisfy appellants' intent standard, a plaintiff must "show that the mapmakers acted with a *predominant intent* to achieve partisan advantage," which can be shown "by direct evidence or by circumstantial evidence that other neutral and legitimate redistricting criteria were subordinated to the goal of achieving partisan advantage."

"Predominant intent" to disadvantage the plaintiff's political group refers to the relative importance of that goal as compared with all the other goals that the map seeks to pursue—contiguity of districts, compactness of districts, observance of the lines of political subdivision, protection of incumbents of all parties, cohesion of natural racial and ethnic neighborhoods, compliance with requirements of the Voting Rights Act of 1965 regarding racial distribution, etc. Appellants contend that their intent test *must* be discernible and manageable because it has been borrowed from our racial gerrymandering cases.

Applying a "predominant intent" test to *racial* gerrymandering is easier and less disruptive. The Constitution clearly contemplates districting by political entities, see Article I, § 4, and unsurprisingly that turns out to be root-and-branch a matter of politics. By contrast, the purpose of segregating voters on the basis of race is not a lawful one, and is much more rarely encountered. Determining whether the shape of a particular district is so substantially affected by the presence of a rare and constitutionally suspect motive as to invalidate it is quite different from determining whether it is so substantially affected by the excess of an ordinary and lawful motive as to invalidate it. Moreover, the fact that partisan districting is a lawful and common practice means that there is almost *always* room for an election-impeding lawsuit contending that partisan advantage was the predominant motivation; not so for claims of racial gerrymandering. Finally, courts might be justified in accepting a modest degree of unmanageability to enforce a constitutional command which (like the Fourteenth Amendment obligation to refrain from racial discrimination) is clear; whereas they are not justified in inferring a judicially enforceable constitutional obligation (the obligation not to apply *too much* partisanship in districting) which is both dubious and severely unmanageable.

The effects prong of appellants' proposal is loosely based on our cases applying § 2 of the Voting Rights Act to discrimination by race. But a person's politics is rarely as readily discernible—and *never* as permanently discernible—as a person's race. Political affiliation is not an immutable characteristic, but may shift from one election to the next; and even within a given election, not all voters follow the party line. We dare say (and hope) that the political party which puts forward an utterly incompetent candidate will lose even in its registration stronghold. These facts make it impossible to assess the effects of partisan gerrymandering, to fashion a standard for evaluating a violation, and finally to craft a remedy.

Assuming, however, that the effects of partisan gerrymandering can be determined, appellants' test would invalidate the districting only when it prevents a majority of the electorate from electing a majority of representatives. Before considering whether this particular standard is judicially manageable we question whether it is judicially discernible in the sense of being relevant to some constitutional violation. Deny it as appellants may (and do), this standard rests upon the principle that groups (or at least political-action groups) have a right to proportional representation. But the Constitution contains no such principle. It guarantees equal protection of the law to persons, not equal representation in government to equivalently sized groups. It nowhere says that farmers or urban dwellers, Christian fundamentalists or Jews, Republicans or Democrats, must be accorded political strength proportionate to their numbers.

Even if the standard were relevant, however, it is not judicially manageable. To begin with, how is a party's majority status to be established? Appellants propose using the results of statewide races as the benchmark of party support. But as their own complaint describes, in the 2000 Pennsylvania statewide elections some Republicans won and some Democrats won. Moreover, to think that majority status in statewide races establishes majority status for district contests, one would have to believe that the only factor determining voting behavior at all levels is political affiliation. That is assuredly not true.

But if we could identify a majority party, we would find it impossible to ensure that that party wins a majority of seats—unless we radically revise the States' traditional structure for elections. In any winner-take-all district system, there can be no guarantee, no matter how the district lines are drawn, that a majority of party votes state-wide will produce a majority of seats for that party. The point is proved by the 2000 congressional elections in Pennsylvania, which, according to appellants' own pleadings, were conducted under a ju-dicially drawn district map "free from partisan gerrymandering." On this "neutral playing field," the Democrats' statewide majority of the major-party vote (50.6%) translated into a minority of seats (10, ver-sus 11 for the Republicans). Whether by reason of partisan districting or not, party constituents may always wind up "packed" in some dis-tricts and "cracked" throughout others. Consider, for example, a leg-islature that draws district lines with no objectives in mind except compactness and respect for the lines of political subdivisions. Under that system, political groups that tend to cluster (as is the case with Democratic voters in cities) would be systematically affected by what might be called a "natural" packing effect.

Eighteen years of essentially pointless litigation have persuaded us that *Bandemer* is incapable of principled application. We would there-fore overrule that case, and decline to adjudicate these political ger-rymandering claims.

FEDERALISM

The Constitution's horizontal separation of powers among the three federal branches provides one essential structural protection of liberty. Federalism—the Constitution's vertical separation of powers between the federal government and state governments—provides another.

The Two Faces of Federalism

Federalism is usually thought of as preserving the realm in which state governments may act. But, as then-Professor Antonin Scalia explained in this speech, it also requires recognition of the federal government's proper authorities.

Scalia presented this speech at the Federalist Society's first national symposium, held at Yale Law School in the spring of 1982.[1] Months later, President Reagan appointed Scalia to the D.C. Circuit.

When I began to prepare some thoughts for this conference on federalism, I got out my handy *vade mecum* copy of the *Federalist Papers* to see what they might have to say about the subject. In reading the relevant portions, I found that they were not talking about what I expected this group to be addressing. In fact it was quite clear that if a resurrected and updated Alexander Hamilton had been invited to this conference, the subjects he would have expected to hear addressed are quite different from—and the tenor of his own remarks would have been quite the opposite of—what we have heard over the past few days.

The underlying explanation for this duality of meaning in the word "federalism" is expressed in a vaudeville routine which many of you may know. The straight line is "How's your wife?" and the response is "Compared to what?" That question, "Compared to what?," is important in all the affairs of life, not excluding federalism. In meeting to discuss federalism, we have to bear in mind that it is a form of government midway between two extremes. At one extreme, the autonomy, the disunity, the conflict of independent states; at the other, the uniformity, the inflexibility, the monotony of one centralized government. Federalism is meant to be a compromise between the two. As such, it is a stick that can be used to beat either dog. When Alexander Hamilton exalted its virtues, he meant it as a criticism of colonial disunity; we mean it today—in this group, at least—as a criticism of central control.

Conservatives have tended to take this non-Hamiltonian perspective for at least the past half century, opposing the national government's intervention and extolling the benefits of state and local control. It is interesting to speculate why this is so. One reason, perhaps, is simply an unthinking extension of notions of natural autonomy that are quite appropriate with regard to the power of the state over the individual into the quite different field of the priority of one coercive governmental unit over another. The individual possesses, as the Declaration of Independence points out, a God-given freedom, which rightly counsels an attitude of suspicion if not hostility toward novel impositions of governmental constraint. By contrast, no particular governmental or authoritarian unit can claim any natural right to rule—except, perhaps, the family, whose rights our law has generally protected through the individuals who compose it. The decision concerning which level of government should have the last word is, therefore, a pragmatic one, to be determined by the practicalities of the matter. To be sure, decision at a lower level of government tends to maximize overall satisfaction, by permitting diversity instead of submerging large regional majorities beneath a narrow national vote. But that is a practical rather than a transcendental concern, to be laid beside other practical concerns such as the need for national rather than local enforcement of certain prescriptions. It justifies a predisposition toward state and local control—but not, I think, the degree of generalized hostility toward national law which has become a common feature of conservative thought.

A better reason for conservatives' antagonism toward federalism (in the Hamiltonian sense) is the fact that conservatives have simply been out-gunned at the federal level for half a century. Since the 1930s, the policies that have come from that source have been policies that conservatives disfavor. That is surely an understandable tactical reason for opposition to the exercise of federal power. Unfortunately, a tactic employed for half a century tends to develop into a philosophy. And an anti-federalist philosophy on the part of conservatives seems to me simply wrong. The result of it is that conservatives have been fighting a two-front war on only one front—or at least fighting it purely defensively on one of the two fronts. When liberals are in power, they do not shrink from using the federal structure for what they consider to be sound governmental goals. But when conservatives take charge, the most they hope to do is to keep anything from happening. I understand that in some of the offices of the current administration there are signs on the wall that read, "Don't just stand there; undo something." That seems to me an inadequate approach.

Consider, for example, economic regulation—an area in which it is clear that the Founding Fathers meant the federal government to restrain the centrifugal tendencies of the states. Conservatives believe that the free market has the ability to order things in the most efficient manner, and should generally be allowed to operate free of government intervention. That is a *positive* policy, not the absence of one. Yet I do not know a single federal statute that seeks to enact that policy. Numerous laws impose federal regulation to some degree and then go on to say, "and the States will not interfere," but I know of no federal statute that simply says, "the States shall not regulate." To the extent that such a policy has been imposed, it has been by the courts through the negative Commerce Clause. (I do not happen to think that a good idea—but that is another question.) Why does it not even occur to those who believe strongly in a policy of market freedom to have it adopted by federal legislation in those segments of the economy that are truly national? Let me mention a few areas where one would at least expect this to be debated.

Anyone from a city that has recently gotten "wired" knows of the extraordinary exactions that are imposed upon cable by municipalities. Competing applicants for the franchise are set to out-bidding one another in the promise of "freebies" (although, as we know, someone is paying for them). They offer "free" channels for the schools, "free" channels for the city council, "free" channels for public access, and much more. I do not think the most dyed-in-the-wool anti-federalist among you would deny that the federal government has *power* to establish the regulatory environment for cable—which is, realistically, part of an interstate delivery system that brings information and entertainment from the production studios of New York and California to the individual home. And there are, indeed, proposals that various national restrictions be placed upon cable operations; but I am unaware of any proposed federal requirement that cable be—in one respect or another—simply left alone.

The administration floated a proposal some time back (I do not know what happened to it) to deny federal housing funds to cities with rent controls. The theory was that cities should not be paid to remedy a housing shortage that is largely of their own creation. But if the theory is correct, and if local housing is the federal government's proper concern, then why has no one even *floated* a federal law that says, "no rent controls" period?

I could multiply the areas in which one would expect economic conservatives to seek establishment of a federal policy excluding state regulation: The prohibition in some building codes of construction materials that are universally recognized to be safe, and whose only sin is that they are not labor-intensive. State-court creation of new tort theories of "enterprise liability" or of design defect which subject interstate businesses to greatly increased damages. State antitrust laws which permit treble-damage actions by indirect purchasers that the federal antitrust law has been held to exclude. State "anti-escape" laws that penalize (through the obligation to compensate workers) businesses that choose to close plants and move to another state.

I am not suggesting that federal action barring state regulation would be a good thing in all of these fields. In some, it seems to me, the national power exists, but the national interest is not sufficient to justify intervention. The point I wish to make, however, is that with all these targets out there—and with what has generally been regarded as a conservative economic mood in Washington—one would have expected at least a few targets to be shot at. The inaction has less to do with the merits than with the unfortunate tendency of conservatives to regard the federal government, at least in its purely domestic activities, as something to be resisted, or better yet (when conservatives are in power) undone, rather than as a legitimate and useful instrument of policy. Such an attitude is ultimately self-defeating, since it converts the instrument into a tool that cuts only one way.

I urge you, then—as Hamilton would have urged you—to keep in mind that the federal government is not bad but good. The trick is to use it wisely.

Our System of Dual Sovereignty—
Printz v. United States (1997)

Majority opinion (joined by Chief Justice Rehnquist and Justices O'Connor, Kennedy, and Thomas)

Some of the provisions of the Brady Handgun Violence Prevention Act, enacted in 1993, required state and local law enforcement officers to conduct background checks on prospective handgun purchasers and to perform certain related tasks. Law enforcement officers from counties in Montana and Arizona challenged the provisions. By a vote of 5 to 4, the Court, in a majority opinion by Justice Scalia, ruled that Congress may not command state officers to administer or enforce a federal regulatory program.

It is incontestible that the Constitution established a system of dual sovereignty. Although the States surrendered many of their powers to the new Federal Government, they retained "a residuary and inviolable sovereignty." The Federalist No. 39. This is reflected throughout the Constitution's text, including (to mention only a few examples) the prohibition on any involuntary reduction or combination of a State's territory, Art. IV, § 3; the Judicial Power Clause, Art. III, § 2, and the Privileges and Immunities Clause, Art. IV, § 2, which speak of the "Citizens" of the States; the amendment provision, Article V, which requires the votes of three-fourths of the States to amend the Constitution; and the Guarantee Clause, Art. IV, § 4, which "presupposes the continued existence of the states and . . . those means and instrumentalities which are the creation of their sovereign and reserved rights."[1] Residual state sovereignty was also implicit, of course, in the Constitution's conferral upon Congress of not all governmental powers, but only discrete, enumerated ones, Art. I, § 8, which implication was rendered express by the Tenth Amendment's assertion that "[t]he powers not delegated to the

United States by the Constitution, nor prohibited by it to the States, are reserved to the States respectively, or to the people."

The Framers' experience under the Articles of Confederation had persuaded them that using the States as the instruments of federal governance was both ineffectual and provocative of federal-state conflict. Preservation of the States as independent political entities being the price of union, and "the practicality of making laws, with coercive sanctions, for the States as political bodies" having been, in Madison's words, "exploded on all hands,"[2] the Framers rejected the concept of a central government that would act upon and through the States, and instead designed a system in which the State and Federal Governments would exercise concurrent authority over the people—who were, in Hamilton's words, "the only proper objects of government." The Federalist No. 15. We have set forth the historical record in more detail elsewhere, and need not repeat it here. It suffices to repeat the conclusion: "the Framers explicitly chose a Constitution that confers upon Congress the power to regulate individuals, not States."[3] The great innovation of this design was that "our citizens would have two political capacities, one state and one federal, each protected from incursion by the other"—"a legal system unprecedented in form and design, establishing two orders of government, each with its own direct relationship, its own privity, its own set of mutual rights and obligations to the people who sustain it and are governed by it."[4] The Constitution thus contemplates that a State's government will represent and remain accountable to its own citizens. As Madison expressed it: "the local or municipal authorities form distinct and independent portions of the supremacy, no more subject, within their respective spheres, to the general authority than the general authority is subject to them, within its own sphere." The Federalist No. 39.

This separation of the two spheres is one of the Constitution's structural protections of liberty. "Just as the separation and independence of the coordinate branches of the Federal Government serve to prevent the accumulation of excessive power in any one branch, a healthy balance of power between the States and the Federal Government will reduce the risk of tyranny and abuse from either front."5 To quote Madison once again:

> In the compound republic of America, the power surrendered by the people is first divided between two distinct governments, and then the portion allotted to each subdivided among distinct and separate departments. Hence a double security arises to the rights of the people. The different governments will control each other, at the same time that each will be controlled by itself. [The Federalist No. 51.]

The power of the Federal Government would be augmented immeasurably if it were able to impress into its service—and at no cost to itself—the police officers of the 50 States.

We have thus far discussed the effect that federal control of state officers would have upon the first element of the "double security" alluded to by Madison: the division of power between State and Federal Governments. It would also have an effect upon the second element: the separation and equilibration of powers between the three branches of the Federal Government itself. The Constitution does not leave to speculation who is to administer the laws enacted by Congress; the President, it says, "shall take Care that the Laws be faithfully executed," Art. II, § 3, personally and through officers whom he appoints (save for such inferior officers as Congress may authorize to be appointed by the "Courts of Law" or by "the Heads of Departments" who are themselves Presidential appointees), Art. II, § 2. The Brady Act effectively transfers this responsibility to thousands of CLEOs* in the 50 States, who are left to implement the program without meaningful Presidential control (if indeed meaningful Presidential control is possible without the power to appoint and remove). The insistence of the Framers upon unity in the Federal Executive—to ensure both vigor and accountability—is well known. That unity would be shattered, and the power of the President would

---

* Chief law enforcement officers.

be subject to reduction, if Congress could act as effectively without the President as with him, by simply requiring state officers to execute its laws.

The Federal Government may neither issue directives requiring the States to address particular problems, nor command the States' officers, or those of their political subdivisions, to administer or enforce a federal regulatory program. It matters not whether policymaking is involved, and no case-by-case weighing of the burdens or benefits is necessary; such commands are fundamentally incompatible with our constitutional system of dual sovereignty.

There Is No Dormant Commerce Clause—
Comptroller of Treasury of Maryland v. Wynne (2015)

Dissent (joined by Justice Thomas)

Although the Commerce Clause of the Constitution provides only that "Congress shall have Power . . . To regulate Commerce with foreign Nations, and among the several States, and with the Indian Tribes," the Court has long read into the Commerce Clause an additional command that, in the absence of congressional action, prohibits state actions that discriminate against interstate commerce. In this case, the Court held, by a vote of 5 to 4, that a feature of Maryland's income-tax system violated the "dormant" or "negative" Commerce Clause. Justice Scalia disagreed.

The fundamental problem with our negative Commerce Clause cases is that the Constitution does not contain a negative Commerce Clause. It contains only a Commerce Clause. Unlike the negative Commerce Clause adopted by the judges, the real Commerce Clause adopted by the People merely empowers Congress to "regulate Commerce with foreign Nations, and among the several States, and with the Indian Tribes." The Clause says nothing about prohibiting state laws that burden commerce. Much less does it say anything about authorizing judges to set aside state laws *they believe* burden commerce. The clearest sign that the negative Commerce Clause is a judicial fraud is the utterly illogical holding that congressional consent enables States to enact laws that would otherwise constitute impermissible burdens upon interstate commerce. How could congressional consent lift a constitutional prohibition?

The Court's efforts to justify this judicial economic veto come to naught. The Court claims that the doctrine "has deep roots." So it does, like many weeds. But age alone does not make up for brazen invention. And the doctrine in any event is not quite as old as the Court makes it seem. The idea that the Commerce Clause of its own

force limits state power "finds no expression" in discussions surrounding the Constitution's ratification.[1] For years after the adoption
of the Constitution, States continually made regulations that burdened interstate commerce (like pilotage laws and quarantine laws)
without provoking any doubts about their constitutionality. This
Court's earliest allusions to a negative Commerce Clause came only
in dicta*—ambiguous dicta, at that—and were vigorously contested
at the time. Our first clear *holding* setting aside a state law under the
negative Commerce Clause came after the Civil War, more than 80
years after the Constitution's adoption. Since then, we have tended
to revamp the doctrine every couple of decades upon finding existing decisions unworkable or unsatisfactory. The negative Commerce
Clause applied today has little in common with the negative Commerce Clause of the 19th century, except perhaps for incoherence.

The failings of negative Commerce Clause doctrine go beyond its
lack of a constitutional foundation, as today's decision well illustrates.

One glaring defect of the negative Commerce Clause is its lack of
governing principle. Neither the Constitution nor our legal traditions offer guidance about how to separate improper state interference with commerce from permissible state taxation or regulation of
commerce. So we must make the rules up as we go along. That is
how we ended up with the bestiary of ad hoc tests and ad hoc exceptions that we apply nowadays, including the substantial nexus test,
the fair apportionment test, and the fair relation test, the interest-on-
state-bonds exception, and the sales-taxes-on-mail-orders exception.

Another conspicuous feature of the negative Commerce Clause is
its instability. Because no principle anchors our development of this
doctrine—and because the line between wise regulation and burden-
some interference changes from age to economic age—one can never
tell when the Court will make up a new rule or throw away an old
one.

A final defect of our Synthetic Commerce Clause cases is their

---

* The term *dicta*, the plural of *dictum*, is drawn from the Latin phrase *obiter dictum*, meaning
"said in passing," and refers to parts of an opinion that are not integral to the reasoning supporting the holding.

incompatibility with the judicial role. The doctrine does not call upon us to perform a conventional judicial function, like interpreting a legal text, discerning a legal tradition, or even applying a stable body of precedents. It instead requires us to balance the needs of commerce against the needs of state governments. That is a task for legislators, not judges.*

---

* In the final part of his dissent, Justice Scalia stated that "for reasons of *stare decisis*" he would nonetheless "vote to set aside a tax under the negative Commerce Clause if (but only if) it discriminates on its face against interstate commerce or cannot be distinguished from a tax this Court has already held unconstitutional." Justice Thomas declined to join this part of the dissent.

Civil Liberties

———

This section concerns the civil liberties set forth in the Bill of Rights and the Fourteenth Amendment. On disputes concerning free speech, religion, abortion, guns, and many other issues, this section contains many of the majority opinions and dissents for which Justice Scalia is most widely known.

The field of civil liberties is arguably where a judge's temptation to ignore or re-write legal text in order to achieve what the judge regards as just is strongest. In A Matter of Interpretation,[1] *Justice Scalia explained that the case-law method of education in American law schools invites future judges to indulge this temptation, as it indoctrinates them early on into thinking that judging "consists of playing common-law judge, which in turn consists of playing king—devising, out of the brilliance of one's own mind, those laws that ought to govern mankind." As he memorably put it:*

This system of making law by judicial opinion, and making law by distinguishing earlier cases, is what every American law student, every newborn American lawyer, first sees when he opens his eyes. And the impression remains for life. His image of the great judge—the Holmes, the Cardozo—is the man (or woman) who has the intelligence to discern the best rule of law for the case at hand and then the skill to perform the broken-field running through earlier cases that leaves him free to impose that rule: distinguishing one prior case on the left, straight-arming another one on the right, high-stepping away from another precedent about to tackle him from the rear, until (bravo!) he reaches the goal— good law. That image of the great judge remains with the former law student when he himself becomes a judge, and thus the common-law tradition is passed on.

But, Justice Scalia argues, the mind-set of the common-law judge is ill suited to the task of discerning the meaning of constitutional text and, indeed, "frustrates the whole purpose of a written constitution."

FREE SPEECH

The Freedom of Speech

In March 2012, in his Hugo L. Black Lecture on Freedom of Expression at Wesleyan University, Justice Scalia explained how the originalist approach to constitutional interpretation applies to the Free Speech Clause of the First Amendment.

Let me explain how to apply originalist methodology to the speech guarantee of the First Amendment. I start where originalists always start: with the text. "Congress shall make no law . . . abridging the freedom of speech, or of the press." A good example of how originalist and non-originalist interpretations differ can be seen by applying this text to laws providing causes of action for libel. There is no doubt that at the time it was adopted in 1791 no one thought that this provision invalidated laws against libel—which existed then and have continued to exist ever since. The issue is an easy one for originalists: libel laws are constitutional. The famous case of *New York Times v. Sullivan* (1964), much beloved by the press, is a classic example of non-originalist interpretation. That case held that suit would not lie for libel of a public figure, unless the libel was in bad faith—that is, with knowledge, or reason to know, that it was false. There is no doubt that libel of a public figure was unprotected by the First Amendment in 1791 (and it remains unprotected speech, by the way, in England). But the Warren Court determined, as the Framers had not, that allowing good-faith libel of public figures would be good for democracy, and so the First Amendment was revised accordingly.

Justice Hugo Black voted along with the majority in that case, though he would have gone even further to say that *no* libel, not even bad-faith libel, was outside the scope of "the freedom of speech." Here are a few excerpts from his opinion:

I vote to reverse exclusively on the ground that the *Times* and the individual defendants had an absolute, unconditional constitutional right to publish in the *Times* advertisement their criticisms of the Montgomery agencies and officials. State libel laws threaten the very existence of an American press virile enough to publish unpopular views on public affairs and bold enough to criticize the conduct of public officials. In my opinion, the Federal Constitution has dealt with this deadly danger to the press in the only way possible without leaving the press open to destruction—by granting the press an absolute immunity for criticism of the way public officials do their public duty.

How Justice Black arrived at this view is summed up in an interview he gave in 1962:

I am for the First Amendment from the first word to the last. I believe it means what it says, and it says to me, "Government shall keep its hands off religion. Government shall not attempt to control the ideas a man has. Government shall not attempt to establish a religion of any kind. Government shall not abridge freedom of the press or speech. It shall let anybody talk in this country."

As I said earlier, originalists are textualists—they begin with the text. So you might expect me to agree with Justice Black. But the flaw in his reasoning is that the First Amendment does *not* say that government shall not abridge freedom of speech. It says that government shall not abridge "*the* freedom of speech"—that is, that freedom of speech which was the understood right of Englishmen. Thus, there are several types of speech or categories of speech unprotected by the First Amendment because the Framing generation never understood them to fall within "the freedom of speech." Libel is one of them. Another is obscenity. Justice Black would not acknowledge that exception either. He wrote in one dissenting opinion:

In my view the First Amendment denies Congress the power to act as censor and determine what books our citizens may read and what pictures they may watch. But for the foreseeable future this Court must sit as a Board of Supreme Censors, sifting through books and magazines and watching movies because some official fears they deal too explicitly with sex. I can imagine no more distasteful, useless, and time-consuming task for the members of this Court than perusing this material to determine whether it has "redeeming social value." This absurd spectacle could be avoided if we would adhere to the literal command of the First Amendment that "Congress shall make no law . . . abridging the freedom of speech, or of the press."

Now, I agree with Justice Black that it is "distasteful, useless, and time-consuming" for the Court to sort through obscene materials deciding what should and should not be allowed. But it is non-originalist jurisprudence that has made this a difficult chore, by adding to the requirement that the material appeal to a prurient interest in sex the requirements that it do so "as a whole," that it "portray sexual conduct in a patently offensive way," and that "taken as a whole, it not have serious literary, artistic, political, or scientific value." In any case, it is only Justice Black's "literal" reading of the First Amendment (which as I have said is not really very literal) that enables him to avoid the difficulty.

There are other examples of speech that is unprotected by the First Amendment because "the freedom of speech" was not understood to cover it. Incitement to violence and fighting words, for example. Other speech, such as criminal conspiracy and solicitation or fraud, has not yet come before my court in a First Amendment case, but since these forms of speech have long been criminalized without serious First Amendment challenge, I doubt we would find that the First Amendment was understood to protect them.

Under an originalist approach, not only is speech unprotected at the Founding unprotected today, but speech *protected* at the Founding *remains* protected today. Exemplifying that point is a recent Supreme Court case, *Brown v. Entertainment Merchants Association*, which involved a California law restricting the sale or rental of violent video games to minors. First, the Court (in an opinion I wrote) re-affirmed the principle I mentioned earlier, that "the basic principles of freedom of speech do not vary" with a new and different communication medium. Next it noted that the First Amendment excludes from its protection certain limited categories of historically unprotected speech, such as obscenity, incitement, and fighting words. But speech about violence was not among those historically unprotected categories. The California legislature was not free to create its own new category of unprotected speech—speech about violence—by weighing the value of such speech against its social costs. That balance was already struck by the Founding generation, and we are not free to re-weigh it on a continual basis. The California statute was invalid.

Thus far, I have spoken mostly about the original meaning of "the freedom of speech," but even in free-speech cases, that is not the only part of the First Amendment that the originalist approach helps elucidate. In some of those cases, it may be fairly easy to determine that the speech at issue is protected by the First Amendment but much harder to tell whether the government has *abridged* that freedom. In *National Endowment for the Arts v. Finley*, a majority of my court made things very difficult for itself in upholding as constitutional a federal statute that allowed government subsidies only for art that was determined to be decent and in line with American values. The court engaged in what I considered extreme mental and linguistic gymnastics to conclude that the law did not discriminate against artists based on the viewpoint expressed in their art. For me, that vote was much easier. Of course the law discriminated based on the views expressed by the artist! And if the National Endowment for the Arts had been deciding whether to fine or punish the artists, the law would certainly have been unconstitutional. But instead, the NEA was deciding only whether the artists should receive *government subsidies* for their work. When the Bill of Rights was passed, as now, *to abridge* meant "to contract, to diminish; to deprive of." Simply put, when the government decides not to pay you for your speech, it is not *abridging* the freedom of speech within the meaning of the First Amendment.

Peaceful Speech Outside Abortion Clinics—
Hill v. Colorado (2000)

Dissent *(joined by Justice Thomas)*

A statute enacted in Colorado in 1993 impaired the ability of pro-life "sidewalk counselors" to use the streets and sidewalks near abortion clinics to communicate with women and girls entering the clinics. The Supreme Court ruled by a 6–3 vote that the statute did not violate the First Amendment rights of the sidewalk counselors. Justice Scalia strongly objected to the Court's holding.

The Court today concludes that a regulation requiring speakers on the public thoroughfares bordering medical facilities to speak from a distance of eight feet is "not a regulation of speech," but "a regulation of the places where some speech may occur," and that a regulation directed to only certain categories of speech (protest, education, and counseling) is not "content-based." For these reasons, it says, the regulation is immune from the exacting scrutiny we apply to content-based suppression of speech in the public forum. The Court then determines that the regulation survives the less rigorous scrutiny afforded content-neutral time, place, and manner restrictions because it is narrowly tailored to serve a government interest—protection of citizens' "right to be let alone"—that has explicitly been disclaimed by the State, probably for the reason that, as a basis for suppressing peaceful private expression, it is patently incompatible with the guarantees of the First Amendment.

None of these remarkable conclusions should come as a surprise. What is before us, after all, is a speech regulation directed against the opponents of abortion, and it therefore enjoys the benefit of the "ad hoc nullification machine"[1] that the Court has set in motion to push aside whatever doctrines of constitutional law stand in the way of that highly favored practice. Having deprived abortion opponents of the political right to persuade the electorate that abortion should be restricted by law, the Court today continues and expands its assault upon their individual right to persuade women contemplating abortion that what they are doing is wrong.

Colorado's statute makes it a criminal act knowingly to approach within 8 feet of another person on the public way or sidewalk area within 100 feet of the entrance door of a health care facility for the purpose of passing a leaflet to, displaying a sign to, or engaging in oral protest, education, or counseling with such person. Whatever may be said about the restrictions on the other types of expressive activity, the regulation as it applies to oral communications is obviously and undeniably content-based. A speaker wishing to approach another for the purpose of communicating *any* message except one of protest, education, or counseling may do so without first securing the other's consent. Whether a speaker must obtain permission before approaching within eight feet—and whether he will be sent to prison for failing to do so—depends entirely on *what he intends to say* when he gets there. I have no doubt that this regulation would be deemed content-based *in an instant* if the case before us involved anti-war protesters, or union members seeking to "educate" the public about the reasons for their strike. "It is," we would say, "the content of the speech that determines whether it is within or without the statute's blunt prohibition." But the jurisprudence of this Court has a way of changing when abortion is involved.

"The vice of content-based legislation—what renders it deserving of the high standard of strict scrutiny—is not that it is always used for invidious, thought-control purposes, but that it lends itself to use for those purposes."[2] A restriction that operates only on speech that communicates a message of protest, education, or counseling presents exactly this risk. When applied, as it is here, at the entrance to medical facilities, it is a means of impeding speech against abortion. The Court's confident assurance that the statute poses no special threat to First Amendment freedoms because it applies alike to "used car salesmen, animal rights activists, fundraisers, environmentalists, and missionaries" is a wonderful replication (except for its lack of sarcasm) of Anatole France's observation that "The law, in its majestic equality, forbids the rich as well as the poor to sleep under bridges." This Colorado law is no more targeted at used car salesmen, animal rights activists, fundraisers, environmentalists, and missionaries than French vagrancy law was targeted at the rich. We know what the Colorado legislators, by their careful selection of content ("protest, education, and counseling"), were taking aim at, for they set it forth in the statute itself: the "right to protest or counsel *against* certain medical procedures" on the sidewalks and streets surrounding health care facilities.

It blinks reality to regard this statute, in its application to oral communications, as anything other than a content-based restriction upon speech in the public forum. As such, it must survive that stringent mode of constitutional analysis our cases refer to as "strict scrutiny," which requires that the restriction be narrowly tailored to serve a compelling state interest. Since the Court does not even attempt to support the regulation under this standard, I shall discuss it only briefly. Suffice it to say that if protecting people from unwelcome communications (the governmental interest the Court posits) is a compelling state interest, the First Amendment is a dead letter. And if forbidding peaceful, nonthreatening, but uninvited speech from a distance closer than eight feet is a "narrowly tailored" means of preventing the obstruction of entrance to medical facilities (the governmental interest the State asserts), narrow tailoring must refer not to the standards of Versace, but to those of Omar the tentmaker.

The Court purports to derive from our cases a principle limiting the protection the Constitution affords the speaker's right to direct "offensive messages" at "unwilling" audiences in the public forum. There is no such principle. We have upheld limitations on a speaker's exercise of his right to speak on the public streets *when that speech intrudes into the privacy of the home. Frisby v. Schultz* (1988) upheld a content-neutral municipal ordinance prohibiting picketing outside a residence or dwelling. The ordinance, we concluded, was justified by, and narrowly tailored to advance, the government's interest in the "protection of residential privacy." Our opinion rested upon the "unique nature of the home"; "the home," we said, "is different." The Court today elevates the abortion clinic to the status of the home.

The public forum involved here—the public spaces outside of health care facilities—has become, by necessity and by virtue of this Court's decisions, a forum of last resort for those who oppose abortion. The possibility of limiting abortion by legislative means—even abortion of a live-and-kicking child that is almost entirely out of the womb—has been rendered impossible by our decisions from *Roe v. Wade* (1973) to *Stenberg v. Carhart* (2000).* For those who share an abiding moral or religious conviction (or, for that matter, simply a biological appreciation) that abortion is the taking of a human life, there is no option but to persuade women, one by one, not to make that choice. And as a general matter, the most effective place, if not the only place, where that persuasion can occur, is outside the entrances to abortion facilities. By upholding these restrictions on speech in this place the Court ratifies the State's attempt to make even that task an impossible one.

Those whose concern is for the physical safety and security of clinic patients, workers, and doctors should take no comfort from today's decision. Individuals or groups intent on bullying or frightening women out of an abortion, or doctors out of performing that procedure, will not be deterred by Colorado's statute; bullhorns and screaming from eight feet away will serve their purposes well. But those who would accomplish their moral and religious objectives by peaceful and civil means, by trying to persuade individual women of the rightness of their cause, will be deterred; and that is not a good thing in a democracy. This Court once recognized, as the Framers surely did, that the freedom to speak and persuade is inseparable from, and antecedent to, the survival of self-government. The Court today rotates that essential safety valve on our democracy one-half turn to the right, and no one who seeks safe access to health care facilities in Colorado or elsewhere should feel that her security has by this decision been enhanced.

Does the deck seem stacked? You bet. As I have suggested throughout this opinion, today's decision is not an isolated distortion

---

* In *Stenberg v. Carhart*, issued the same day as *Hill v. Colorado*, the Court ruled by a vote of 5 to 4 that a state ban on partial-birth abortion violated the Constitution.

of our traditional constitutional principles, but is one of many aggressively proabortion novelties announced by the Court in recent years. Today's distortions, however, are particularly blatant. Restrictive views of the First Amendment that have been in dissent since the 1930s suddenly find themselves in the majority. "Uninhibited, robust, and wide open" debate is replaced by the power of the state to protect an unheard-of "right to be let alone" on the public streets. I dissent.

Political Speech of Corporations—
Austin v. Michigan Chamber of Commerce (1990)

Dissent

A Michigan law prohibited corporations (other than media corporations) from using general corporate funds for independent expenditures for or against any candidate in elections for state office. By a vote of 6 to 3, the Supreme Court ruled that the law did not violate the First Amendment rights of the Michigan Chamber of Commerce (a nonprofit corporation). In addition to joining Justice Kennedy's dissent, Justice Scalia issued his own dissent.

"Attention all citizens. To assure the fairness of elections by preventing disproportionate expression of the views of any single powerful group, your Government has decided that the following associations of persons shall be prohibited from speaking or writing in support of any candidate: _____." In permitting Michigan to make private corporations the first object of this Orwellian announcement, the Court today endorses the principle that too much speech is an evil that the democratic majority can proscribe. I dissent because that principle is contrary to our case law and incompatible with the absolutely central truth of the First Amendment: that government cannot be trusted to assure, through censorship, the "fairness" of political debate.

The Court's opinion says that political speech of corporations can be regulated because "state law grants [them] special advantages" and because this "unique state-conferred corporate structure . . . facilitates the amassing of large treasuries." This analysis seeks to create one good argument by combining two bad ones. Those individuals who form that type of voluntary association known as a corporation are, to be sure, given special advantages—notably, the immunization of their personal fortunes from liability for the actions of the association—that the State is under no obligation to confer. But so are other associations and private individuals given all sorts of special advantages that the State need not confer, ranging from tax breaks to contract awards to public employment to outright cash subsidies. It is rudimentary that the State cannot exact as the price of those special advantages the forfeiture of First Amendment rights. The categorical suspension of the right of any person, or of any association of persons, to speak out on political matters must be justified by a compelling state need. That is why the Court puts forward its second bad argument, the fact that corporations "amass large treasuries." But that alone is also not sufficient justification for the suppression of political speech, unless one thinks it would be lawful to prohibit men and women whose net worth is above a certain figure from endorsing political candidates. Neither of these two flawed arguments is improved by combining them and saying, as the Court in effect does, that "since the State gives special advantages to these voluntary associations, and since they thereby amass vast wealth, they may be required to abandon their right of political speech."

Perhaps the Michigan law before us here has an unqualifiedly noble objective—to "equalize" the political debate by preventing disproportionate expression of corporations' points of view. But governmental abridgment of liberty is always undertaken with the very best of announced objectives (dictators promise to bring order, not tyranny), and often with the very best of genuinely intended objectives (zealous policemen conduct unlawful searches in order to put dangerous felons behind bars). The premise of our Bill of Rights, however, is that there are some things—even some seemingly *desirable* things—that government cannot be trusted to do. The very first of these is establishing the restrictions upon speech that will assure "fair" political debate. The incumbent politician who says he welcomes full and fair debate is no more to be believed than the entrenched monopolist who says he welcomes full and fair competition. Perhaps the Michigan Legislature was genuinely trying to assure a "balanced" presentation of political views; on the other hand, perhaps it was trying to give unincorporated unions (a not insubstantial force in Michigan) political advantage over major employers. Or perhaps it was trying to assure a "balanced" presentation because it knows that with evenly balanced speech incumbent officeholders generally win. The fundamental approach of the First Amendment, I had always thought, was to assume the worst, and to rule the regulation of political speech "for fairness' sake" simply out of bounds.

Despite all the talk about "corruption and the appearance of corruption"—evils that are not significantly implicated and that can be avoided in many other ways—it is entirely obvious that the object of the law we have approved today is not to prevent wrongdoing but to prevent speech. Since those private associations known as corporations have so much money, they will speak so much more, and their views will be given inordinate prominence in election campaigns. This is not an argument that our democratic traditions allow— neither with respect to individuals associated in corporations nor with respect to other categories of individuals whose speech may be "unduly" extensive (because they are rich) or "unduly" persuasive (because they are movie stars) or "unduly" respected (because they are clergymen). The premise of our system is that there is no such thing as too much speech—that the people are not foolish but intelligent, and will separate the wheat from the chaff. As conceded in Lincoln's aphorism about fooling "all of the people some of the time," that premise will not invariably accord with reality; but it will assuredly do so much more frequently than the premise the Court today embraces: that a healthy democratic system can survive the legislative power to prescribe how much political speech is too much, who may speak, and who may not.

The Right to Criticize the Government—
McConnell v. Federal Election Commission (2003)

Dissent

The Bipartisan Campaign Reform Act of 2002 (more commonly known as McCain-Feingold) made numerous changes to existing federal campaign-finance law. In a complicated set of opinions totaling nearly 300 pages, a five-justice majority of the Supreme Court rejected most of the constitutional challenges to the provisions of the Act. Justice Scalia broadly dissented from these holdings.

This is a sad day for the freedom of speech. Who could have imagined that the same Court which, within the past four years, has sternly disapproved of restrictions upon such inconsequential forms of expression as virtual child pornography, tobacco advertising, dissemination of illegally intercepted communications, and sexually explicit cable programming would smile with favor upon a law that cuts to the heart of what the First Amendment is meant to protect: the right to criticize the government. For that is what the most offensive provisions of this legislation are all about. We are governed by Congress, and this legislation prohibits the criticism of Members of Congress by those entities most capable of giving such criticism loud voice: national political parties and corporations, both of the commercial and the not-for-profit sort. It forbids pre-election criticism of incumbents by corporations, even not-for-profit corporations, by use of their general funds; and forbids national-party use of "soft" money to fund "issue ads" that incumbents find so offensive.

To be sure, the legislation is evenhanded: It similarly prohibits criticism of the candidates who oppose Members of Congress in their reelection bids. But as everyone knows, this is an area in which evenhandedness is not fairness. If *all* electioneering were evenhandedly prohibited, incumbents would have an enormous advantage.

Likewise, if incumbents and challengers are limited to the same quantity of electioneering, incumbents are favored. In other words, *any* restriction upon a type of campaign speech that is equally available to challengers and incumbents tends to favor incumbents.

Beyond that, however, the present legislation *targets* for prohibition certain categories of campaign speech that are particularly harmful to incumbents. Is it accidental, do you think, that incumbents raise about three times as much "hard money"—the sort of funding generally *not* restricted by this legislation—as do their challengers? Or that lobbyists (who seek the favor of incumbents) give 92 percent of their money in "hard" contributions? Is it an oversight, do you suppose, that the so-called "millionaire provisions" raise the contribution limit for a candidate running against an individual who devotes to the campaign (as challengers often do) great personal wealth, but do not raise the limit for a candidate running against an individual who devotes to the campaign (as incumbents often do) a massive election "war chest"? And is it mere happenstance, do you estimate, that national-party funding, which is severely limited by the Act, is more likely to assist cash-strapped challengers than flush-with-hard-money incumbents? Was it unintended, by any chance, that incumbents are free personally to receive some soft money and even to solicit it for other organizations, while national parties are not?

Today's cavalier attitude toward regulating the financing of speech frustrates the fundamental purpose of the First Amendment. In any economy operated on even the most rudimentary principles of division of labor, effective public communication requires the speaker to make use of the services of others. An author may write a novel, but he will seldom publish and distribute it himself. A freelance reporter may write a story, but he will rarely edit, print, and deliver it to subscribers. To a government bent on suppressing speech, this mode of organization presents opportunities: Control any cog in the machine, and you can halt the whole apparatus. License printers, and it matters little whether authors are still free to write. Restrict the sale of books, and it matters little who prints them. Predictably, repressive regimes have exploited these principles by attacking all levels of the production and dissemination of ideas.

Division of labor requires a means of mediating exchange, and in a commercial society, that means is supplied by money. The publisher pays the author for the right to sell his book; it pays its staff who print and assemble the book; it demands payments from booksellers who bring the book to market. This, too, presents opportunities for repression: Instead of regulating the various parties to the enterprise individually, the government can suppress their ability to coordinate by regulating their use of money. What good is the right to print books without a right to buy works from authors? Or the right to publish newspapers without the right to pay deliverymen? The right to speak would be largely ineffective if it did not include the right to engage in financial transactions that are the incidents of its exercise.

This is not to say that *any* regulation of money is a regulation of speech. The government may apply general commercial regulations to those who use money for speech if it applies them evenhandedly to those who use money for other purposes. But where the government singles out money used to fund speech as its legislative object, it is acting against speech as such, no less than if it had targeted the paper on which a book was printed or the trucks that deliver it to the bookstore.

It should be obvious, then, that a law limiting the amount a person can spend to broadcast his political views is a direct restriction on speech. That is no different from a law limiting the amount a newspaper can pay its editorial staff or the amount a charity can pay its leafletters. It is equally clear that a limit on the amount a candidate can *raise* from any one individual for the purpose of speaking is also a direct limitation on speech. That is no different from a law limiting the amount a publisher can accept from any one shareholder or lender, or the amount a newspaper can charge any one advertiser or customer.

Another proposition which could explain at least some of the results of today's opinion is that the First Amendment right to spend money for speech does not include the right to combine with others in spending money for speech. Such a proposition fits uncomfortably with the concluding words of our Declaration of Independence: "And for the support of this Declaration, . . . we mutually pledge to each other our Lives, *our Fortunes* and our sacred Honor." (Emphasis added.) The freedom to associate with others for the dissemination of ideas—not just by singing or speaking in unison, but by pooling financial resources for expressive purposes—is part of the freedom of speech.

If it were otherwise, Congress would be empowered to enact legislation requiring newspapers to be sole proprietorships, banning their use of partnership or corporate form. That sort of restriction would be an obvious violation of the First Amendment, and it is incomprehensible why the conclusion should change when what is at issue is the pooling of funds for the most important (and most perennially threatened) category of speech: electoral speech. The principle that such financial association does not enjoy full First Amendment protection threatens the existence of all political parties.

The last proposition that might explain at least some of today's casual abridgment of free-speech rights is this: that the particular form of association known as a corporation does not enjoy full First Amendment protection. Of course the text of the First Amendment does not limit its application in this fashion, even though "by the end of the eighteenth century the corporation was a familiar figure in American economic life."[1] Nor is there any basis in reason why First Amendment rights should not attach to corporate associations—and we have said so. In *First National Bank of Boston v. Bellotti* (1978), we held unconstitutional a state prohibition of corporate speech designed to influence the vote on referendum proposals. We said:

> There is practically universal agreement that a major purpose of [the First] Amendment was to protect the free discussion of governmental affairs. If the speakers here were not corporations, no one would suggest that the State could silence their proposed speech. It is the type of speech indispensable to decisionmaking in a democracy, and this is no less true because the speech comes from a corporation rather than an individual. The inherent worth

of the speech in terms of its capacity for informing the public does not depend upon the identity of its source, whether corporation, association, union, or individual.

In *NAACP v. Button* (1963), we held that the NAACP could assert First Amendment rights "on its own behalf, . . . though a corporation," and that the activities of the corporation were "modes of expression and association protected by the First and Fourteenth Amendments." In *Pacific Gas & Electric Co. v. Public Utilities Commission of California* (1986), we held unconstitutional a state effort to compel corporate speech. "The identity of the speaker," we said, "is not decisive in determining whether speech is protected. Corporations and other associations, like individuals, contribute to the discussion, debate, and the dissemination of information and ideas that the First Amendment seeks to foster."

In the modern world, giving the government power to exclude corporations from the political debate enables it effectively to muffle the voices that best represent the most significant segments of the economy and the most passionately held social and political views. People who associate—who pool their financial resources—for purposes of economic enterprise overwhelmingly do so in the corporate form; and with increasing frequency, incorporation is chosen by those who associate to defend and promote particular ideas—such as the American Civil Liberties Union and the National Rifle Association, parties to these cases. Imagine, then, a government that wished to suppress nuclear power—or oil and gas exploration, or automobile manufacturing, or gun ownership, or civil liberties—and that had the power to prohibit corporate advertising against its proposals. To be sure, the individuals involved in, or benefited by, those industries, or interested in those causes, could (given enough time) form political action committees or other associations to make their case. But the organizational form in which those enterprises already *exist*, and in which they can most quickly and most effectively get their message across, is the corporate form. The First Amendment does not in my view permit the restriction of that political speech. And the same holds true for corporate electoral speech: A candidate should not be insulated from the most effective speech that the major participants in the economy and major incorporated interest groups can generate.

But what about the danger to the political system posed by "amassed wealth"? The most direct threat from that source comes in the form of undisclosed favors and payoffs to elected officials—which have already been criminalized, and will be rendered no more discoverable by the legislation at issue here. The use of corporate wealth (like individual wealth) to speak to the electorate is unlikely to "distort" elections—*especially* if disclosure requirements *tell* the people where the speech is coming from. The premise of the First Amendment is that the American people are neither sheep nor fools, and hence fully capable of considering both the substance of the speech presented to them and its proximate and ultimate source. If that premise is wrong, our democracy has a much greater problem to overcome than merely the influence of amassed wealth. Given the premises of democracy, there is no such thing as *too much* speech.

It cannot be denied, however, that corporate (like noncorporate) allies will have greater access to the officeholder, and that he will tend to favor the same causes as those who support him (which is usually *why* they supported him). That is the nature of politics—if not indeed human nature—and how this can properly be considered "corruption" (or "the appearance of corruption") with regard to corporate allies and not with regard to other allies is beyond me. If the Bill of Rights had intended an exception to the freedom of speech in order to combat this malign proclivity of the officeholder to agree with those who agree with him, and to speak more with his supporters than his opponents, it would surely have said so. It did not do so, I think, because the juice is not worth the squeeze. Evil corporate (and private affluent) influences are well enough checked (so long as adequate campaign-expenditure disclosure rules exist) by the politician's fear of being portrayed as "in the pocket" of so-called moneyed interests. The incremental benefit obtained by muzzling corporate speech is more than offset by loss of the information and persuasion that corporate speech can contain. That, at least, is the assumption of a constitutional guarantee which prescribes that Congress shall make no law abridging the freedom of speech.

But let us not be deceived. While the Government's briefs and arguments before this Court focused on the horrible "appearance of corruption," the most passionate floor statements during the debates on this legislation pertained to so-called attack ads, which the Constitution surely protects, but which Members of Congress analogized to "crack cocaine," "drive-by shootings," and "air pollution." There is good reason to believe that the ending of negative campaign ads was the principal attraction of the legislation. A Senate sponsor said, "I hope that we will not allow our attention to be distracted from the real issues at hand—how to raise the tenor of the debate in our elections and give people real choices. No one benefits from negative ads. They don't aid our Nation's political dialog." He assured the body that "you cut off the soft money, you are going to see a lot less of that [attack ads]. Prohibit unions and corporations, and you will see a lot less of that. If you demand full disclosure for those who pay for those ads, you are going to see a lot less of that."

Which brings me back to where I began: This litigation is about preventing criticism of the government. I cannot say for certain that many, or some, or even any, of the Members of Congress who voted for this legislation did so not to produce "fairer" campaigns, but to mute criticism of their records and facilitate reelection. Indeed, I will stipulate that all those who voted for [this law] believed they were acting for the good of the country. There remains the problem of the Charlie Wilson Phenomenon, named after Charles Wilson, former president of General Motors, who is supposed to have said during the Senate hearing on his nomination as Secretary of Defense that "what's good for General Motors is good for the country." Those in power, even giving them the benefit of the greatest good will, are inclined to believe that what is good for them is good for the country.

The first instinct of power is the retention of power, and, under a Constitution that requires periodic elections, that is best achieved by the suppression of election-time speech. We have witnessed merely the second scene of Act I of what promises to be a lengthy tragedy.

In scene 3 the Court, having abandoned most of the First Amendment weaponry that *Buckley* left intact, will be even less equipped to resist the incumbents' writing of the rules of political debate. The federal election campaign laws, which are already (as today's opinions show) so voluminous, so detailed, so complex, that no ordinary citizen dare run for office, or even contribute a significant sum, without hiring an expert adviser in the field, can be expected to grow more voluminous, more detailed, and more complex in the years to come—and always, always, with the objective of reducing the excessive amount of speech.

Political Patronage—*Rutan v. Republican Party of Illinois* (1990)

Dissent (joined by Chief Justice Rehnquist and Justice Kennedy)*

In 1980, Illinois governor James Thompson ordered a hiring freeze in the state agencies under his control. Any exceptions to the hiring freeze required the governor's express permission. Individuals who believed that they had suffered from the hiring freeze sued. They claimed that the governor was basing his exceptions to the hiring freeze on whether an applicant supported the Republican Party and that the resulting system of political patronage violated their First Amendment rights.

By a 5–4 vote, the Supreme Court ruled that the First Amendment bars a government entity from basing hiring and promotion decisions for low-level employees on party affiliation or support.

Today the Court establishes the constitutional principle that party membership is not a permissible factor in the dispensation of government jobs, except those jobs for the performance of which party affiliation is an "appropriate requirement." It is hard to say precisely (or even generally) what that exception means, but if there is any category of jobs for whose performance party affiliation is not an appropriate requirement, it is the job of being a judge, where partisanship is not only unneeded but positively undesirable. It is, however, rare that a federal administration of one party will appoint a judge from another party. And it has always been rare. Thus, the new principle that the Court today announces will be enforced by a corps of judges (the Members of this Court included) who overwhelmingly owe their office to its violation. Something must be wrong here, and I suggest it is the Court.

The merit principle for government employment is probably the

---

* Justice O'Connor joined other parts of the dissent.

most favored in modern America, having been widely adopted by civil service legislation at both the state and federal levels. But there is another point of view, described in characteristically Jacksonian fashion by an eminent practitioner of the patronage system, George Washington Plunkitt of Tammany Hall:

> I ain't up on sillygisms, but I can give you some arguments that nobody can answer.
>
> First, this great and glorious country was built up by political parties; second, parties can't hold together if their workers don't get offices when they win; third, if the parties go to pieces, the government they built up must go to pieces, too; fourth, then there'll be hell to pay.

It may well be that the Good Government Leagues of America were right, and that Plunkitt, James Michael Curley, and their ilk were wrong; but that is not entirely certain. As the merit principle has been extended and its effects increasingly felt; as the Boss Tweeds, the Tammany Halls, the Pendergast Machines, the Byrd Machines, and the Daley Machines have faded into history; we find that political leaders at all levels increasingly complain of the helplessness of elected government, unprotected by "party discipline," before the demands of small and cohesive interest groups.

The choice between patronage and the merit principle—or, to be more realistic about it, the choice between the desirable mix of merit and patronage principles in widely varying federal, state, and local political contexts—is not so clear that I would be prepared, as an original matter, to chisel a single, inflexible prescription into the Constitution.

The provisions of the Bill of Rights were designed to restrain transient majorities from impairing long-recognized personal liberties. They did not create by implication novel individual rights overturning accepted political norms. Thus, when a practice not expressly prohibited by the text of the Bill of Rights bears the endorsement of a long tradition of open, widespread, and unchallenged use that dates back to the beginning of the Republic, we have no proper basis for striking it down. Such a venerable and accepted tradition is not to be laid on the examining table and scrutinized for its conformity to some abstract principle of First Amendment adjudication devised by this Court. To the contrary, such traditions are themselves the stuff out of which the Court's principles are to be formed. They are, in these uncertain areas, the very points of reference by which the legitimacy or illegitimacy of *other* practices is to be figured out. When it appears that the latest "rule," or "three-part test," or "balancing test" devised by the Court has placed us on a collision course with such a landmark practice, it is the former that must be recalculated by us, and not the latter that must be abandoned by our citizens. I know of no other way to formulate a constitutional jurisprudence that reflects, as it should, the principles adhered to, over time, by the American people, rather than those favored by the personal (and necessarily shifting) philosophical dispositions of a majority of this Court.

Violent Video Games—*Brown v. Entertainment Merchants Association* (2011)

Majority opinion (joined by Justices Kennedy, Ginsburg, Sotomayor, and Kagan)

A California law enacted in 2005 prohibited the sale or rental of "violent video games" to minors. The Supreme Court ruled by a vote of 7 to 2* that the law violated the First Amendment.

We consider whether a California law imposing restrictions on violent video games comports with the First Amendment.

The Free Speech Clause exists principally to protect discourse on public matters, but we have long recognized that it is difficult to distinguish politics from entertainment, and dangerous to try. "Everyone is familiar with instances of propaganda through fiction. What is one man's amusement, teaches another's doctrine."[1] Like the protected books, plays, and movies that preceded them, video games communicate ideas—and even social messages—through many familiar literary devices (such as characters, dialogue, plot, and music) and through features distinctive to the medium (such as the player's interaction with the virtual world). That suffices to confer First Amendment protection. Under our Constitution, "esthetic and moral judgments about art and literature are for the individual to make, not for the Government to decree, even with the mandate or approval of a majority."[2] And whatever the challenges of applying the Constitution to ever-advancing technology, "the basic principles of freedom of speech and the press, like the First Amendment's command, do not vary" when a new and different medium for communication appears.[3]

---

* Justice Alito, joined by Chief Justice Roberts, wrote an opinion concurring in the judgment. Justice Thomas and Justice Breyer filed separate dissents.

The most basic of those principles is this: "As a general matter, government has no power to restrict expression because of its message, its ideas, its subject matter, or its content."[4] There are of course exceptions. "From 1791 to the present, the First Amendment has permitted restrictions upon the content of speech in a few limited areas, and has never included a freedom to disregard these traditional limitations."[5] These limited areas—such as obscenity, incitement, and fighting words—represent "well-defined and narrowly limited classes of speech, the prevention and punishment of which have never been thought to raise any Constitutional problem."[6]

California wishes to create a wholly new category of content-based regulation that is permissible only for speech directed at children. No doubt a State possesses legitimate power to protect children from harm, but that does not include a free-floating power to restrict the ideas to which children may be exposed. California's argument would fare better if there were a longstanding tradition in this country of specially restricting children's access to depictions of violence, but there is none. Certainly the *books* we give children to read—or read to them when they are younger—contain no shortage of gore. Grimm's Fairy Tales, for example, are grim indeed. As her just deserts for trying to poison Snow White, the wicked queen is made to dance in red hot slippers "till she fell dead on the floor, a sad example of envy and jealousy." Cinderella's evil stepsisters have their eyes pecked out by doves. And Hansel and Gretel (children!) kill their captor by baking her in an oven.

High-school reading lists are full of similar fare. Homer's Odysseus blinds Polyphemus the Cyclops by grinding out his eye with a heated stake. In the *Inferno*, Dante and Virgil watch corrupt politicians struggle to stay submerged beneath a lake of boiling pitch, lest they be skewered by devils above the surface. And Golding's *Lord of the Flies* recounts how a schoolboy called Piggy is savagely murdered *by other children* while marooned on an island.

This is not to say that minors' consumption of violent entertainment has never encountered resistance. In the 1800s, dime novels depicting crime and "penny dreadfuls" (named for their price and content) were blamed in some quarters for juvenile delinquency.

When motion pictures came along, they became the villains instead. "The days when the police looked upon dime novels as the most dangerous of textbooks in the school for crime are drawing to a close. They say the moving picture machine tends even more than did the dime novel to turn the thoughts of the easily influenced to paths which sometimes lead to prison."[7] For a time, our Court did permit broad censorship of movies because of their capacity to be "used for evil,"[8] but we eventually reversed course. Radio dramas were next, and then came comic books. Many in the late 1940s and early 1950s blamed comic books for fostering a "preoccupation with violence and horror" among the young, leading to a rising juvenile crime rate.[9] But efforts to convince Congress to restrict comic books failed. And, of course, after comic books came television and music lyrics.

California claims that video games present special problems because they are "interactive," in that the player participates in the violent action on screen and determines its outcome. The latter feature is nothing new: Since at least the publication of The Adventures of You: Sugarcane Island in 1969, young readers of choose-your-own-adventure stories have been able to make decisions that determine the plot by following instructions about which page to turn to. As for the argument that video games enable participation in the violent action, that seems to us more a matter of degree than of kind. As Judge Posner has observed, all literature is interactive. "The better it is, the more interactive. Literature when it is successful draws the reader into the story, makes him identify with the characters, invites him to judge them and quarrel with them, to experience their joys and sufferings as the reader's own."[10]

California's effort to regulate violent video games is the latest episode in a long series of failed attempts to censor violent entertainment for minors. While we have pointed out above that some of the evidence brought forward to support the harmfulness of video games is unpersuasive, we do not mean to demean or disparage the concerns that underlie the attempt to regulate them—concerns that may and doubtless do prompt a good deal of parental oversight. We have no business passing judgment on the view of the California Legislature that violent video games (or, for that matter, any other forms of speech) corrupt the young or harm their moral development. Our task is only to say whether or not such works constitute a "well-defined and narrowly limited class of speech, the prevention and punishment of which have never been thought to raise any Constitutional problem"[11] (the answer plainly is no); and if not, whether the regulation of such works is justified by that high degree of necessity we have described as a compelling state interest (it is not). Even where the protection of children is the object, the constitutional limits on governmental action apply.

California's legislation straddles the fence between (1) addressing a serious social problem and (2) helping concerned parents control their children. Both ends are legitimate, but when they affect First Amendment rights they must be pursued by means that are neither seriously underinclusive nor seriously overinclusive. As a means of protecting children from portrayals of violence, the legislation is seriously underinclusive, not only because it excludes portrayals other than video games, but also because it permits a parental or avuncular veto. And as a means of assisting concerned parents it is seriously overinclusive because it abridges the First Amendment rights of young people whose parents (and aunts and uncles) think violent video games are a harmless pastime. And the overbreadth in achieving one goal is not cured by the underbreadth in achieving the other. Legislation such as this, which is neither fish nor fowl, cannot survive strict scrutiny.

Hate Speech—*R.A.V. v. City of St. Paul* (1992)

Majority opinion (joined by Chief Justice Rehnquist and Justices Kennedy, Souter, and Thomas)

A teenager, identified in this case only by his initials R.A.V., was prosecuted under the City of St. Paul's hate-crime ordinance for allegedly burning a cross on the lawn of a black family. All of the justices agreed that the ordinance violated the First Amendment, but they disagreed on why.

In the predawn hours of June 21, 1990, petitioner and several other teenagers allegedly assembled a crudely made cross by taping together broken chair legs. They then allegedly burned the cross inside the fenced yard of a black family that lived across the street from the house where petitioner was staying. Although this conduct could have been punished under any of a number of laws, one of the two provisions under which respondent City of St. Paul chose to charge petitioner (then a juvenile) was the St. Paul Bias Motivated Crime Ordinance (1990), which provides:

> Whoever places on public or private property a symbol, object, appellation, characterization or graffiti, including, but not limited to, a burning cross or Nazi swastika, which one knows or has reasonable grounds to know arouses anger, alarm or resentment in others on the basis of race, color, creed, religion or gender commits disorderly conduct and shall be guilty of a misdemeanor.

The First Amendment generally prevents government from proscribing speech or even expressive conduct because of disapproval of the ideas expressed. Content-based regulations are presumptively invalid. From 1791 to the present, however, our society, like other free but civilized societies, has permitted restrictions upon the content of speech in a few limited areas, which are "of such slight social value as a step to truth that any benefit that may be derived from them is clearly outweighed by the social interest in order and morality."[1] We have recognized that "the freedom of speech" referred to by the First Amendment does not include a freedom to disregard these traditional limitations.

We have sometimes said that these categories of expression are "not within the area of constitutionally protected speech" or that the "protection of the First Amendment does not extend" to them. Such statements must be taken in context, however, and are no more literally true than is the occasionally repeated shorthand characterizing obscenity "as not being speech at all." What they mean is that these areas of speech can, consistently with the First Amendment, be regulated *because of their constitutionally proscribable* content (obscenity, defamation, etc.)—not that they are categories of speech entirely invisible to the Constitution, so that they may be made the vehicles for content discrimination unrelated to their distinctively proscribable content. Thus, the government may proscribe libel; but it may not make the further content discrimination of proscribing *only* libel critical of the government.

The proposition that a particular instance of speech can be proscribable on the basis of one feature (*e.g.*, obscenity) but not on the basis of another (*e.g.*, opposition to the city government) is commonplace and has found application in many contexts. We have long held, for example, that nonverbal expressive activity can be banned because of the action it entails, but not because of the ideas it expresses—so that burning a flag in violation of an ordinance against outdoor fires could be punishable, whereas burning a flag in violation of an ordinance against dishonoring the flag is not.

In other words, the exclusion of "fighting words" from the scope of the First Amendment simply means that, for purposes of that Amendment, the unprotected features of the words are, despite their verbal character, essentially a "nonspeech" element of communication. Fighting words are thus analogous to a noisy sound truck: Each is, as Justice Frankfurter recognized, a "mode of speech";[2] both can be used to convey an idea; but neither has, in and of itself, a claim upon the First Amendment. As with the sound truck, however, so also with fighting words: The government may not regulate use based on hostility—or favoritism—towards the underlying message expressed.

When the basis for the content discrimination consists entirely of the very reason the entire class of speech at issue is proscribable, no significant danger of idea or viewpoint discrimination exists. Such a reason, having been adjudged neutral enough to support exclusion of the entire class of speech from First Amendment protection, is also neutral enough to form the basis of distinction within the class. To illustrate: A State might choose to prohibit only that obscenity which is the most patently offensive *in its prurience*—*i.e.*, that which involves the most lascivious displays of sexual activity. But it may not prohibit, for example, only that obscenity which includes offensive *political* messages.

In its practical operation, moreover, the ordinance goes even beyond mere content discrimination, to actual viewpoint discrimination. Displays containing some words—odious racial epithets, for example—would be prohibited to proponents of all views. But "fighting words" that do not themselves invoke race, color, creed, religion, or gender—aspersions upon a person's mother, for example—would seemingly be usable *ad libitum** in the placards of those arguing *in favor* of racial, color, etc. tolerance and equality, but could not be used by that speaker's opponents. One could hold up a sign saying, for example, that all "anti-Catholic bigots" are misbegotten; but not that all "papists" are, for that would insult and provoke violence "on the basis of religion." St. Paul has no such authority to license one side of a debate to fight freestyle, while requiring the other to follow Marquis of Queensbury Rules.

The dispositive question in this case, therefore, is whether content discrimination is reasonably necessary to achieve St. Paul's compelling interests; it plainly is not. An ordinance not limited to the favored topics, for example, would have precisely the same beneficial effect. In fact the only interest distinctively served by the content

* At one's pleasure.

limitation is that of displaying the city council's special hostility towards the particular biases thus singled out. That is precisely what the First Amendment forbids.

Let there be no mistake about our belief that burning a cross in someone's front yard is reprehensible. But St. Paul has sufficient means at its disposal to prevent such behavior without adding the First Amendment to the fire.

RELIGIOUS LIBERTY

The First Amendment begins by setting forth the dual guarantees of religious liberty known as the Establishment Clause and the Free Exercise Clause: "Congress shall make no law respecting an establishment of religion, or prohibiting the free exercise thereof." The Supreme Court has deemed these guarantees to apply against the states (via the Fourteenth Amendment) as well as against the federal government.

Prayer at Public Ceremonies— Lee v. Weisman (1992)

Dissent (joined by Chief Justice Rehnquist and Justices White and Thomas)

The Supreme Court ruled, by a 5–4 vote, that nonsectarian benedictions and invocations at public high school and middle school graduation ceremonies violate the Establishment Clause because the school district's control of the ceremonies "places public pressure, as well as peer pressure, on attending students to stand as a group or, at least, maintain respectful silence" during the prayers. In his dissent, Justice Scalia complained that the majority's "psychojourney" wandered far astray from our nation's constitutional tradition of nonsectarian prayer at public celebrations.

In holding that the Establishment Clause prohibits invocations and benedictions at public school graduation ceremonies, the Court—with nary a mention that it is doing so—lays waste a tradition that is as old as public school graduation ceremonies themselves and that is a component of an even more longstanding American tradition of nonsectarian prayer to God at public celebrations generally. As its instrument of destruction, the bulldozer of its social engineering, the Court invents a boundless, and boundlessly manipulable, test of psychological coercion. Today's opinion shows more forcefully than volumes of argumentation why our nation's protection, that fortress which is our Constitution, cannot possibly rest upon the changeable philosophical predilections of the Justices of this Court, but must have deep foundations in the historic practices of our people.

Justice Holmes's aphorism that "a page of history is worth a volume of logic" applies with particular force to our Establishment Clause jurisprudence. As we have recognized, our interpretation of the Establishment Clause should "comport with what history reveals was the contemporaneous understanding of its guarantees."[1] "The line we must draw between the permissible and the impermissible is one which accords with history and faithfully reflects the understanding of the Founding Fathers."[2] "Historical evidence sheds light not only on what the draftsmen intended the Establishment Clause to mean, but also on how they thought that Clause applied" to contemporaneous practices.[3] Thus, "the existence from the beginning of the Nation's life of a practice, while not conclusive of its constitutionality is a fact of considerable import in the interpretation" of the Establishment Clause.[4]

The history and tradition of our nation are replete with public ceremonies featuring prayers of thanksgiving and petition. Illustrations of this point have been amply provided in our prior opinions, but since the Court is so oblivious to our history as to suggest that the Constitution restricts "preservation and transmission of religious beliefs to the private sphere," it appears necessary to provide another brief account.

From our nation's origin, prayer has been a prominent part of governmental ceremonies and proclamations. The Declaration of Independence, the document marking our birth as a separate people, "appeal[ed] to the Supreme Judge of the world for the rectitude of our intentions" and avowed "a firm reliance on the protection of divine Providence." In his first inaugural address, after swearing his oath of office on a Bible, George Washington deliberately made a prayer a part of his first official act as president:

> It would be peculiarly improper to omit in this first official act
> my fervent supplications to that Almighty Being who rules over

the universe, who presides in the councils of nations, and whose providential aids can supply every human defect, that His benediction may consecrate to the liberties and happiness of the people of the United States a Government instituted by themselves for these essential purposes.

Such supplications have been a characteristic feature of inaugural addresses ever since. Thomas Jefferson, for example, prayed in his first inaugural address: "May that Infinite Power which rules the destinies of the universe lead our councils to what is best, and give them a favorable issue for your peace and prosperity." In his second inaugural address, Jefferson acknowledged his need for divine guidance and invited his audience to join his prayer:

I shall need, too, the favor of that Being in whose hands we are, who led our fathers, as Israel of old, from their native land and planted them in a country flowing with all the necessaries and comforts of life; who has covered our infancy with His providence and our riper years with His wisdom and power, and to whose goodness I ask you to join in supplications with me that He will so enlighten the minds of your servants, guide their councils, and prosper their measures that whatsoever they do shall result in your good, and shall secure to you the peace, friendship, and approbation of all nations.

Similarly, James Madison, in his first inaugural address, placed his confidence

in the guardianship and guidance of that Almighty Being whose power regulates the destiny of nations, whose blessings have been so conspicuously dispensed to this rising Republic, and to whom we are bound to address our devout gratitude for the past, as well as our fervent supplications and best hopes for the future.

Most recently, President Bush,* continuing the tradition established by President Washington, asked those attending his inaugura-
tion to bow their heads, and made a prayer his first official act as
president.

Our national celebration of Thanksgiving likewise dates back to
President Washington. As we recounted in *Lynch*:[5]

> The day after the First Amendment was proposed, Congress
> urged President Washington to proclaim "a day of public thanks-
> giving and prayer, to be observed by acknowledging with grate-
> ful hearts the many and signal favours of Almighty God."
> President Washington proclaimed November 26, 1789, a day of
> thanksgiving to "offer our prayers and supplications to the Great
> Lord and Ruler of Nations, and beseech Him to pardon our na-
> tional and other transgressions."

This tradition of Thanksgiving Proclamations—with their religious theme of prayerful gratitude to God—has been adhered to by
almost every president.

The other two branches of the federal government also have a
long-established practice of prayer at public events. Congressional
sessions have opened with a chaplain's prayer ever since the First
Congress. And this Court's own sessions have opened with the invocation "God save the United States and this Honorable Court" since
the days of Chief Justice Marshall.

In addition to this general tradition of prayer at public ceremonies, there exists a more specific tradition of invocations and benedictions at public school graduation exercises. By one account, the first
public high school graduation ceremony took place in Connecticut
in July 1868—the very month, as it happens, that the Fourteenth
Amendment (the vehicle by which the Establishment Clause has been
applied against the States) was ratified—when "15 seniors from the
Norwich Free Academy marched in their best Sunday suits and
dresses into a church hall and waited through majestic music and long

---

* Referring to George H. W. Bush.

prayers."[6] As the Court obliquely acknowledges in describing the "customary features" of high school graduations, the invocation and benediction have long been recognized to be "as traditional as any other parts of the [school] graduation program and are widely established."[7]

I find it a sufficient embarrassment that our Establishment Clause jurisprudence regarding holiday displays has come to "require scrutiny more commonly associated with interior decorators than with the judiciary."[8] But interior decorating is a rock-hard science compared to psychology practiced by amateurs. A few citations of "research in psychology" that have no particular bearing upon the precise issue here cannot disguise the fact that the Court has gone beyond the realm where judges know what they are doing. The Court's argument that state officials have "coerced" students to take part in the invocation and benediction at graduation ceremonies is, not to put too fine a point on it, incoherent.

The Court's notion that a student who simply *sits* in "respectful silence" during the invocation and benediction (when all others are standing) has somehow joined—or would somehow be perceived as having joined—in the prayers is nothing short of ludicrous. We indeed live in a vulgar age. But surely "our social conventions" have not coarsened to the point that anyone who does not stand on his chair and shout obscenities can reasonably be deemed to have assented to everything said in his presence. Since the Court does not dispute that students exposed to prayer at graduation ceremonies retain (despite "subtle coercive pressures") the free will to sit, there is absolutely no basis for the Court's decision. It is fanciful enough to say that "a reasonable dissenter," standing head erect in a class of bowed heads, "could believe that the group exercise signified her own participation or approval of it." It is beyond the absurd to say that she could entertain such a belief while pointedly declining to rise.

The deeper flaw in the Court's opinion does not lie in its wrong answer to the question whether there was state-induced "peer-pressure" coercion; it lies, rather, in the Court's making violation of the Establishment Clause hinge on such a precious question. The coercion that was a hallmark of historical establishments of religion was coercion of religious orthodoxy and of financial support by force of law and threat of penalty. Typically, attendance at the state church was required; only clergy of the official church could lawfully perform sacraments; and dissenters, if tolerated, faced an array of civil disabilities. Thus, for example, in the colony of Virginia, where the Church of England had been established, ministers were required by law to conform to the doctrine and rites of the Church of England; and all persons were required to attend church and observe the Sabbath, were tithed for the public support of Anglican ministers, and were taxed for the costs of building and repairing churches.

The Establishment Clause was adopted to prohibit such an establishment of religion at the federal level (and to protect state establishments of religion from federal interference). I will further acknowledge for the sake of argument that, as some scholars have argued, by 1790, the term "establishment" had acquired an additional meaning—"financial support of religion generally, by public taxation"—that reflected the development of "general or multiple" establishments, not limited to a single church.[9] But that would still be an establishment coerced *by force of law*. And I will further concede that our constitutional tradition, from the Declaration of Independence and the first inaugural address of Washington, quoted earlier, down to the present day, has, with a few aberrations, ruled out of order government-sponsored endorsement of religion—even when no legal coercion is present, and indeed even when no ersatz, "peer-pressure" psycho-coercion is present—where the endorsement is sectarian, in the sense of specifying details upon which men and women who believe in a benevolent, omnipotent Creator and Ruler of the world are known to differ (for example, the divinity of Christ). But there is simply no support for the proposition that the officially sponsored nondenominational invocation and benediction read by Rabbi Gutterman—with no one legally coerced to recite them—violated the Constitution of the United States. To the contrary, they are so characteristically American they could have come from the pen of George Washington or Abraham Lincoln himself.

Thus, while I have no quarrel with the Court's general proposition that the Establishment Clause "guarantees that government may not coerce anyone to support or participate in religion or its exercise," I see no warrant for expanding the concept of coercion beyond acts backed by threat of penalty—a brand of coercion that, happily, is readily discernible to those of us who have made a career of reading the disciples of Blackstone, rather than of Freud. The Framers were indeed opposed to coercion of religious worship by the national government; but, as their own sponsorship of nonsectarian prayer in public events demonstrates, they understood that "speech is not coercive; the listener may do as he likes."[10]

The reader has been told much in this case about the personal interest of Mr. Weisman and his daughter, and very little about the personal interests on the other side. They are not inconsequential. Church and state would not be such a difficult subject if religion were, as the Court apparently thinks it to be, some purely personal avocation that can be indulged entirely in secret, like pornography, in the privacy of one's room. For most believers, it is *not* that, and has never been. Religious men and women of almost all denominations have felt it necessary to acknowledge and beseech the blessing of God as a people, and not just as individuals, because they believe in the "protection of divine Providence," as the Declaration of Independence put it, not just for individuals but for societies; because they believe God to be, as Washington's first Thanksgiving Proclamation put it, the "Great Lord and Ruler of Nations." One can believe in the effectiveness of such public worship, or one can deprecate and deride it. But the longstanding American tradition of prayer at official ceremonies displays with unmistakable clarity that the Establishment Clause does not forbid the government to accommodate it.

The narrow context of the present case involves a community's celebration of one of the milestones in its young citizens' lives, and it is a bold step for this Court to seek to banish from that occasion, and from thousands of similar celebrations throughout this land, the expression of gratitude to God that a majority of the community wishes to make. The issue before us today is not the abstract philosophical question whether the alternative of frustrating this desire of a religious majority is to be preferred over the alternative of imposing "psychological coercion," or a feeling of exclusion, upon nonbelievers. Rather, the question is *whether a mandatory choice in favor of the former has been imposed by the United States Constitution.* As the age-old practices of our people show, the answer to that question is not at all in doubt.

I must add one final observation: The Founders of our Republic knew the fearsome potential of sectarian religious belief to generate civil dissension and civil strife. And they also knew that nothing, absolutely nothing, is so inclined to foster among religious believers of various faiths a toleration—no, an affection—for one another than voluntarily joining in prayer together, to the God whom they all worship and seek. Needless to say, no one should be compelled to do that, but it is a shame to deprive our public culture of the opportunity, and indeed the encouragement, for people to do it voluntarily. The Baptist or Catholic who heard and joined in the simple and inspiring prayers of Rabbi Gutterman on this official and patriotic occasion was inoculated from religious bigotry and prejudice in a manner that cannot be replicated. To deprive our society of that important unifying mechanism in order to spare the nonbeliever what seems to me the minimal inconvenience of standing, or even sitting in respectful nonparticipation, is as senseless in policy as it is unsupported in law.

The Establishment Clause Ghoul—*Lamb's Chapel v. Center Moriches Union Free School District* (1993)

Concurrence in the judgment (joined by Justice Thomas)

In this case, the Supreme Court unanimously ruled that a school district violated a local church's First Amendment free-speech rights when it opened school facilities for general use for community activities but refused to allow the church to use the facilities for a religiously oriented film series. The nine justices also agreed that allowing such use would not violate the Establishment Clause, but Justice Scalia objected to the majority's invocation of the so-called Lemon *test in reaching that conclusion. Under the* Lemon *test—set forth in the Supreme Court's 1971 ruling in* Lemon v. Kurtzman—*a law satisfies the Establishment Clause only if it has a secular purpose, has a principal or primary effect that neither advances nor inhibits religion, and does not cause an excessive entanglement of government with religion. Justice Scalia had previously condemned the* Lemon *test as a "formulaic abstraction" that is "not derived from, but positively conflicts with, our long-accepted constitutional traditions."*[1]

Like some ghoul in a late-night horror movie that repeatedly sits up in its grave and shuffles abroad, after being repeatedly killed and buried, *Lemon* stalks our Establishment Clause jurisprudence once again, frightening the little children and school attorneys of Center Moriches Union Free School District. Its most recent burial, only last term, was, to be sure, not fully six feet under: Our decision in *Lee v. Weisman* conspicuously avoided using the supposed "test" but also declined the invitation to repudiate it. Over the years, however, no fewer than five of the currently sitting Justices have, in their own opinions, personally driven pencils through the creature's heart (the author of today's opinion repeatedly), and a sixth has joined an opinion doing so.

The secret of the *Lemon* test's survival, I think, is that it is so easy to kill. It is there to scare us (and our audience) when we wish it to do so, but we can command it to return to the tomb at will. When we wish to strike down a practice it forbids, we invoke it; when we wish to uphold a practice it forbids, we ignore it entirely. Sometimes, we take a middle course, calling its three prongs "no more than helpful signposts." Such a docile and useful monster is worth keeping around, at least in a somnolent state; one never knows when one might need him.

For my part, I agree with the long list of constitutional scholars who have criticized *Lemon* and bemoaned the strange Establishment Clause geometry of crooked lines and wavering shapes its intermittent use has produced. I will decline to apply *Lemon*—whether it validates or invalidates the government action in question—and therefore cannot join the opinion of the Court today.

I cannot join for yet another reason: the Court's statement that the proposed use of the school's facilities is constitutional because (among other things) it would not signal endorsement of religion in general. What a strange notion, that a Constitution which itself gives "religion in general" preferential treatment (I refer to the Free Exercise Clause) forbids endorsement of religion in general. The attorney general of New York not only agrees with that strange notion, he has an explanation for it: "Religious advocacy," he writes, "serves the community only in the eyes of its adherents and yields a benefit only to those who already believe." That was not the view of those who adopted our Constitution, who believed that the public virtues inculcated by religion are a public good. It suffices to point out that during the summer of 1789, when it was in the process of drafting the First Amendment, Congress enacted the Northwest Territory Ordinance that the Confederation Congress had adopted in 1787—Article III of which provides: "Religion, morality, and knowledge, *being necessary to good government and the happiness of mankind,* schools and the means of education shall forever be encouraged." Unsurprisingly, then, indifference to "religion in general" is *not* what our cases, both old and recent, demand.

Ten Commandments Displays—
McCreary County v. ACLU (2005)

*Dissent (joined by Chief Justice Rehnquist and Justice Thomas)**

In this case, the Supreme Court ruled by a 5–4 vote that displays of the Ten Commandments in courthouses in two Kentucky counties violated the Establishment Clause. In his dissent, Justice Scalia argued that the majority's core premise—that the Establishment Clause mandates government neutrality between religion and non-religion—is alien to the American model of the relationship between church and state: "Those who wrote the Constitution believed that morality was essential to the well-being of society and that encouragement of religion was the best way to foster morality."

On September 11, 2001, I was attending in Rome, Italy, an international conference of judges and lawyers, principally from Europe and the United States. That night and the next morning virtually all of the participants watched, in their hotel rooms, the address to the nation by the president of the United States concerning the murderous attacks upon the Twin Towers and the Pentagon, in which thousands of Americans had been killed. The address ended, as presidential addresses often do, with the prayer "God bless America." The next afternoon I was approached by one of the judges from a European country, who, after extending his profound condolences for my country's loss, sadly observed: "How I wish that the head of state of my country, at a similar time of national tragedy and distress, could conclude his address 'God bless _____.' It is of course absolutely forbidden."

That is one model of the relationship between church and state— a model spread across Europe by the armies of Napoleon, and re-

---

* Justice Kennedy joined parts of Justice Scalia's dissent but not the part that contains the excerpted passages.

flected in the Constitution of France, which begins, "France is [a] . . . secular . . . Republic." Religion is to be strictly excluded from the public forum. This is not, and never was, the model adopted by America. George Washington added to the form of presidential oath prescribed by the Constitution the concluding words "so help me God." The Supreme Court under John Marshall opened its sessions with the prayer "God save the United States and this Honorable Court." The First Congress instituted the practice of beginning its legislative sessions with a prayer. The same week that Congress submitted the Establishment Clause as part of the Bill of Rights for ratification by the States, it enacted legislation providing for paid chaplains in the House and Senate. The day after the First Amendment was proposed, the same Congress that had proposed it requested the president to proclaim "a day of public thanksgiving and prayer, to be observed, by acknowledging, with grateful hearts, the many and signal favours of Almighty God." President Washington offered the first Thanksgiving Proclamation shortly thereafter, devoting November 26, 1789, on behalf of the American people "to the service of that great and glorious Being who is the beneficent author of all the good that was, that is, or that will be," thus beginning a tradition of offering gratitude to God that continues today. The same Congress also reenacted the Northwest Territory Ordinance of 1787, Article III of which provided: "Religion, morality, and knowledge, being necessary to good government and the happiness of mankind, schools and the means of education shall forever be encouraged." And of course the First Amendment itself accords religion (and no other manner of belief) special constitutional protection.

These actions of our First President and Congress and the Marshall Court were not idiosyncratic; they reflected the beliefs of the period. Those who wrote the Constitution believed that morality was essential to the well-being of society and that encouragement of religion was the best way to foster morality. The "fact that the Founding Fathers believed devotedly that there was a God and that the unalienable rights of man were rooted in Him is clearly evidenced in their writings, from the Mayflower Compact to the Constitution itself."[1] President Washington opened his presidency with a prayer and reminded his fellow citizens at the conclusion of it that "reason and experience both forbid us to expect that National morality can prevail in exclusion of religious principle." President John Adams wrote to the Massachusetts Militia: "We have no government armed with power capable of contending with human passions unbridled by morality and religion. Our Constitution was made only for a moral and religious people. It is wholly inadequate to the government of any other." Thomas Jefferson concluded his second inaugural address by inviting his audience to pray:

> I shall need, too, the favor of that Being in whose hands we are, who led our fathers, as Israel of old, from their native land and planted them in a country flowing with all the necessaries and comforts of life; who has covered our infancy with His providence and our riper years with His wisdom and power and to whose goodness I ask you to join in supplications with me that He will so enlighten the minds of your servants, guide their councils, and prosper their measures that whatsoever they do shall result in your good, and shall secure to you the peace, friendship, and approbation of all nations.

James Madison, in his first inaugural address, likewise placed his confidence "in the guardianship and guidance of that Almighty Being whose power regulates the destiny of nations, whose blessings have been so conspicuously dispensed to this rising Republic, and to whom we are bound to address our devout gratitude for the past, as well as our fervent supplications and best hopes for the future."

Nor have the views of our people on this matter significantly changed. Presidents continue to conclude the presidential oath with the words "so help me God." Our legislatures, state and national, continue to open their sessions with prayer led by official chaplains. The sessions of this Court continue to open with the prayer "God save the United States and this Honorable Court." Invocation of the Almighty by our public figures, at all levels of government, remains commonplace. Our coinage bears the motto "IN GOD WE TRUST." And our Pledge of Allegiance contains the acknowledgment that we are a nation "under God." As one of our Supreme Court opinions rightly observed, "We are a religious people whose institutions presuppose a Supreme Being."[2]

With all of this reality (and much more) staring it in the face, how can the Court *possibly* assert that "the First Amendment mandates governmental neutrality between religion and nonreligion" and that "manifesting a purpose to favor adherence to religion generally" is unconstitutional? Who says so? Surely not the words of the Constitution. Surely not the history and traditions that reflect our society's constant understanding of those words. Surely not even the current sense of our society, recently reflected in an act of Congress adopted *unanimously* by the Senate and with only five nays in the House of Representatives, criticizing a Court of Appeals opinion that had held "under God" in the Pledge of Allegiance unconstitutional. Nothing stands behind the Court's assertion that governmental affirmation of the society's belief in God is unconstitutional except the Court's own say-so, citing as support only the unsubstantiated say-so of earlier Courts going back no farther than the mid-twentieth century. And it is, moreover, a thoroughly discredited say-so. It is discredited, to begin with, because a majority of the Justices on the current Court (including at least one member of today's majority) have, in separate opinions, repudiated the brain-spun "*Lemon* test" that embodies the supposed principle of neutrality between religion and irreligion. And it is discredited because the Court has not had the courage (or the foolhardiness) to apply the neutrality principle consistently.

Besides appealing to the demonstrably false principle that the government cannot favor religion over irreligion, today's opinion suggests that the posting of the Ten Commandments violates the principle that the government cannot favor one religion over another. That is indeed a valid principle where public aid or assistance to religion is concerned, or where the free exercise of religion is at issue, but it necessarily applies in a more limited sense to public acknowledgment of the Creator. If religion in the public forum had to be entirely non-denominational, there could be no religion in the public forum at all. One cannot say the word "God" or "the Almighty," one cannot offer public supplication or thanksgiving, without contradicting the beliefs of some people that there are many gods, or that God or the gods pay no attention to human affairs. With respect to public acknowledgment of religious belief, it is entirely clear from our nation's historical practices that the Establishment Clause permits this disregard of polytheists and believers in unconcerned deities, just as it permits the disregard of devout atheists.

Historical practices thus demonstrate that there is a distance between the acknowledgment of a single Creator and the establishment of a religion. The former is, as *Marsh v. Chambers* (1983) put it, "a tolerable acknowledgment of beliefs widely held among the people of this country." The three most popular religions in the United States, Christianity, Judaism, and Islam—which combined account for 97.7 percent of all believers—are monotheistic. All of them, moreover (Islam included), believe that the Ten Commandments were given by God to Moses, and are divine prescriptions for a virtuous life. Publicly honoring the Ten Commandments is thus indistinguishable, insofar as discriminating against other religions is concerned, from publicly honoring God. Both practices are recognized across such a broad and diverse range of the population—from Christians to Muslims—that they cannot be reasonably understood as a government endorsement of a particular religious viewpoint.

Finally, I must respond to Justice Stevens' assertion that I would "marginalize the belief systems of more than seven million Americans" who adhere to religions that are not monotheistic. Surely that is a gross exaggeration. The beliefs of those citizens are entirely protected by the Free Exercise Clause, and by those aspects of the Establishment Clause that do not relate to government acknowledgment of the Creator. Invocation of God despite their beliefs is permitted not because nonmonotheistic religions cease to be religions recognized by the religion clauses of the First Amendment, but because governmental invocation of God is not an establishment. Justice Stevens fails to recognize that in the context of public acknowledgments of God there are legitimate *competing* interests: On the one hand, the interest of that minority in not feeling "excluded"; but on the other, the interest of the overwhelming majority of religious believers in being able to give God thanks and supplication *as a people*, and with respect to our national endeavors. Our national tradition has resolved that conflict in favor of the majority. It is not for this Court to change a disposition that accounts, many Americans think, for the phenomenon remarked upon in a quotation attributed to various authors, including Bismarck, but which I prefer to associate with Charles de Gaulle: "God watches over little children, drunkards, and the United States of America."

Neutral and General Laws—
Employment Division v. Smith (1990)

Majority opinion (joined by Chief Justice Rehnquist and Justices White, Stevens, and Kennedy)

This case arose when Alfred Smith and Galen Black, members of the Native American Church, ingested the psychoactive substance peyote for sacramental purposes. Their possession of peyote violated Oregon law. They were fired from their jobs with a private drug-rehabilitation organization as a result, and they were determined to be ineligible for unemployment benefits because they had been fired for work-related misconduct. An Oregon court reversed that determination on the ground that the denial of benefits violated their rights under the Free Exercise Clause.

The Supreme Court ruled by a vote of 6 to 3* that Oregon did not violate Smith's and Black's Free Exercise rights. In his majority opinion for five justices, Justice Scalia held that a "neutral law of general applicability" does not violate the Free Exercise Clause even if it heavily burdens a person's exercise of religion. Oregon banned possession of peyote as part of its general criminal prohibition on possession of controlled substances. That ban therefore did not violate Smith's and Black's rights under the Free Exercise Clause, even though it prevented their sacramental use of peyote.

Justice Scalia rejected an alternative test under which governmental actions that substantially burden a religious practice would have to be justified by a compelling governmental interest. Any society that adopted and faithfully applied such a test would, he argued, make each conscience "a law unto itself" and thus be "courting anarchy." Exemptions protective of religious liberty are, he said, matters for the political process to enact, not for the courts to devise. (In the aftermath of the Court's ruling, Oregon enacted an exemption for religious use of peyote.)

Congress reacted against the Court's decision by enacting the Religious

---

* Justice O'Connor was part of the six-justice majority that ruled in favor of Oregon, but she did not join Justice Scalia's opinion.

Freedom Restoration Act of 1993, which undertook to impose as a statutory matter the alternative test that Justice Scalia had rejected. (In its 1997 decision in City of Boerne v. Flores, *the Supreme Court ruled by a vote of 6 to 3, with Justice Scalia in the majority, that RFRA could not constitutionally be applied against the states.)*

This case requires us to decide whether the Free Exercise Clause of the First Amendment permits the State of Oregon to include religiously inspired peyote use within the reach of its general criminal prohibition on use of that drug, and thus permits the State to deny unemployment benefits to persons dismissed from their jobs because of such religiously inspired use.

The Free Exercise Clause of the First Amendment, which has been made applicable to the States by incorporation into the Fourteenth Amendment, provides that "Congress shall make no law respecting an establishment of religion, or *prohibiting the free exercise thereof.*" The free exercise of religion means, first and foremost, the right to believe and profess whatever religious doctrine one desires. Thus, the First Amendment obviously excludes all "governmental regulation of religious beliefs as such."[1] The government may not compel affirmation of religious belief, punish the expression of religious doctrines it believes to be false, impose special disabilities on the basis of religious views or religious status, or lend its power to one or the other side in controversies over religious authority or dogma.

But the "exercise of religion" often involves not only belief and profession but the performance of (or abstention from) physical acts: assembling with others for a worship service, participating in sacramental use of bread and wine, proselytizing, abstaining from certain foods or certain modes of transportation. It would be true, we think (though no case of ours has involved the point), that a state would be "prohibiting the free exercise [of religion]" if it sought to ban such acts or abstentions only when they are engaged in for religious reasons, or only because of the religious belief that they display. It would doubtless be unconstitutional, for example, to ban the casting of "statues that are to be used for worship purposes," or to prohibit bowing down before a golden calf.

Smith and Black, however, seek to carry the meaning of "prohibiting the free exercise [of religion]" one large step further. They contend that their religious motivation for using peyote places them beyond the reach of a criminal law that is not specifically directed at their religious practice, and that is concededly constitutional as applied to those who use the drug for other reasons. They assert, in other words, that "prohibiting the free exercise [of religion]" includes requiring any individual to observe a generally applicable law that requires (or forbids) the performance of an act that his religious belief forbids (or requires). As a textual matter, we do not think the words must be given that meaning. It is no more necessary to regard the collection of a general tax, for example, as "prohibiting the free exercise [of religion]" by those citizens who believe support of organized government to be sinful than it is to regard the same tax as "abridging the freedom . . . of the press" of those publishing companies that must pay the tax as a condition of staying in business. It is a permissible reading of the text, in the one case as in the other, to say that, if prohibiting the exercise of religion (or burdening the activity of printing) is not the object of the tax, but merely the incidental effect of a generally applicable and otherwise valid provision, the First Amendment has not been offended.

Our decisions reveal that the latter reading is the correct one. We have never held that an individual's religious beliefs excuse him from compliance with an otherwise valid law prohibiting conduct that the State is free to regulate. On the contrary, the record of more than a century of our free exercise jurisprudence contradicts that proposition. As described succinctly by Justice Frankfurter in *Minersville School District Board of Education v. Gobitis* (1940):

Conscientious scruples have not, in the course of the long struggle for religious toleration, relieved the individual from obedience to a general law not aimed at the promotion or restriction of religious beliefs. The mere possession of religious convictions which contradict the relevant concerns of a political society does not relieve the citizen from the discharge of political responsibilities.

We first had occasion to assert that principle in *Reynolds v. United States* (1879), where we rejected the claim that criminal laws against polygamy could not be constitutionally applied to those whose religion commanded the practice. "Laws," we said,

> are made for the government of actions, and while they cannot interfere with mere religious belief and opinions, they may with practices. Can a man excuse his practices to the contrary because of his religious belief? To permit this would be to make the professed doctrines of religious belief superior to the law of the land, and in effect to permit every citizen to become a law unto himself.

Subsequent decisions have consistently held that the right of free exercise does not relieve an individual of the obligation to comply with a valid and neutral law of general applicability on the ground that the law proscribes (or prescribes) conduct that his religion prescribes (or proscribes).

Smith and Black urge us to hold, quite simply, that when otherwise prohibitable conduct is accompanied by religious convictions, not only the convictions but the conduct itself must be free from governmental regulation. We have never held that, and decline to do so now. There being no contention that Oregon's drug law represents an attempt to regulate religious beliefs, the communication of religious beliefs, or the raising of one's children in those beliefs, the rule to which we have adhered ever since *Reynolds* plainly controls.

The government's ability to enforce generally applicable prohibitions of socially harmful conduct, like its ability to carry out other aspects of public policy, "cannot depend on measuring the effects of a governmental action on a religious objector's spiritual development."[2] To make an individual's obligation to obey such a law contingent upon the law's coincidence with his religious beliefs, except where the State's interest is "compelling"—permitting him, by virtue of his beliefs, "to become a law unto himself"[3]—contradicts both constitutional tradition and common sense.

The "compelling government interest" requirement seems benign, because it is familiar from other fields. But using it as the standard that must be met before the government may accord different treatment on the basis of race, or before the government may regulate the content of speech, is not remotely comparable to using it for the purpose asserted here. What it produces in those other fields—equality of treatment, and an unrestricted flow of contending speech—are constitutional norms; what it would produce here—a private right to ignore generally applicable laws—is a constitutional anomaly.

Nor is it possible to limit the impact of their proposal by requiring a "compelling state interest" only when the conduct prohibited is "central" to the individual's religion. It is no more appropriate for judges to determine the "centrality" of religious beliefs before applying a "compelling interest" test in the free exercise field than it would be for them to determine the "importance" of ideas before applying the "compelling interest" test in the free speech field. What principle of law or logic can be brought to bear to contradict a believer's assertion that a particular act is "central" to his personal faith? Judging the centrality of different religious practices is akin to the unacceptable "business of evaluating the relative merits of differing religious claims."[4] As we reaffirmed only last term, "it is not within the judicial ken to question the centrality of particular beliefs or practices to a faith, or the validity of particular litigants' interpretation of those creeds."[5]

If the "compelling interest" test is to be applied at all, then, it must be applied across the board, to all actions thought to be religiously commanded. Moreover, if "compelling interest" really means what it says (and watering it down here would subvert its rigor in the other fields where it is applied), many laws will not meet the test. Any society adopting such a system would be courting anarchy, but that danger increases in direct proportion to the society's diversity of religious beliefs, and its determination to coerce or suppress none of them. Precisely because "we are a cosmopolitan nation made up of people of almost every conceivable religious preference"[6] and precisely because we value and protect that religious divergence, we cannot afford the luxury of deeming *presumptively invalid*, as applied to the religious objector, every regulation of conduct that does not protect an interest of the highest order. The rule Smith and Black favor would open the prospect of constitutionally required religious exemptions from civic obligations of almost every conceivable kind—ranging from compulsory military service, to the payment of taxes, to health and safety regulation such as manslaughter and child neglect laws, compulsory vaccination laws, drug laws, and traffic laws, to social welfare legislation such as minimum wage laws, child labor laws, animal cruelty laws, environmental protection laws, and laws providing for equality of opportunity for the races. The First Amendment's protection of religious liberty does not require this.

Values that are protected against government interference through enshrinement in the Bill of Rights are not thereby banished from the political process. Just as a society that believes in the negative protection accorded to the press by the First Amendment is likely to enact laws that affirmatively foster the dissemination of the printed word, so also a society that believes in the negative protection accorded to religious belief can be expected to be solicitous of that value in its legislation as well. It is therefore not surprising that a number of States have made an exception to their drug laws for sacramental peyote use. But to say that a nondiscriminatory religious-practice exemption is permitted, or even that it is desirable, is not to say that it is constitutionally required, and that the appropriate occasions for its creation can be discerned by the courts. It may fairly be said that leaving accommodation to the political process will place at a relative disadvantage those religious practices that are not widely engaged in; but that unavoidable consequence of democratic government must be preferred to a system in which each conscience is a law unto itself or in which judges weigh the social importance of all laws against the centrality of all religious beliefs.

Equal Treatment of Religious Believers—
Locke v. Davey (2004)

Dissent (joined by Justice Thomas)

Under the State of Washington's Promise Scholarship Program, students who received scholarships for college expenses could use the scholarships for any course of study except the pursuit of a devotional theology degree. Joshua Davey sued when he learned that he could not use his Promise Scholarship for that purpose. By a vote of 7 to 2, the Supreme Court held that Washington's exclusion of the pursuit of a devotional theology degree from its otherwise inclusive scholarship program did not violate the Free Exercise Clause. In his dissent, Justice Scalia argued that the Free Exercise Clause does not allow the government to single out religions for disfavored treatment.

We articulated the principle that governs this case more than fifty years ago in *Everson v. Board of Education* (1947):

> New Jersey cannot hamper its citizens in the free exercise of their own religion. Consequently, it cannot exclude individual Catholics, Lutherans, Mohammedans, Baptists, Jews, Methodists, Non-believers, Presbyterians, or the members of any other faith, because of their faith, or lack of it, from receiving the benefits of public welfare legislation.

When the state makes a public benefit generally available, that benefit becomes part of the baseline against which burdens on religion are measured; and when the state withholds that benefit from some individuals solely on the basis of religion, it violates the Free Exercise Clause no less than if it had imposed a special tax.

That is precisely what the State of Washington has done here. It has created a generally available public benefit, whose receipt is conditioned only on academic performance, income, and attendance at an accredited school. It has then carved out a solitary course of study for exclusion: theology. No field of study but religion is singled out for disfavor in this fashion. Davey is not asking for a special benefit to which others are not entitled. He seeks only *equal* treatment—the right to direct his scholarship to his chosen course of study, a right every other Promise Scholar enjoys.

The Court's reference to historical "popular uprisings against procuring taxpayer funds to support church leaders" is therefore quite misplaced. That history involved not the inclusion of religious ministers in public benefits programs like the one at issue here, but laws that singled them out for financial aid. For example, the Virginia bill at which Madison's Remonstrance was directed provided: "For the support of Christian teachers a sum payable for tax on the property within this Commonwealth is hereby assessed." Laws supporting the clergy in other States operated in a similar fashion. One can concede the Framers' hostility to funding the clergy *specifically*, but that says nothing about whether the clergy had to be excluded from benefits the state made available to all. No one would seriously contend, for example, that the Framers would have barred ministers from using public roads on their way to church.

The Court makes no serious attempt to defend the program's neutrality, and instead identifies two features thought to render its discrimination less offensive. The first is the lightness of Davey's burden. The Court offers no authority for approving facial discrimination against religion simply because its material consequences are not severe. I might understand such a test if we were still in the business of reviewing facially neutral laws that merely happen to burden some individual's religious exercise, but we are not. See *Employment Division v. Smith* (1990). Discrimination *on the face of a statute* is something else. The indignity of being singled out for special burdens on the basis of one's religious calling is so profound that the concrete harm produced can never be dismissed as insubstantial. The Court has not required proof of "substantial" concrete harm with other forms of discrimination, and it should not do so here.

Even if there were some threshold quantum-of-harm requirement, surely Davey has satisfied it. The First Amendment, after all, guarantees *free* exercise of religion, and when the state exacts a financial penalty of almost $3,000 for religious exercise—whether by tax or by forfeiture of an otherwise available benefit—religious practice is anything *but* free.

The other reason the Court thinks this particular facial discrimination less offensive is that the scholarship program was not motivated by animus toward religion. The Court does not explain why the legislature's motive matters, and I fail to see why it should. If a state deprives a citizen of trial by jury or passes an *ex post facto* law, we do not pause to investigate whether it was actually trying to accomplish the evil the Constitution prohibits. It is sufficient that the citizen's rights have been infringed.

The Court has not approached other forms of discrimination this way. When we declared racial segregation unconstitutional, we did not ask whether the state had originally adopted the regime not out of "animus" against blacks, but because of a well-meaning but misguided belief that the races would be better off apart. It was sufficient to note the current effect of segregation on racial minorities. Similarly, the Court does not excuse statutes that facially discriminate against women just because they are the vestigial product of a well-intentioned view of women's appropriate social role.

It may be that Washington's original purpose in excluding the clergy from public benefits was benign, and the same might be true of its purpose in maintaining the exclusion today. But those singled out for disfavor can be forgiven for suspecting more invidious forces at work. Let there be no doubt: This case is about discrimination against a religious minority. Most citizens of this country identify themselves as professing some religious belief, but the state's policy poses no obstacle to practitioners of only a tepid, civic version of faith. Those the statutory exclusion actually affects—those whose belief in their religion is so strong that they dedicate their study and their lives to its ministry—are a far narrower set. One need not delve too far into modern popular culture to perceive a trendy disdain for deep religious conviction. In an era when the Court is so quick to come to the aid of other disfavored groups, its indifference in this case, which involves a form of discrimination to which the Constitution actually speaks, is exceptional.

Today's holding is limited to training the clergy, but its logic is readily extendible, and there are plenty of directions to go. What next? Will we deny priests and nuns their prescription-drug benefits on the ground that taxpayers' freedom of conscience forbids medicating the clergy at public expense? This may seem fanciful, but recall that France has proposed banning religious attire from schools, invoking interests in secularism no less benign than those the Court embraces today. When the public's freedom of conscience is invoked to justify denial of equal treatment, benevolent motives shade into indifference and ultimately into repression. Having accepted the justification in this case, the Court is less well equipped to fend it off in the future. I respectfully dissent.

RIGHT TO BEAR ARMS

Individual Right to Possess a Handgun— *District of Columbia v. Heller* (2008)

Majority opinion (joined by Chief Justice Roberts and Justices Kennedy, Thomas, and Alito)

Dick Heller, a special police officer who was authorized to carry a handgun while on duty in the District of Columbia, applied for a registration certificate to keep a handgun at home. D.C. law generally prohibited the possession of handguns and also prohibited the registration of handguns, so the District of Columbia denied Heller's application.

By a vote of 5 to 4, the Court ruled that D.C.'s ban on handgun possession in the home violated the Second Amendment.

Law professor Randy Barnett, a prominent proponent of originalism, hailed Justice Scalia's "sweeping and masterful" majority opinion as "the culmination of his ambition to place the original meaning of the text at the center of constitutional law."

We consider whether a District of Columbia prohibition on the possession of usable handguns in the home violates the Second Amendment to the Constitution.

The Second Amendment provides: "A well regulated Militia, being necessary to the security of a free State, the right of the people to keep and bear Arms, shall not be infringed." In interpreting this text, we are guided by the principle that "the Constitution was written to be understood by the voters; its words and phrases were used in their normal and ordinary as distinguished from technical meaning."[1]

The Second Amendment is naturally divided into two parts: its prefatory clause and its operative clause. The former does not limit the latter grammatically, but rather announces a purpose. The

Amendment could be rephrased, "Because a well regulated Militia is necessary to the security of a free State, the right of the people to keep and bear Arms shall not be infringed." Although this structure of the Second Amendment is unique in our Constitution, other legal documents of the Founding era, particularly individual-rights provisions of state constitutions, commonly included a prefatory statement of purpose.

Logic demands that there be a link between the stated purpose and the command. The Second Amendment would be nonsensical if it read, "A well regulated Militia, being necessary to the security of a free State, the right of the people to petition for redress of grievances shall not be infringed." That requirement of logical connection may cause a prefatory clause to resolve an ambiguity in the operative clause. But apart from that clarifying function, a prefatory clause does not limit or expand the scope of the operative clause. "It is nothing unusual in acts for the enacting part to go beyond the preamble; the remedy often extends beyond the particular act or mischief which first suggested the necessity of the law."[2] Therefore, while we will begin our textual analysis with the operative clause, we will return to the prefatory clause to ensure that our reading of the operative clause is consistent with the announced purpose.

Some have made the argument, bordering on the frivolous, that only those arms in existence in the 18th century are protected by the Second Amendment. We do not interpret constitutional rights that way. Just as the First Amendment protects modern forms of communications, and the Fourth Amendment applies to modern forms of search, the Second Amendment extends to all instruments that constitute bearable arms, even those that were not in existence at the time of the Founding.

We turn to the phrases "keep arms" and "bear arms." Johnson defined "keep" as, most relevantly, "to retain; not to lose," and "to have in custody."[3] Webster defined it as "to hold; to retain in one's power or possession."[4] No party has apprised us of an idiomatic meaning of "keep Arms." Thus, the most natural reading of "keep Arms" in the Second Amendment is to "have weapons."

At the time of the Founding, as now, to "bear" meant to "carry."

When used with "arms," however, the term has a meaning that refers to carrying for a particular purpose—confrontation. In *Muscarello v. United States* (1998), in the course of analyzing the meaning of "carries a firearm" in a federal criminal statute, Justice Ginsburg wrote that "surely a most familiar meaning is, as the Constitution's Second Amendment indicates: wear, bear, or carry upon the person or in the clothing or in a pocket, for the purpose of being armed and ready for offensive or defensive action in a case of conflict with another person." We think that Justice Ginsburg accurately captured the natural meaning of "bear arms." Although the phrase implies that the carrying of the weapon is for the purpose of "offensive or defensive action," it in no way connotes participation in a structured military organization.

From our review of Founding-era sources, we conclude that this natural meaning was also the meaning that "bear arms" had in the 18th century. In numerous instances, "bear arms" was unambiguously used to refer to the carrying of weapons outside of an organized militia. The most prominent examples are those most relevant to the Second Amendment: Nine state constitutional provisions written in the 18th century or the first two decades of the 19th, which enshrined a right of citizens to "bear arms in defense of themselves and the state" or "bear arms in defense of himself and the state." It is clear from those formulations that "bear arms" did not refer only to carrying a weapon in an organized military unit. Justice James Wilson interpreted the Pennsylvania Constitution's arms-bearing right, for example, as a recognition of the natural right of defense "of one's person or house"—what he called the law of "self preservation."[5] That was also the interpretation of those state constitutional provisions adopted by pre–Civil War state courts. These provisions demonstrate—again, in the most analogous linguistic context—that "bear arms" was not limited to the carrying of arms in a militia.

Our interpretation is confirmed by analogous arms-bearing rights in state constitutions that preceded and immediately followed adoption of the Second Amendment. Four States adopted analogues to the Federal Second Amendment in the period between independence and the ratification of the Bill of Rights. Two of them—Pennsylvania and Vermont—clearly adopted individual rights unconnected to militia service. Pennsylvania's Declaration of Rights of 1776 said: "That the people have a right to bear arms *for the defence of themselves* and the state." In 1777, Vermont adopted the identical provision, except for inconsequential differences in punctuation and capitalization.

North Carolina also codified a right to bear arms in 1776: "That the people have a right to bear arms, for the defence of the State." This could plausibly be read to support only a right to bear arms in a militia—but that is a peculiar way to make the point in a constitution that elsewhere repeatedly mentions the militia explicitly. Many colonial statutes required individual arms-bearing for public-safety reasons—such as the 1770 Georgia law that "for the security and *defence of this province* from internal dangers and insurrections" required those men who qualified for militia duty individually "to carry fire arms" "to places of public worship." That broad public-safety understanding was the connotation given to the North Carolina right by that State's Supreme Court in 1843.

The 1780 Massachusetts Constitution presented another variation on the theme: "The people have a right to keep and to bear arms for the common defence." Once again, if one gives narrow meaning to the phrase "common defence" this can be thought to limit the right to the bearing of arms in a state-organized military force. But once again the State's highest court thought otherwise. Writing for the court in an 1825 libel case, Chief Justice Parker wrote: "The liberty of the press was to be unrestrained, but he who used it was to be responsible in cases of its abuse; like the right to keep fire arms, which does not protect him who uses them for annoyance or destruction." The analogy makes no sense if firearms could not be used for any individual purpose at all.

Between 1789 and 1820, nine States adopted Second Amendment analogues. Four of them—Kentucky, Ohio, Indiana, and Missouri—referred to the right of the people to "bear arms in defence of themselves and the State." Another three States—Mississippi, Connecticut, and Alabama—used the even more individualistic phrasing that each citizen has the "right to bear arms in defence of himself and the

State." Finally, two States—Tennessee and Maine—used the "common defence" language of Massachusetts. That of the nine state constitutional protections for the right to bear arms enacted immediately after 1789 at least seven unequivocally protected an individual citizen's right to self-defense is strong evidence that that is how the Founding generation conceived of the right.

The historical narrative that petitioners must endorse would thus treat the Federal Second Amendment as an odd outlier, protecting a right unknown in state constitutions or at English common law, based on little more than an overreading of the prefatory clause.

Like most rights, the right secured by the Second Amendment is not unlimited. From Blackstone through the 19th-century cases, commentators and courts routinely explained that the right was not a right to keep and carry any weapon whatsoever in any manner whatsoever and for whatever purpose. For example, the majority of the 19th-century courts to consider the question held that prohibitions on carrying concealed weapons were lawful under the Second Amendment or state analogues. Although we do not undertake an exhaustive historical analysis today of the full scope of the Second Amendment, nothing in our opinion should be taken to cast doubt on longstanding prohibitions on the possession of firearms by felons and the mentally ill, or laws forbidding the carrying of firearms in sensitive places such as schools and government buildings, or laws imposing conditions and qualifications on the commercial sale of arms.

We also recognize another important limitation on the right to keep and carry arms: that the sorts of weapons protected were those "in common use at the time."[6] We think that limitation is fairly supported by the historical tradition of prohibiting the carrying of "dangerous and unusual weapons."[7]

It may be objected that if weapons that are most useful in military service—M-16 rifles and the like—may be banned, then the Second Amendment right is completely detached from the prefatory clause. But as we have said, the conception of the militia at the time of the Second Amendment's ratification was the body of all citizens capable of military service, who would bring the sorts of lawful weapons that they possessed at home to militia duty. It may well be true today that a militia, to be as effective as militias in the 18th century, would require sophisticated arms that are highly unusual in society at large. Indeed, it may be true that no amount of small arms could be useful against modern-day bombers and tanks. But the fact that modern developments have limited the degree of fit between the prefatory clause and the protected right cannot change our interpretation of the right.

We turn finally to the law at issue here. As we have said, the law totally bans handgun possession in the home. It also requires that any lawful firearm in the home be disassembled or bound by a trigger lock at all times, rendering it inoperable.

As the quotations earlier in this opinion demonstrate, the inherent right of self-defense has been central to the Second Amendment right. The handgun ban amounts to a prohibition of an entire class of "arms" that is overwhelmingly chosen by American society for that lawful purpose. The prohibition extends, moreover, to the home, where the need for defense of self, family, and property is most acute. Under any of the standards of scrutiny that we have applied to enumerated constitutional rights, banning from the home "the most preferred firearm in the nation to keep and use for protection of one's home and family"[8] would fail constitutional muster.

The very enumeration of the right takes out of the hands of government—even the Third Branch of Government—the power to decide on a case-by-case basis whether the right is *really worth* insisting upon. A constitutional guarantee subject to future judges' assessments of its usefulness is no constitutional guarantee at all. Constitutional rights are enshrined with the scope they were understood to have when the people adopted them, whether or not future legislatures or (yes) even future judges think that scope too broad. We would not apply an "interest-balancing"[9] approach to the prohibition of a peaceful neo-Nazi march through Skokie. The First Amendment contains the freedom-of-speech guarantee that the people ratified, which included exceptions for obscenity, libel, and disclosure of state secrets, but not for the expression of extremely unpopular and wrong-headed views. The Second Amendment is no different.

Like the First, it is the very *product* of an interest-balancing by the people. And whatever else it leaves to future evaluation, it surely elevates above all other interests the right of law-abiding, responsible citizens to use arms in defense of hearth and home.

We are aware of the problem of handgun violence in this country, and we take seriously the concerns raised by the many *amici* who believe that prohibition of handgun ownership is a solution. The Constitution leaves the District of Columbia a variety of tools for combating that problem, including some measures regulating handguns. But the enshrinement of constitutional rights necessarily takes certain policy choices off the table. These include the absolute prohibition of handguns held and used for self-defense in the home. Undoubtedly some think that the Second Amendment is outmoded in a society where our standing army is the pride of our Nation, where well-trained police forces provide personal security, and where gun violence is a serious problem. That is perhaps debatable, but what is not debatable is that it is not the role of this Court to pronounce the Second Amendment extinct.

SUBSTANTIVE DUE PROCESS

The Due Process Clause of the Fifth Amendment, applicable against the federal government, provides that "[n]o person shall . . . be deprived of life, liberty, or property, without due process of law." The Due Process Clause of the Fourteenth Amendment, applicable against the states, similarly provides: "nor shall any State deprive any person of life, liberty, or property, without due process of law." By their terms, both provisions afford purely procedural protections: the government must provide "due process of law" when it deprives a person of "life, liberty, or property."

By contrast, under the concept of "substantive due process," there are some liberties, the Court has said, that the Due Process Clauses protect against deprivation, no matter how much process is provided.

Justice Scalia fought forcefully, but often unsuccessfully, against the Court's expanding applications of substantive due process.

Abortion—*Planned Parenthood v. Casey* (1992)

Concurrence in the judgment in part and dissent in part
(joined by Chief Justice Rehnquist and Justices White and Thomas)

In 1973, the Court ruled in Roe v. Wade *that the Due Process Clause of the Fourteenth Amendment protects a right to abortion. When this case challenging various provisions of Pennsylvania law (e.g., informed consent) reached the Court in 1992, it was widely anticipated that the Court would overrule* Roe *and restore abortion policy to the legislative processes in the states. Instead, in their controlling joint opinion, Justices O'Connor, Kennedy, and Souter refused to overrule* Roe. *(At the same time, they ruled that most of the challenged provisions of Pennsylvania law were constitutionally permissible.)*

Justice Scalia vigorously objected to the Court's failure to overturn Roe.

The States may, if they wish, permit abortion on demand, but the Constitution does not *require* them to do so. The permissibility of abortion, and the limitations upon it, are to be resolved like most important questions in our democracy: by citizens trying to persuade one another and then voting. A State's choice between two positions on which reasonable people can disagree is constitutional even when (as is often the case) it intrudes upon a "liberty" in the absolute sense. Laws against bigamy, for example—which entire societies of reasonable people disagree with—intrude upon men and women's liberty to marry and live with one another. But bigamy happens not to be a liberty specially protected by the Constitution.

That is, quite simply, the issue in these cases: not whether the power of a woman to abort her unborn child is a "liberty" in the absolute sense; or even whether it is a liberty of great importance to many women. Of course it is both. The issue is whether it is a liberty protected by the Constitution of the United States. I am sure it is not. I reach that conclusion not because of anything so exalted as my views concerning the "concept of existence, of meaning, of the universe, and of the mystery of human life."[1] Rather, I reach it for the same reason I reach the conclusion that bigamy is not constitutionally protected—because of two simple facts: (1) the Constitution says absolutely nothing about it, and (2) the longstanding traditions of American society have permitted it to be legally proscribed.

The Court's description of the place of *Roe v. Wade* (1973) in the social history of the United States is unrecognizable. Not only did *Roe* not, as the Court suggests, *resolve* the deeply divisive issue of abortion; it did more than anything else to nourish it, by elevating it to the national level, where it is infinitely more difficult to resolve. National politics were not plagued by abortion protests, national abortion lobbying, or abortion marches on Congress, before *Roe v. Wade* was decided. Profound disagreement existed among our citizens over the issue—as it does over other issues, such as the death penalty—but that disagreement was being worked out at the state level. As with many other issues, the division of sentiment within each State was not as closely balanced as it was among the population of the Nation as a whole, meaning not only that more people would be satisfied with the results of state-by-state resolution, but also that those results would be more stable. Pre-*Roe*, moreover, political compromise was possible.

Roe's mandate for abortion on demand destroyed the compromises of the past, rendered compromise impossible for the future, and required the entire issue to be resolved uniformly, at the national level. At the same time, *Roe* created a vast new class of abortion consumers and abortion proponents by eliminating the moral opprobrium that had attached to the act. ("If the Constitution *guarantees* abortion, how can it be bad?"—not an accurate line of thought, but a natural one.) Many favor all of those developments, and it is not for me to say that they are wrong. But to portray *Roe* as the statesmanlike "settlement" of a divisive issue, a jurisprudential Peace of Westphalia that is worth preserving, is nothing less than Orwellian. *Roe* fanned into life an issue that has inflamed our national politics in general, and has obscured with its smoke the selection of Justices to this Court, in particular, ever since. And by keeping us in the abortion-umpiring business, it is the perpetuation of that disruption, rather than of any *Pax Roeana*, that the Court's new majority decrees.

In truth, I am as distressed as the Court is about the "political pressure" directed to the Court: the marches, the mail, the protests aimed at inducing us to change our opinions. How upsetting it is, that so many of our citizens (good people, not lawless ones, on both sides of this abortion issue, and on various sides of other issues as well) think that we Justices should properly take into account their views, as though we were engaged not in ascertaining an objective law, but in determining some kind of social consensus. The Court would profit, I think, from giving less attention to the *fact* of this distressing phenomenon, and more attention to the *cause* of it. That cause permeates today's opinion: a new mode of constitutional adjudication that relies not upon text and traditional practice to determine the law, but upon what the Court calls "reasoned judgment," which turns out to be nothing but philosophical predilection and moral intuition. All manner of "liberties," the Court tells us, inhere in the Constitution, and are enforceable by this Court—not just those mentioned in the text or established in the traditions of our society.

What makes all this relevant to the bothersome application of "political pressure" against the Court are the twin facts that the

American people love democracy and the American people are not fools. As long as this Court thought (and the people thought) that we Justices were doing essentially lawyers' work up here—reading text and discerning our society's traditional understanding of that text—the public pretty much left us alone. Texts and traditions are facts to study, not convictions to demonstrate about. But if in reality, our process of constitutional adjudication consists primarily of making *value judgments*; if we can ignore a long and clear tradition clarifying an ambiguous text, as we did, for example, five days ago in declaring unconstitutional invocations and benedictions at public high school graduation ceremonies;[2] if, as I say, our pronouncement of constitutional law rests primarily on value judgments, then a free and intelligent people's attitude towards us can be expected to be (*ought* to be) quite different. The people know that their value judgments are quite as good as those taught in any law school—maybe better. If, indeed, the "liberties" protected by the Constitution are, as the Court says, undefined and unbounded, then the people *should* demonstrate, to protest that we do not implement *their* values instead of *ours*. Not only that, but the confirmation hearings for new Justices *should* deteriorate into question-and-answer sessions in which Senators go through a list of their constituents' most favored and most disfavored alleged constitutional rights, and seek the nominee's commitment to support or oppose them. Value judgments, after all, should be voted on, not dictated; and if our Constitution has somehow accidentally committed them to the Supreme Court, at least we can have a sort of plebiscite each time a new nominee to that body is put forward.

There is a poignant aspect to today's opinion. Its length, and what might be called its epic tone, suggest that its authors believe they are bringing to an end a troublesome era in the history of our Nation, and of our Court. "It is the dimension" of authority, they say, to "call the contending sides of national controversy to end their national division by accepting a common mandate rooted in the Constitution."

There comes vividly to mind a portrait by Emanuel Leutze that hangs in the Harvard Law School: Roger Brooke Taney, painted in 1859, the 82nd year of his life, the 24th of his Chief Justiceship, the second after his opinion in *Dred Scott*. He is in black, sitting in a shadowed red armchair, left hand resting upon a pad of paper in his lap, right hand hanging limply, almost lifelessly, beside the inner arm of the chair. He sits facing the viewer, and staring straight out. There seems to be on his face, and in his deep-set eyes, an expression of profound sadness and disillusionment. Perhaps he always looked that way, even when dwelling upon the happiest of thoughts. But those of us who know how the luster of his great Chief Justiceship came to be eclipsed by *Dred Scott* cannot help believing that he had that case—its already apparent consequences for the Court, and its soon-to-be-played-out consequences for the Nation—burning on his mind. I expect that, two years earlier, he, too, had thought himself "calling the contending sides of national controversy to end their national division by accepting a common mandate rooted in the Constitution."

It is no more realistic for us in this litigation than it was for him in that to think that an issue of the sort they both involved—an issue involving life and death, freedom and subjugation—can be "speedily and finally settled" by the Supreme Court, as President James Buchanan, in his inaugural address, said the issue of slavery in the territories would be. Quite to the contrary, by foreclosing all democratic outlet for the deep passions this issue arouses, by banishing the issue from the political forum that gives all participants, even the losers, the satisfaction of a fair hearing and an honest fight, by continuing the imposition of a rigid national rule instead of allowing for regional differences, the Court merely prolongs and intensifies the anguish.

We should get out of this area, where we have no right to be, and where we do neither ourselves nor the country any good by remaining.

Marriage—*Obergefell v. Hodges* (2015)

Dissent (joined by Justice Thomas)

By a 5–4 vote, the Court ruled that state laws that define marriage as the union of a man and a woman violate both the Due Process Clause and the Equal Protection Clause of the Fourteenth Amendment. In addition to joining each of the dissenting opinions filed by Chief Justice Roberts, Justice Thomas, and Justice Alito, Justice Scalia issued his own dissenting opinion.

The substance of today's decree is not of immense personal importance to me. The law can recognize as marriage whatever sexual attachments and living arrangements it wishes, and can accord them favorable civil consequences, from tax treatment to rights of inheritance. Those civil consequences—and the public approval that conferring the name of marriage evidences—can perhaps have adverse social effects, but no more adverse than the effects of many other controversial laws. So it is not of special importance to me what the law says about marriage. It is of overwhelming importance, however, who it is that rules me. Today's decree says that my Ruler, and the Ruler of 320 million Americans coast-to-coast, is a majority of the nine lawyers on the Supreme Court. The opinion in these cases is the furthest extension in fact—and the furthest extension one can even imagine—of the Court's claimed power to create "liberties" that the Constitution and its Amendments neglect to mention. This practice of constitutional revision by an unelected committee of nine, always accompanied (as it is today) by extravagant praise of liberty, robs the People of the most important liberty they asserted in the Declaration of Independence and won in the Revolution of 1776: the freedom to govern themselves.

Until the courts put a stop to it, public debate over same-sex marriage displayed American democracy at its best. Individuals on both sides of the issue passionately, but respectfully, attempted to persuade their fellow citizens to accept their views. Americans considered the arguments and put the question to a vote. The electorates of 11 States, either directly or through their representatives, chose to expand the traditional definition of marriage. Many more decided not to. Win or lose, advocates for both sides continued pressing their cases, secure in the knowledge that an electoral loss can be negated by a later electoral win. That is exactly how our system of government is supposed to work.

The Constitution places some constraints on self-rule—constraints adopted by the People themselves when they ratified the Constitution and its Amendments. Forbidden are laws "impairing the Obligation of Contracts," denying "Full Faith and Credit" to the "public Acts" of other States, prohibiting the free exercise of religion, abridging the freedom of speech, infringing the right to keep and bear arms, authorizing unreasonable searches and seizures, and so forth. Aside from these limitations, those powers "reserved to the States respectively, or to the people" can be exercised as the States or the People desire. These cases ask us to decide whether the Fourteenth Amendment contains a limitation that requires the States to license and recognize marriages between two people of the same sex. Does it remove that issue from the political process?

Of course not. It would be surprising to find a prescription regarding marriage in the Federal Constitution since, as the author of today's opinion reminded us only two years ago (in an opinion joined by the same Justices who join him today):

> Regulation of domestic relations is an area that has long been regarded as a virtually exclusive province of the States.

> The Federal Government, through our history, has deferred to state-law policy decisions with respect to domestic relations.[1]

But we need not speculate. When the Fourteenth Amendment was ratified in 1868, every State limited marriage to one man and one woman, and no one doubted the constitutionality of doing so. That resolves these cases. When it comes to determining the meaning of a vague constitutional provision—such as "due process of law" or "equal protection of the laws"—it is unquestionable that the People who ratified that provision did not understand it to prohibit a practice that remained both universal and uncontroversial in the years after ratification. We have no basis for striking down a practice that is not expressly prohibited by the Fourteenth Amendment's text, and that bears the endorsement of a long tradition of open, widespread, and unchallenged use dating back to the Amendment's ratification. Since there is no doubt whatever that the People never decided to prohibit the limitation of marriage to opposite-sex couples, the public debate over same-sex marriage must be allowed to continue.

But the Court ends this debate, in an opinion lacking even a thin veneer of law. Buried beneath the mummeries and straining-to-be-memorable passages of the opinion is a candid and startling assertion: No matter *what* it was the People ratified, the Fourteenth Amendment protects those rights that the Judiciary, in its "reasoned judgment," thinks the Fourteenth Amendment ought to protect. That is so because "the generations that wrote and ratified the Bill of Rights and the Fourteenth Amendment did not presume to know the extent of freedom in all of its dimensions. . . ." One would think that sentence would continue: ". . . and therefore they provided for a means by which the People could amend the Constitution," or perhaps ". . . and therefore they left the creation of additional liberties, such as the freedom to marry someone of the same sex, to the People, through the never-ending process of legislation." But no. What logically follows, in the majority's judge-empowering estimation, is: "and so they entrusted to future generations a charter protecting the right of all persons to enjoy liberty as we learn its meaning." The "we," needless to say, is the nine of us. "History and tradition guide and discipline [our] inquiry but do not set its outer boundaries." Thus, rather than focusing on the People's understanding of "liberty"—at the time of ratification or even today—the majority focuses on four "principles and traditions" that, *in the majority's view*, prohibit States from defining marriage as an institution consisting of one man and one woman.

This is a naked judicial claim to legislative—indeed, super-legislative—power; a claim fundamentally at odds with our system of government. Except as limited by a constitutional prohibition agreed to by the People, the States are free to adopt whatever laws they like, even those that offend the esteemed Justices' "reasoned judgment." A system of government that makes the People subordinate to a committee of nine unelected lawyers does not deserve to be called a democracy.

Judges are selected precisely for their skill as lawyers; whether they reflect the policy views of a particular constituency is not (or should not be) relevant. Not surprisingly then, the Federal Judiciary is hardly a cross-section of America. Take, for example, this Court, which consists of only nine men and women, all of them successful lawyers who studied at Harvard or Yale Law School. Four of the nine are natives of New York City. Eight of them grew up in east- and west-coast States. Only one hails from the vast expanse in-between. Not a single Southwesterner or even, to tell the truth, a genuine Westerner (California does not count). Not a single evangelical Christian (a group that comprises about one quarter of Americans), or even a Protestant of any denomination. The strikingly unrepresentative character of the body voting on today's social upheaval would be irrelevant if they were functioning as *judges*, answering the legal question whether the American people had ever ratified a constitutional provision that was understood to proscribe the traditional definition of marriage. But of course the Justices in today's majority are not voting on that basis; *they say they are not*. And to allow the policy question of same-sex marriage to be considered and resolved by a select, patrician, highly unrepresentative panel of nine is to violate a principle even more fundamental than no taxation without representation: no social transformation without representation.

But what really astounds is the hubris reflected in today's judicial Putsch. The five Justices who compose today's majority are entirely comfortable concluding that every State violated the Constitution for all of the 135 years between the Fourteenth Amendment's ratification and Massachusetts' permitting of same-sex marriages in 2003. They have discovered in the Fourteenth Amendment a "fundamental right" overlooked by every person alive at the time of ratification, and almost everyone else in the time since. They see what lesser legal minds—minds like Thomas Cooley, John Marshall Harlan, Oliver Wendell Holmes, Jr., Learned Hand, Louis Brandeis, William Howard Taft, Benjamin Cardozo, Hugo Black, Felix Frankfurter, Robert Jackson, and Henry Friendly—could not. They are certain that the People ratified the Fourteenth Amendment to bestow on them the power to remove questions from the democratic process when that is called for by their "reasoned judgment." These Justices *know* that limiting marriage to one man and one woman is contrary to reason; they *know* that an institution as old as government itself, and accepted by every nation in history until 15 years ago, cannot possibly be supported by anything other than ignorance or bigotry. And they are willing to say that any citizen who does not agree with that, who adheres to what was, until 15 years ago, the unanimous judgment of all generations and all societies, stands against the Constitution.

Hubris is sometimes defined as o'erweening pride; and pride, we know, goeth before a fall. The Judiciary is the "least dangerous" of the federal branches because it has "neither Force nor Will, but merely judgment; and must ultimately depend upon the aid of the executive arm" and the States, "even for the efficacy of its judgments." The Federalist No. 78. With each decision of ours that takes from the People a question properly left to them—with each decision that is unabashedly based not on law, but on the "reasoned judgment" of a bare majority of this Court—we move one step closer to being reminded of our impotence.

Punitive Damages—
BMW of North America v. Gore (1996)

Dissent (joined by Justice Thomas)

Justice Scalia's objections to substantive due process applied equally to conservative causes, such as limiting punitive damages, that he might well have favored as a matter of policy.

In 1990, Dr. Ira Gore Jr. bought a new black BMW sports sedan. Nine months later, he discovered that it had been re-painted before he bought it. He sued BMW for fraud for its failure to disclose the re-painting. At trial, it was learned that BMW had a policy of not informing its dealers of pre-delivery damage to new cars when the cost of repair was less than 3 percent of the car's retail price. The jury awarded Gore $4,000 in compensatory damages and $4 million in punitive damages. On appeal, the Alabama Supreme Court reduced the punitive award to $2 million.

By a 5–4 vote, the U.S. Supreme Court ruled that the $2 million award of punitive damages was "grossly excessive," in violation of BMW's rights under the Due Process Clause of the Fourteenth Amendment. Justice Scalia responded with this dissent.*

Today we see the latest manifestation of this Court's recent and increasingly insistent "concern about punitive damages that run wild."[1] Since the Constitution does not make that concern any of our business, the Court's activities in this area are an unjustified incursion into the province of state governments.

In earlier cases that were the prelude to this decision, I set forth my view that a state trial procedure that commits the decision whether to impose punitive damages, and the amount, to the discretion of the jury, subject to some judicial review for "reasonableness," furnishes a defendant with all the process that is "due." I do not re-

---

* Justice Ginsburg, joined by Chief Justice Rehnquist, penned a separate dissent.

gard the Fourteenth Amendment's Due Process Clause as a secret repository of substantive guarantees against "unfairness"—neither the unfairness of an excessive civil compensatory award, nor the unfairness of an "unreasonable" punitive award. What the Fourteenth Amendment's procedural guarantee assures is an opportunity to contest the reasonableness of a damages judgment in state court; but there is no federal guarantee a damages award actually *be* reasonable.

The Constitution provides no warrant for federalizing yet another aspect of our Nation's legal culture (no matter how much in need of correction it may be), and the application of the Court's new rule of constitutional law is constrained by no principle other than the Justices' subjective assessment of the "reasonableness" of the award in relation to the conduct for which it was assessed.

At the time of adoption of the Fourteenth Amendment, it was well understood that punitive damages represent the assessment by the jury, as the voice of the community, of the measure of punishment the defendant deserved. Today's decision, though dressed up as a legal opinion, is really no more than a disagreement with the community's sense of indignation or outrage expressed in the punitive award of the Alabama jury, as reduced by the State Supreme Court. It reflects not merely, as the concurrence candidly acknowledges, "a judgment about a matter of degree," but a judgment about the appropriate degree of indignation or outrage, which is hardly an analytical determination.

EQUAL PROTECTION

The Disease as Cure

Antonin Scalia was a law professor at the University of Chicago in 1978 when he took part in a symposium at Washington University Law School on "The Quest for Equality." His remarks were published in the Washington University Law Quarterly *in 1979 under the title "The Disease as Cure: 'In Order to Get Beyond Racism, We Must First Take Account of Race.'"[1] Other future jurists who took part in that symposium included Robert H. Bork and Ruth Bader Ginsburg.*

When John Minor Wisdom* speaks of "restorative justice," I am reminded of the story about the Lone Ranger and his "faithful Indian companion" Tonto. If you recall the famous radio serial, you know that Tonto never said much, but what he did say was (disguised beneath a Hollywood-Indian dialect) wisdom of an absolutely Solomonic caliber. On one occasion, it seems that the Lone Ranger was galloping along with Tonto, heading eastward, when they saw coming toward them a large band of Mohawk Indians in full war dress. The Lone Ranger reins in his horse, turns to Tonto, and asks, "Tonto, what should we do?" Tonto says, "Ugh, ride-um west." So they wheel around and gallop off to the west until suddenly they encounter a large band of Sioux heading straight toward them. The Lone Ranger asks, "Tonto, what should we do?" Tonto says, "Ugh, ride-um north." So they turn around and ride north, and, sure enough, there's a whole tribe of Iroquois headed straight toward them. The Ranger asks, "Tonto, what should we do?" And Tonto says, "Ugh, ride-um south," which they do until they see a war party of Apaches coming right for them. The Lone Ranger

---

* Judge John Minor Wisdom served on the United States Court of Appeals for the Fifth Circuit. Professor Scalia is commenting on a dissenting opinion he wrote.

asks, "Tonto, what should we do?" And Tonto says, "Ugh, what you mean, *we*, white man?"*

I have somewhat the same feeling when John Minor Wisdom talks of the evils that "we" whites have done to blacks and that "we" must now make restoration for. My father came to this country when he was a teenager. Not only had he never profited from the sweat of any black man's brow, I don't think he had ever seen a black man. There are, of course, many white ethnic groups that came to this country in great numbers relatively late in its history—Italians, Jews, Irish, Poles—who not only took no part in, and derived no profit from, the major historic suppression of the currently acknowledged minority groups, but were, in fact, themselves the object of discrimination by the dominant Anglo-Saxon majority. If I can recall in my lifetime the obnoxious "White Trade Only" signs in shops in Washington, D.C., others can recall "Irish Need Not Apply" signs in Boston, three or four decades earlier. To be sure, in relatively recent years some or all of these groups have been the beneficiaries of discrimination against blacks, or have themselves practiced discrimination. But to compare their racial debt—I must use that term, since the concept of "restorative justice" implies it; there is no creditor without a debtor—with that of those who plied the slave trade, and who maintained a formal caste system for many years thereafter, is to confuse a mountain with a molehill. Yet curiously enough, we find that in the system of restorative justice established by the Wisdoms and the Powells and the Whites,† it is precisely these groups that do most of the restoring. It is they who, to a disproportionate degree, are the competitors with the urban blacks and Hispanics for jobs, housing,

---

* At the 1986 Senate Judiciary Committee confirmation hearing on his Supreme Court nomination, one senator asked Scalia whether his "use of an Indian dialect would offend the Indians." Scalia replied: "I am fully aware of that sensitivity, Senator, which was why, when I began the story, I made it clear that Tonto's wisdom was always Solomonic, but it was disguised beneath what I referred to there as a Hollywood-Indian dialect. That [i.e., *Hollywood-Indian dialect*] is a disparaging term. I am fully aware that Indians do not talk that way. It is how Hollywood portrayed them. I thought I made it very clear in what I wrote that Indians do not talk that way but that is the way that Hollywood wrongfully portrays them."

† Justices Lewis F. Powell Jr. and Byron R. White were members of the Supreme Court and took part in the Court's 1978 decision in *Regents of the University of California v. Bakke*, which Professor Scalia directly criticizes in other passages in this article.

education—all those things that enable one to scramble to the top of the social heap where one can speak eloquently (and quite safely) of restorative justice.

To remedy this inequity, I have developed a modest proposal, which I call RJHS—the Restorative Justice Handicapping System. Under my system each individual in society would be assigned at birth Restorative Justice Handicapping Points, determined on the basis of his or her ancestry. Obviously, the highest number of points must go to what we may loosely call the Aryans—the Powells, the Whites, the Stewarts, the Burgers,* and, in fact (curiously enough), the entire composition of the present Supreme Court, with the exception of Justice Marshall. This grouping of North European races obviously played the greatest role in the suppression of the American black. But unfortunately, what was good enough for Nazi Germany is not good enough for our purposes. We must further divide the Aryans into sub-groups. As I have suggested, the Irish (having arrived later) probably owe less of a racial debt than the Germans, who in turn surely owe less of a racial debt than the English. It will, to be sure, be difficult drawing precise lines and establishing the correct number of handicapping points, but having reviewed the Supreme Court's jurisprudence on abortion, I am convinced that our justices would not shrink from the task.

Of course, the mere identification of the various degrees of debtor-races is only part of the job. One must in addition account for the dilution of bloodlines by establishing, for example, a half-Italian, half-Irish handicapping score. There are those who will scoff at this as a refinement impossible of achievement, but I am confident it can be done, and can even be extended to take account of dilution of blood in creditor-races as well. Indeed, I am informed (though I have not had the stomach to check) that a system to achieve the latter objective is already in place in federal agencies—specifying, for example, how much dilution of blood deprives one of his racial-creditor status as a "Hispanic" under affirmative-action programs. Moreover, it should not be forgotten that we have a rich body of statutory and

* Referring to Justice Potter Stewart and Chief Justice Warren E. Burger.

case law from the Old South to which we can turn for guidance in this exacting task.

But I think it unnecessary to describe the Restorative Justice Handicapping System any further. I trust you find it thoroughly offensive, as I do. It, and the racist concept of restorative justice of which it is merely the concrete expression, is fundamentally contrary to the principles that govern, and should govern, our society. I owe no man anything, nor he me, because of the blood that flows in our veins. To go down that road (or I should say to return down that road), even behind a banner as gleaming as restorative justice, is to make a frightening mistake. This is not to say that I have no obligation to my fellow citizens who are black. I assuredly do—not because of their race or because of any special debt that my bloodline owes to theirs, but because they have (many of them) special needs, and they are (all of them) my countrymen and (as I believe) my brothers. This means that I am entirely in favor of according the poor inner-city child, who happens to be black, advantages and preferences not given to my own children because they don't need them. But I am not willing to prefer the son of a prosperous and well-educated black doctor or lawyer—solely because of his race—to the son of a recent refugee from Eastern Europe who is working as a manual laborer to get his family ahead. The affirmative-action system now in place will produce the latter result because it is based upon concepts of racial indebtedness and racial entitlement rather than individual worth and individual need; that is to say, because it is racist.

Racial Preferences in Government Contracting— *City of Richmond v. J. A. Croson Co.* (1989)

Concurrence in the judgment

In 1983, the city council of Richmond, Virginia, adopted a "Minority Business Utilization Plan." Under that plan, prime contractors on the city's construction contracts had to subcontract at least 30 percent of the dollar amount of the contract to minority business enterprises (unless those prime contractors were themselves minority business enterprises).

By a vote of 6 to 3, the Court ruled that the plan violated the Equal Protection Clause. Justice O'Connor's lead opinion garnered a majority on some but not all parts. Justice Scalia wrote separately.

I do not agree with Justice O'Connor's dictum suggesting that, despite the Fourteenth Amendment, state and local governments may in some circumstances discriminate on the basis of race in order (in a broad sense) "to ameliorate the effects of past discrimination." The benign purpose of compensating for social disadvantages, whether they have been acquired by reason of prior discrimination or otherwise, can no more be pursued by the illegitimate means of racial discrimination than can other assertedly benign purposes we have repeatedly rejected. The difficulty of overcoming the effects of past discrimination is as nothing compared with the difficulty of eradicating from our society the source of those effects, which is the tendency—fatal to a Nation such as ours—to classify and judge men and women on the basis of their country of origin or the color of their skin. A solution to the first problem that aggravates the second is no solution at all. I share the view expressed by Alexander Bickel that "the lesson of the great decisions of the Supreme Court and the lesson of contemporary history have been the same for at least a generation: discrimination on the basis of race is illegal, immoral, unconstitutional, inherently wrong, and destructive of democratic society."[1] At least where state or local action is at issue, only a social emergency rising to the level of imminent danger to life and limb—for example, a prison race riot, requiring temporary segregation of inmates—can justify an exception to the principle embodied in the Fourteenth Amendment that "our Constitution is colorblind, and neither knows nor tolerates classes among citizens," *Plessy v. Ferguson* (1896) (Harlan, J., dissenting).

Racial discrimination against any group finds a more ready expression at the state and local than at the federal level. To the children of the Founding Fathers, this should come as no surprise. An acute awareness of the heightened danger of oppression from political factions in small, rather than large, political units dates to the very beginning of our national history. As James Madison observed in support of the proposed Constitution's enhancement of national powers:

> The smaller the society, the fewer probably will be the distinct parties and interests composing it; the fewer the distinct parties and interests, the more frequently will a majority be found of the same party; and the smaller the number of individuals composing a majority, and the smaller the compass within which they are placed, the more easily will they concert and execute their plan of oppression. Extend the sphere and you take in a greater variety of parties and interests; you make it less probable that a majority of the whole will have a common motive to invade the rights of other citizens; or if such a common motive exists, it will be more difficult for all who feel it to discover their own strength and to act in unison with each other. [The Federalist No. 10.]

The prophecy of these words came to fruition in Richmond in the enactment of a set-aside clearly and directly beneficial to the dominant political group, which happens also to be the dominant racial group. The same thing has no doubt happened before in other cities (though the racial basis of the preference has rarely been made textually explicit)—and blacks have often been on the receiving end of the injustice. Where injustice is the game, however, turnabout is not fair play.

In my view there is only one circumstance in which the States may act *by race* to undo the effects of past discrimination: where that is necessary to eliminate their own maintenance of a system of unlawful racial classification. If, for example, a state agency has a discriminatory pay scale compensating black employees in all positions at 20% less than their nonblack counterparts, it may assuredly promulgate an order raising the salaries of "all black employees" to eliminate the differential.

A State can, of course, act to undo the effects of past discrimination in many permissible ways that do not involve classification by race. In the particular field of state contracting, for example, it may adopt a preference for small businesses, or even for new businesses—which would make it easier for those previously excluded by discrimination to enter the field. Such programs may well have racially disproportionate impact, but they are not based on race. And, of course, a State may undo the effects of past discrimination in the sense of giving the identified victim of state discrimination that which it wrongfully denied him—for example, giving to a previously rejected black applicant the job that, by reason of discrimination, had been awarded to a white applicant, even if this means terminating the latter's employment. In such a context, the white jobholder is not being selected for disadvantageous treatment because of his race, but because he was wrongfully awarded a job to which another is entitled. That is worlds apart from the system here, in which those to be disadvantaged are identified solely by race.

In his final book, Professor Bickel wrote:

> A racial quota derogates the human dignity and individuality of all to whom it is applied; it is invidious in principle as well as in practice. Moreover, it can easily be turned against those it purports to help. The history of the racial quota is a history of subjugation, not beneficence. Its evil lies not in its name, but in its

effects: a quota is a divider of society, a creator of castes, and it is all the worse for its racial base, especially in a society desperately striving for an equality that will make race irrelevant.[2]

Those statements are true and increasingly prophetic. Apart from their societal effects, however, which are "in the aggregate disastrous,"[3] it is important not to lose sight of the fact that even "benign" racial quotas have individual victims, whose very real injustice we ignore whenever we deny them enforcement of their right not to be disadvantaged on the basis of race.

It is plainly true that in our society blacks have suffered discrimination immeasurably greater than any directed at other racial groups. But those who believe that racial preferences can help to "even the score" display, and reinforce, a manner of thinking by race that was the source of the injustice and that will, if it endures within our society, be the source of more injustice still. The relevant proposition is not that it was blacks, or Jews, or Irish who were discriminated against, but that it was individual men and women, "created equal," who were discriminated against. And the relevant resolve is that that should never happen again. Racial preferences appear to "even the score" (in some small degree) only if one embraces the proposition that our society is appropriately viewed as divided into races, making it right that an injustice rendered in the past to a black man should be compensated for by discriminating against a white. Nothing is worth that embrace. Since blacks have been disproportionately disadvantaged by racial discrimination, any race-neutral remedial program aimed at the disadvantaged *as such* will have a disproportionately beneficial impact on blacks. Only such a program, and not one that operates on the basis of race, is in accord with the letter and the spirit of our Constitution.

Racial Preferences in Higher-Education Admissions— *Grutter v. Bollinger* (2003)

Dissent in relevant part (joined by Justice Thomas)

The University of Michigan's law school pursued an admission policy that aimed at ensuring a "critical mass" of "underrepresented" minority students— "like African-Americans, Hispanics, and Native Americans"—in order to "obtain the educational benefits that flow from a diverse student body." As a state institution, the law school is subject to constitutional constraints. By a vote of 5 to 4, the Court held that the law school's use of race in its admission decisions did not violate the Equal Protection Clause.

In addition to joining dissents written by Chief Justice Rehnquist and Justice Thomas, Justice Scalia briefly explained his disagreement with the majority.

The "educational benefit" that the University of Michigan seeks to achieve by racial discrimination consists, according to the Court, of "cross-racial understanding" and "better preparation of students for an increasingly diverse workforce and society," all of which is necessary not only for work, but also for good "citizenship." This is not, of course, an "educational benefit" on which students will be graded on their Law School transcript (Works and Plays Well with Others: B+) or tested by the bar examiners (Q: Describe in 500 words or less your cross-racial understanding). For it is a lesson of life rather than law—essentially the same lesson taught to (or rather learned by, for it cannot be "taught" in the usual sense) people three feet shorter and twenty years younger than the full-grown adults at the University of Michigan Law School, in institutions ranging from Boy Scout troops to public-school kindergartens. If properly considered an "educational benefit" at all, it is surely not one that is either uniquely relevant to law school or uniquely "teachable" in a formal educational setting. *And therefore*: If it is appropriate for the University of Michigan Law School to use racial discrimination for the purpose of putting together a "critical mass" that will convey generic lessons in socialization and good citizenship, surely it is no less appropriate—indeed, *particularly* appropriate—for the civil service system of the State of Michigan to do so. There, also, those exposed to "critical masses" of certain races will presumably become better Americans, better Michiganders, better civil servants. And surely private employers cannot be criticized—indeed, should be praised—if they also "teach" good citizenship to their adult employees through a patriotic, all-American system of racial discrimination in hiring. The nonminority individuals who are deprived of a legal education, a civil service job, or any job at all by reason of their skin color will surely understand.

All-Male Military Institutions—
United States v. Virginia (1996)

Dissent

Founded in 1839, the Virginia Military Institute was by 1990 the only single-sex school among Virginia's public institutions of higher learning. The federal government sued to overturn VMI's males-only admission policy. By a vote of 7 to 1 (with Justice Thomas recused), the Court ruled that VMI's policy violated the Equal Protection Clause.

Today the Court shuts down an institution that has served the people of the Commonwealth of Virginia with pride and distinction for over a century and a half.

Much of the Court's opinion is devoted to deprecating the closed-mindedness of our forebears with regard to women's education, and even with regard to the treatment of women in areas that have nothing to do with education. Closed-minded they were—as every age is, including our own, with regard to matters it cannot guess, because it simply does not consider them debatable. The virtue of a democratic system with a First Amendment is that it readily enables the people, over time, to be persuaded that what they took for granted is not so, and to change their laws accordingly. That system is destroyed if the smug assurances of each age are removed from the democratic process and written into the Constitution. So to counterbalance the Court's criticism of our ancestors, let me say a word in their praise: they left us free to change. The same cannot be said of this most illiberal Court, which has embarked on a course of inscribing one after another of the current preferences of the society (and in some cases only the countermajoritarian preferences of the society's law-trained elite) into our Basic Law. Today it enshrines the notion that no substantial educational value is to be served by an all-men's military academy—so that the decision by the people of Virginia to maintain such an institution denies equal protection to women who cannot attend that institution but can attend others. Since it is entirely clear that the Constitution of the United States—the old one—takes no sides in this educational debate, I dissent.

I shall devote most of my analysis to evaluating the Court's opinion on the basis of our current equal protection jurisprudence, which regards this Court as free to evaluate everything under the sun by applying one of three tests: "rational basis" scrutiny, intermediate scrutiny, or strict scrutiny. These tests are no more scientific than their names suggest, and a further element of randomness is added by the fact that it is largely up to us which test will be applied in each case.

I have no problem with a system of abstract tests such as rational basis, intermediate, and strict scrutiny (though I think we can do better than applying strict scrutiny and intermediate scrutiny whenever we feel like it). Such formulas are essential to evaluating whether the new restrictions that a changing society constantly imposes upon private conduct comport with that "equal protection" our society has always accorded in the past. But in my view the function of this Court is to *preserve* our society's values regarding (among other things) equal protection, not to *revise* them; to prevent backsliding from the degree of restriction the Constitution imposed upon democratic government, not to prescribe, on our own authority, progressively higher degrees. For that reason it is my view that, whatever abstract tests we may choose to devise, they cannot supersede—and indeed ought to be crafted *so as to reflect*—those constant and unbroken national traditions that embody the people's understanding of ambiguous constitutional texts. More specifically, it is my view that "when a practice not expressly prohibited by the text of the Bill of Rights bears the endorsement of a long tradition of open, widespread, and unchallenged use that dates back to the beginning of the Republic, we have no proper basis for striking it down."[1]

The all-male constitution of VMI comes squarely within such a governing tradition. Founded by the Commonwealth of Virginia in 1839 and continuously maintained by it since, VMI has always admitted only men. And in that regard it has not been unusual. For almost all of VMI's more than a century and a half of existence, its single-sex status reflected the uniform practice for government-supported military colleges. Another famous Southern institution, The Citadel, has existed as a state-funded school of South Carolina since 1842. And all the federal military colleges—West Point, the Naval Academy at Annapolis, and even the Air Force Academy, which was not established until 1954—admitted only males for most of their history. Their admission of women in 1976 came not by court decree, but because the people, through their elected representatives, decreed a change. In other words, the tradition of having government-funded military schools for men is as well rooted in the traditions of this country as the tradition of sending only men into military combat. The people may decide to change the one tradition, like the other, through democratic processes; but the assertion that either tradition has been unconstitutional through the centuries is not law, but politics-smuggled-into-law.

And the same applies, more broadly, to single-sex education in general, which is threatened by today's decision with the cutoff of all state and federal support. Government-run *non*military educational institutions for the two sexes have until very recently also been part of our national tradition. "It is coeducation, historically, that is a novel educational theory. From grade school through high school, college, and graduate and professional training, much of the Nation's population during much of our history has been educated in sexually segregated classrooms."[2] These traditions may of course be changed by the democratic decisions of the people, as they largely have been.

Today, however, change is forced upon Virginia, and reversion to single-sex education is prohibited nationwide, not by democratic processes but by order of this Court. Even while bemoaning the sorry, bygone days of "fixed notions" concerning women's education, the Court favors current notions so fixedly that it is willing to write them into the Constitution of the United States by application of custom-built "tests." This is not the interpretation of a Constitution, but the creation of one.

ECONOMIC LIBERTIES

Economic Affairs as Human Affairs

In October 1984, then–D.C. Circuit judge Antonin Scalia delivered remarks at the Cato Institute's conference on "Economic Liberties and the Judiciary." His remarks were published in the Cato Journal.[1]

The title of this article—Economic Affairs as Human Affairs—is derived from a phrase I recall from the earliest days of my political awareness. Dwight Eisenhower used to insist, with demonstrably successful effect, that he was "a conservative in economic affairs, but a liberal in human affairs." I am sure he meant it to connote nothing more profound than that he represented the best of both Republican and Democratic tradition. But still, that seemed to me a peculiar way to put it—contrasting economic affairs with human affairs as though economics is a science developed for the benefit of dogs or trees; something that has nothing to do with human beings, with their welfare, aspirations, or freedoms.

That, of course, is a pernicious notion, though it represents a turn of mind that characterizes much American political thought. It leads to the conclusion that economic rights and liberties are qualitatively distinct from, and fundamentally inferior to, other noble human values called civil rights, about which we should be more generous. Unless one is a thoroughgoing materialist, there is some appeal to this. Surely the freedom to dispose of one's property as one pleases, for example, is not as high an aspiration as the freedom to think or write or worship as one's conscience dictates. On closer analysis, however, it seems to me that the difference between economic freedoms and what are generally called civil rights turns out to be a difference of degree rather than of kind. Few of us, I suspect, would have much difficulty choosing between the right to own property and the right to receive a *Miranda* warning.

In any case, in the real world a stark dichotomy between economic freedoms and civil rights does not exist. Human liberties of various types are dependent on one another, and it may well be that the most humble of them is indispensable to the others—the firmament, so to speak, upon which the high spires of the most exalted freedoms ultimately rest. I know no society, today or in any era of history, in which high degrees of intellectual and political freedom have flourished side by side with a high degree of state control over the relevant citizen's economic life. The free market, which presupposes relatively broad economic freedom, has historically been the cradle of broad political freedom, and in modern times the demise of economic freedom has been the grave of political freedom as well. The same phenomenon is observable in the small scales of our private lives. As a practical matter, he who controls my economic destiny controls much more of my life as well. Most salaried professionals do not consider themselves "free" to go about wearing sandals and Nehru jackets, or to write letters on any subjects they please to the *New York Times*.

My concern in this essay, however, is not economic liberty in general, but economic liberty and the judiciary. One must approach this topic with the realization that the courts are (in most contexts, at least) hardly disparaging of economic rights and liberties. Although most of the cases you read of in the newspaper may involve busing, or homosexual rights, or the supervision of school districts and mental institutions, the vast bulk of the courts' civil business consists of the vindication of economic rights between private individuals and against the government. Indeed, even the vast bulk of non-criminal "civil rights" cases are really cases involving economic disputes. The legal basis for the plaintiff's claim may be sex discrimination, but what she is really complaining about is that someone did her out of a job. Even the particular court on which I sit, which because of its location probably gets an inordinately large share of civil cases *not* involving economic rights, still finds that the majority of its business consists of enforcing economic rights against the government—the right to conduct business in an unregulated fashion where Congress has authorized no regulation, or the right to receive a fair return upon capital invested in a rate-regulated business. Indeed, some of the economic interests protected by my court are quite rarefied, such as a business's right to remain free of economic competition from a government licensee whose license is defective in a respect having nothing to do with the plaintiff's interests—for example, one radio station's challenge to the license of a competing station on the basis that the latter will produce electronic interference with a third station.

Fundamental or rarefied, the point is that we, the judiciary, do a lot of protecting of economic rights and liberties. The problem that some see is that this protection in the federal courts runs only by and large against the executive branch and not against the Congress. We will ensure that the executive does not impose any constraints upon economic activity which Congress has not authorized; and that where constraints *are* authorized the executive follows statutorily prescribed procedures and that the executive (and, much more rarely, Congress in its prescriptions) follows constitutionally required procedures. But we will never (well, hardly ever) decree that the substance of the congressionally authorized constraint is unlawful. That is to say, we do not provide a *constitutionalized* protection except insofar as matters of process, as opposed to substantive economic rights, are concerned.

There are those who urge reversal of this practice. The main vehicle available—and the only one I address specifically here—is the Due Process Clause of the Fifth and Fourteenth Amendments, which provides that no person shall be deprived of "life, liberty, or property, without due process of law." Although one might suppose that a reference to "process" places limitations only upon the *manner* in which a thing may be done, and not upon the *doing* of it, since at least the late 1800s the federal courts have in fact interpreted these clauses to prohibit the *substance* of certain governmental action, no matter what fair and legitimate procedures attend that substance. Thus, there has come to develop a judicial vocabulary which refers (seemingly redundantly) to "procedural due process" on the one hand, and (seemingly paradoxically) to "substantive due process" on the other hand. Until the mid-1930s, substantive-due-process rights were extended not merely to what we would now term "civil rights"—for example, the freedom to teach one's child a foreign language if one wishes—but also to a broad range of economic rights—for example, the right to work twelve hours a day if one wishes. Since that time, application of the concept has been consistently expanded in the civil-rights field (*Roe v. Wade* is the most controversial recent extension) but entirely eliminated in the field of economic rights. Some urge that it should be resuscitated.

I pause to note at this point, lest I either be credited with what is good in the present system or blamed for what is bad, that it is not up to me. (I did not have to make that disclaimer a few years ago, when I was a law professor.) The Supreme Court decisions rejecting substantive due process in the economic field are clear, unequivocal, and current, and as an appellate judge I try to do what I'm told. But I will go beyond that disclaimer and say that in my view the position the Supreme Court has arrived at is good—or at least that the suggestion that it change its position is even worse.

As should be apparent from what I said above, my position is not based on the proposition that economic rights are unimportant. Nor do I necessarily quarrel with the specific nature of the particular economic rights that the most sagacious of the proponents of substantive due process would bring within the protection of the Constitution; were I a legislator, I might well vote for them. Rather, my skepticism arises from misgivings about, first, the effect of such expansion on the behavior of courts in other areas quite separate from economic liberty, and second, the ability of the courts to limit their constitutionalizing to those elements of economic liberty that are sensible. I will say a few words about each.

First, the effect of constitutionalizing substantive economic guarantees on the behavior of the courts in other areas: There is an inevitable connection between judges' ability and willingness to craft substantive-due-process guarantees in the economic field and their ability and willingness to do it elsewhere. Many believe—and among those many are some of the same people who urge an expansion of economic due-process rights—that our system already suffers from relatively recent constitutionalizing, and thus judicializing, of social judgments that ought better be left to the democratic process. The courts, they feel, have come to be regarded as an alternate legislature, whose charge differs from that of the ordinary legislature in the respect that while the latter may enact into law good ideas, the former may enact into law only *unquestionably* good ideas, which, since they *are* so unquestionably good, *must* be part of the Constitution. I would not adopt such an extravagant description of the problem. But I do believe that every era raises its own peculiar threat to constitutional democracy, and that the attitude of mind thus caricatured represents the distinctive threat of our times. And I therefore believe that whatever reinforces rather than challenges that attitude is to that extent undesirable. It seems to me that the reversal of a half century of judicial restraint in the economic realm comes within that category. In the long run, and perhaps even in the short run, the reinforcement of mistaken and unconstitutional perceptions of the role of the courts in our system far outweighs whatever evils may have accrued from undue judicial abstention in the economic field.

The response to my concern, I suppose, is that the connection I assert between judicial intervention in the economic realm and in other realms can simply not be shown to exist. We have substantive due process aplenty in the field of civil liberties, even while it has been obliterated in the economic field. My rejoinder is simply an abiding faith that logic will out. Litigants before me often characterize the argument that if the court does *w* (which is desirable) then it must logically do *x*, *y*, and *z* (which are undesirable) as a "parade of horribles"; but in my years at the law I have too often seen the end of the parade come by. There really is an inevitable tug of logical consistency upon human affairs, and especially upon judicial affairs—indeed, that is the only thing that makes the system work. So I must believe that as bad as some feel judicial "activism" has gotten without substantive due process in the economic field, *absent* that memento of judicial humility it might have gotten even worse. And I have little hope that judicial and lawyerly attitudes can be coaxed back to a more restricted view of the courts' role in a democratic society at the same time that we are charging forward on an entirely new front.

Though it is something of an over-simplification, I do not think it unfair to say that this issue presents the moment of truth for many conservatives who have been criticizing the courts in recent years. They must decide whether they really believe, as they have been saying, that the courts are doing too much, or whether they are actually nursing only the less principled grievance that the courts have not been doing what *they* want.

The second reason for my skepticism is the absence of any reason to believe that the courts would limit their constitutionalizing of economic rights to those rights that are sensible. In this regard some conservatives seem to make the same mistake they so persuasively argue the society makes whenever it unthinkingly calls in government regulation to remedy a "market failure." It is first necessary to make sure, they have persuaded us, that the cure is not worse than the disease—that the phenomenon of "government failure," attributable to the fact that the government, like the market, happens to be composed of self-interested human beings, will not leave the last state of the problem worse than the first. It strikes me as peculiar that these same rational free-market proponents will unthinkingly call in the courts as a *deus ex machina* to solve what they perceive as the problems of democratic inadequacy in the field of economic rights. Is there much reason to believe that the courts, if they undertook the task, would do a good job? If economic sophistication is the touchstone, it suffices to observe that these are the folks who developed three-quarters of a century of counterproductive law under the Sherman Act. But perhaps what counts is not economic sophistication, but rather a favoritism—not shared by the political branches of government—toward the institution of property and its protection. I have no doubt that judges once met this qualification. When Madison described them as a "natural aristocracy," I am sure he had in mind an aristocracy of property as well as of manners. But with the proliferation and consequent bureaucratization of the courts, the relative modesty of judicial salaries, and above all the development of lawyers (and hence of judges) through a system of generally available university education which, in this country as in others, more often nurtures collectivist than capitalist philosophy, one would be foolish to look for Daddy Warbucks on the bench.

But, the proponents of constitutionalized economic rights will object, we do not propose an open-ended, unlimited charter to the courts to create economic rights, but would tie the content of those rights to the text of the Constitution and, where the text is itself somewhat open-ended (the Due Process Clause, for example), to established (if recently forgotten) constitutional traditions. As a theoretical matter, that could be done—though it is infinitely more difficult today than it was fifty years ago. Because of the courts' long retirement from the field of constitutional economics, and because of judicial and legislative developments in other fields, the social consensus as to what are the limited, "core" economic rights does not exist today as it perhaps once did. But even if it is theoretically possible for the courts to mark out limits to their intervention, it is hard to be confident that they would do so. We may find ourselves burdened with judicially prescribed economic liberties that are worse than the pre-existing economic bondage. What would you think, for example, of a substantive-due-process, constitutionally guaranteed, economic right of every worker to "just and favourable remuneration ensuring for himself and his family an existence worthy of human dignity"? Many think this a precept of natural law; why not of the Constitution? A sort of constitutionally prescribed (and thus judicially determined) minimum wage. Lest it be thought fanciful, I have taken the formulation of this right verbatim from Article 23 of the United Nations' Universal Declaration of Human Rights.

Finally, let me suggest that the call for creating (or, if you prefer, "re-establishing") economic constitutional guarantees mistakes the nature and effect of the constitutionalizing process. To some degree, a constitutional guarantee is like a commercial loan: you can only get it if, at the time, you don't really need it. The most important, enduring, and stable portions of the Constitution represent such a deep social consensus that one suspects that if they were entirely eliminated, very little would change. And the converse is also true. A guarantee may appear in the words of the Constitution, but when the society ceases to possess an abiding belief in it, it has no living effect. Consider the fate of the principle expressed in the Tenth Amendment that the federal government is a government of limited powers. I do not suggest that constitutionalization has no effect in helping the society to preserve allegiance to its fundamental principles. That is the whole purpose of a constitution. But the allegiance comes first and the preservation afterward.

Most of the constitutionalizing of civil rights that the courts have effected in recent years has been at the margins of well-established and deeply held social beliefs. Even *Brown v. Board of Education*, as significant a step as it might have seemed, was only an elaboration of the consequences of the nation's deep belief in the equality of all persons before the law. Where the Court has tried to go further than that (the unsuccessful attempt to eliminate the death penalty, to take one of the currently less controversial examples), the results have been precarious. Unless I have been on the bench so long that I no longer have any feel for popular sentiment, I do not detect the sort of national commitment to most of the economic liberties generally discussed that would enable even an activist court to constitutionalize them. That lack of sentiment may be regrettable, but to seek to develop it by enshrining the unaccepted principles in the Constitution is to place the cart before the horse.

If you are interested in economic liberties, then, the first step is to recall the society to that belief in their importance which (I have no doubt) the Founders of the Republic shared. That may be no simple task, because the roots of the problem extend as deeply into modern theology as into modern social thought. I remember a conversation with Irving Kristol some years ago, in which he expressed gratitude that his half of the Judeo-Christian heritage had never thought it a sin to be rich. In fact my half never thought it so either. Voluntary poverty, like voluntary celibacy, was a counsel of perfection—but it was not thought that either wealth or marriage was inherently evil, or a condition that the just society should seek to stamp out. But that subtle distinction has assuredly been forgotten, and we live in an age in which many Christians are predisposed to believe that John D. Rockefeller, for all his piety (he founded the University of Chicago as a Baptist institution), is likely to be damned and Che Guevara, for all his non-belief, is likely to be among the elect. This suggests that the task of creating what I might call a constitutional ethos of economic liberty is no easy one. But it is the first task.

Regulatory Takings—*Lucas v. South Carolina Coastal Council* (1992)

Majority opinion (joined by Chief Justice Rehnquist and Justices White, O'Connor, and Thomas)*

The Takings Clause of the Fifth Amendment, which applies against the federal government, provides: "nor shall private property be taken for public use without just compensation." That guarantee, like nearly every other guarantee in the Bill of Rights, has also been deemed to apply against the states via the Fourteenth Amendment.

Beyond direct appropriations of land, the Takings Clause has also long been understood to forbid regulation of land that "goes too far." Drawing the line between permissible and impermissible regulations of land has proven to be a challenging matter.

In 1986, David H. Lucas paid $975,000 for two residential lots on a barrier island in South Carolina. Two years later, South Carolina enacted the Beachfront Management Act, which had the effect of preventing him from building any permanent habitable structures on his lots.

In his majority opinion, Justice Scalia concluded that the state supreme court applied the wrong principles when it determined that Lucas was not entitled to any compensation under the Takings Clause.

P rior to Justice Holmes's exposition in *Pennsylvania Coal Co. v. Mahon* (1922), it was generally thought that the Takings Clause reached only a direct appropriation of property or the functional equivalent of a practical ouster of the owner's possession. Justice Holmes recognized in *Mahon*, however, that if the protection against physical appropriations of private property was to be meaningfully enforced, the government's power to redefine the range of interests included in the ownership of property was necessarily constrained by

---

* Justice Kennedy, concurring in the judgment, provided a sixth vote in favor of Lucas.

constitutional limits. If, instead, the uses of private property were subject to unbridled, uncompensated qualification under the police power, "the natural tendency of human nature [would be] to extend the qualification more and more until at last private property disappear[ed]." These considerations gave birth in that case to the oft-cited maxim that, "while property may be regulated to a certain extent, if regulation goes too far it will be recognized as a taking."

Nevertheless, our decision in *Mahon* offered little insight into when, and under what circumstances, a given regulation would be seen as going "too far" for purposes of the Fifth Amendment. In 70-odd years of succeeding "regulatory takings" jurisprudence, we have generally eschewed any set formula for determining how far is too far, preferring to "engage in . . . essentially ad hoc, factual inquiries."[1] We have, however, described at least two discrete categories of regulatory action as compensable without case-specific inquiry into the public interest advanced in support of the restraint. The first encompasses regulations that compel the property owner to suffer a physical invasion of his property. In general (at least with regard to permanent invasions), no matter how minute the intrusion, and no matter how weighty the public purpose behind it, we have required compensation.

The second situation in which we have found categorical treatment appropriate is where regulation denies all economically beneficial or productive use of land. As we have said on numerous occasions, the Fifth Amendment is violated when land-use regulation "does not substantially advance legitimate state interests *or denies an owner economically viable use of his land.*"[2]

Where the State seeks to sustain regulation that deprives land of all economically beneficial use, we think it may resist compensation only if the logically antecedent inquiry into the nature of the owner's estate shows that the proscribed use interests were not part of his title to begin with. This accords, we think, with our takings jurisprudence, which has traditionally been guided by the understandings of our citizens regarding the content of, and the State's power over, the "bundle of rights" that they acquire when they obtain title to property. It seems to us that the property owner necessarily expects the uses of his property to be restricted, from time to time, by various measures newly enacted by the State in legitimate exercise of its police powers; "as long recognized, some values are enjoyed under an implied limitation and must yield to the police power."[3] And in the case of personal property, by reason of the State's traditionally high degree of control over commercial dealings, he ought to be aware of the possibility that new regulation might even render his property economically worthless (at least if the property's only economically productive use is sale or manufacture for sale). In the case of land, however, we think the notion pressed by the Council that title is somehow held subject to the implied limitation that the State may subsequently eliminate all economically valuable use is inconsistent with the historical compact recorded in the Takings Clause that has become part of our constitutional culture.

Where permanent physical occupation of land is concerned, we have refused to allow the government to decree it anew (without compensation), no matter how weighty the asserted public interests involved—though we assuredly *would* permit the government to assert a permanent easement that was a pre-existing limitation upon the land owner's title. We believe similar treatment must be accorded confiscatory regulations, *i.e.*, regulations that prohibit all economically beneficial use of land: Any limitation so severe cannot be newly legislated or decreed (without compensation), but must inhere in the title itself, in the restrictions that background principles of the State's law of property and nuisance already place upon land ownership. A law or decree with such an effect must, in other words, do no more than duplicate the result that could have been achieved in the courts—by adjacent landowners (or other uniquely affected persons) under the State's law of private nuisance, or by the State under its complementary power to abate nuisances that affect the public generally, or otherwise.

On this analysis, the owner of a lake bed, for example, would not be entitled to compensation when he is denied the requisite permit to engage in a landfilling operation that would have the effect of flooding others' land. Nor the corporate owner of a nuclear generating plant, when it is directed to remove all improvements from its land upon discovery that the plant sits astride an earthquake fault. Such regulatory action may well have the effect of eliminating the land's only economically productive use, but it does not proscribe a productive use that was previously permissible under relevant property and nuisance principles. The use of these properties for what are now expressly prohibited purposes was *always* unlawful, and (subject to other constitutional limitations) it was open to the State at any point to make the implication of those background principles of nuisance and property law explicit. In light of our traditional resort to existing rules or understandings that stem from an independent source such as state law to define the range of interests that qualify for protection as "property" under the Fifth and Fourteenth Amendments, this recognition that the Takings Clause does not require compensation when an owner is barred from putting land to a use that is proscribed by those existing rules or understandings is surely unexceptional.

When, however, a regulation that declares "off-limits" all economically productive or beneficial uses of land goes beyond what the relevant background principles would dictate, compensation must be paid to sustain it.

The "total taking" inquiry we require today will ordinarily entail (as the application of state nuisance law ordinarily entails) analysis of, among other things, the degree of harm to public lands and resources, or adjacent private property, posed by the claimant's proposed activities, the social value of the claimant's activities and their suitability to the locality in question, and the relative ease with which the alleged harm can be avoided through measures taken by the claimant and the government (or adjacent private landowners) alike. The fact that a particular use has long been engaged in by similarly situated owners ordinarily imports a lack of any common-law prohibition (though changed circumstances or new knowledge may make what was previously permissible no longer so). So also does the fact that other landowners, similarly situated, are permitted to continue the use denied to the claimant.

We emphasize that to win its case South Carolina must do more than proffer the legislature's declaration that the uses Lucas desires are inconsistent with the public interest. Instead, as it would be required to do if it sought to restrain Lucas in a common-law action for public nuisance, South Carolina must identify background principles of nuisance and property law that prohibit the uses he now intends in the circumstances in which the property is presently found. Only on this showing can the State fairly claim that, in proscribing all such beneficial uses, the Beachfront Management Act is taking nothing.

Criminal Protections

Criminal law offers a revealing perspective on Justice Scalia's approach to constitutional interpretation. During his tenure, he was one of the Court's strongest voices in the area—sometimes favoring criminal defendants, sometimes ruling against them. Who won his vote turned on which side anchored its argument in the Constitution's text and history.

When people think of transformative criminal law decisions, Mapp v. Ohio (1961) (imposing the exclusionary rule), Miranda v. Arizona (1966) (dictating warnings to be given before interrogating suspects), and decisions limiting capital punishment come to mind. But to Justice Scalia, these decisions transformed pre-existing law precisely because they had no basis in the Constitution. He thus led the charge to confine the reach of Mapp, to critique and limit Miranda, and to hold the line against judicial efforts to eliminate the death penalty.

But if a criminal defendant grounded his claimed right in the Constitution's text and history, there was no more vigilant defender of the right than Justice Scalia. Take the Fourth Amendment and the new risks to privacy created by new technologies. His judicial philosophy led him, in Kyllo v. United States (2001), to recognize constitutional limitations on the government's use of innovative technology to obtain information about what is inside a person's home.

Or take his efforts to honor the language and history of the Sixth Amendment's Confrontation Clause. That quest began with a vigorous dissent in Maryland v. Craig (1990), in which he maintained that the Court had "subordinated" the Constitution's textual demand that the defendant had a right "to be confronted with the witnesses against him" to "currently favored public policy" when it allowed a child witness to testify by one-way closed-circuit television. In Crawford v. Washington (2004), the justice persuaded six colleagues to join his opinion for the Court insisting that out-of-court testimonial statements by witnesses are barred unless the defendant had a prior opportunity to examine the witness and the witness is currently unavailable. The decision led to a sea change in the handling of criminal cases.

Or take the impact of his commitment to the Sixth Amendment's trial by jury. He helped to launch a wholesale shift in the Court's view of sentencing laws. A majority of the Court ultimately came around to his position through three system-changing decisions, one of which (Blakely v. Washington (2004)) he wrote, the others of which he joined. Sentencing laws in the state and federal courts have not been the same since. He also led the charge against vague criminal laws. What started as a dissenting position again became a majority position: in Johnson v. United States (2015), he convinced his colleagues that their past "indulgence of imprecisions that violate the Constitution" had "encouraged" more "imprecisions that violate the Constitution."

The rule of law can indeed be a law of rules, as thousands of criminal defendants have come to appreciate. That Justice Scalia, whose first stint in public service came in a Republican administration promising law-and-order judges, ended up where he did on so many matters of criminal law shows that he worked to follow his principles where they led him.

UNREASONABLE SEARCHES AND SEIZURES

Thermal Imaging—*Kyllo v. United States* (2001)

Majority opinion (joined by Justices Souter, Thomas, Ginsburg, and Breyer)

The Fourth Amendment guarantees "[t]he right of the people to be secure in their persons, houses, papers, and effects, against unreasonable searches and seizures."

Federal agents suspected that Danny Kyllo was growing marijuana in his home with the assistance of high-intensity lamps. They used a thermal imager to scan the home to determine whether it was emitting a level of infrared radiation consistent with the use of such lamps. They conducted the scan from a vehicle parked across the street from the home. The scan took just a few minutes. When the scan revealed hot areas in the home, agents used the scan images to obtain a warrant to search Kyllo's home. They found more than one hundred marijuana plants in it.

Kyllo argued that the search violated his Fourth Amendment rights. Taking "the long view, from the original meaning of the Fourth Amendment forward," the Court, in a majority opinion by Justice Scalia, ruled in favor of Kyllo by a 5–4 vote.

This case presents the question whether the use of a thermal-imaging device aimed at a private home from a public street to detect relative amounts of heat within the home constitutes a "search" within the meaning of the Fourth Amendment.

The Fourth Amendment provides that "[t]he right of the people to be secure in their persons, houses, papers, and effects, against unreasonable searches and seizures, shall not be violated." "At the very core" of the Fourth Amendment "stands the right of a man to retreat into his own home and there be free from unreasonable governmental intrusion."[1] With few exceptions, the question whether a warrantless search of a home is reasonable and hence constitutional must be answered no.

On the other hand, the antecedent question of whether or not a Fourth Amendment "search" has occurred is not so simple under our precedent. The permissibility of ordinary visual surveillance of a home used to be clear because, well into the 20th century, our Fourth Amendment jurisprudence was tied to common-law trespass. Visual surveillance was unquestionably lawful because "the eye cannot by the laws of England be guilty of a trespass."[2] We have since decoupled violation of a person's Fourth Amendment rights from trespassory violation of his property, but the lawfulness of warrantless visual surveillance of a home has still been preserved.

It would be foolish to contend that the degree of privacy secured to citizens by the Fourth Amendment has been entirely unaffected by the advance of technology. For example, the technology enabling human flight has exposed to public view (and hence, we have said, to official observation) uncovered portions of the house and its curtilage that once were private. The question we confront today is what limits there are upon this power of technology to shrink the realm of guaranteed privacy.

We think that obtaining by sense-enhancing technology any information regarding the interior of the home that could not otherwise have been obtained without physical intrusion into a constitutionally protected area constitutes a search—at least where (as here) the technology in question is not in general public use. This assures preservation of that degree of privacy against government that existed when the Fourth Amendment was adopted. On the basis of this criterion, the information obtained by the thermal imager in this case was the product of a search.

We have said that the Fourth Amendment draws "a firm line at the entrance to the house." That line, we think, must be not only firm but also bright—which requires clear specification of those methods of surveillance that require a warrant. While it is certainly possible to conclude from the videotape of the thermal imaging that occurred in this case that no "significant" compromise of the homeowner's privacy has occurred, we must take the long view, from the original meaning of the Fourth Amendment forward.

DNA Swabs—*Maryland v. King* (2013)

Dissent (joined by Justices Ginsburg, Sotomayor, and Kagan)

In 2009, Alonzo King was arrested in Maryland and charged with assault. Police used a cotton swab to take a DNA sample from the inside of his cheeks. That DNA sample was found to match the DNA taken from a rape victim in 2003. King was then charged with and convicted of that rape.

By a 5–4 vote, the Supreme Court ruled that taking and analyzing the cheek swab of King's DNA did not violate his Fourth Amendment rights. Justice Scalia closed his dissent by expressing his "doubt that the proud men who wrote the charter of our liberties would have been so eager to open their mouths for royal inspection."

The Fourth Amendment forbids searching a person for evidence of a crime when there is no basis for believing the person is guilty of the crime or is in possession of incriminating evidence. That prohibition is categorical and without exception; it lies at the very heart of the Fourth Amendment. Whenever this Court has allowed a suspicionless search, it has insisted upon a justifying motive apart from the investigation of crime.

It is obvious that no such noninvestigative motive exists in this case. The Court's assertion that DNA is being taken, not to solve crimes, but to *identify* those in the State's custody, taxes the credulity of the credulous. And the Court's comparison of Maryland's DNA searches to other techniques, such as fingerprinting, can seem apt only to those who know no more than today's opinion has chosen to tell them about how those DNA searches actually work.

At the time of the Founding, Americans despised the British use of so-called "general warrants"—warrants not grounded upon a sworn oath of a specific infraction by a particular individual, and thus not limited in scope and application. The first Virginia Constitution declared that "general warrants, whereby any officer or messenger may be commanded to search suspected places without evidence of a fact committed," or to search a person "whose offence is not particularly described and supported by evidence," "are grievous and oppressive, and ought not be granted." The Maryland Declaration of Rights similarly provided that general warrants were "illegal."

In the ratification debates, Antifederalists sarcastically predicted that the general, suspicionless warrant would be among the Constitution's "blessings." "Brutus" of New York asked why the Federal Constitution contained no provision like Maryland's, and Patrick Henry warned that the new Federal Constitution would expose the citizenry to searches and seizures "in the most arbitrary manner, without any evidence or reason."

Madison's draft of what became the Fourth Amendment answered these charges by providing that the "rights of the people to be secured in their persons . . . from all unreasonable searches and seizures, shall not be violated by warrants issued without probable cause . . . or not particularly describing the places to be searched." As ratified, the Fourth Amendment's Warrant Clause forbids a warrant to "issue" except "upon probable cause," and requires that it be "particula[r]" (which is to say, *individualized*) to "the place to be searched, and the persons or things to be seized." And we have held that, even when a warrant is not constitutionally necessary, the Fourth Amendment's general prohibition of "unreasonable" searches imports the same requirement of individualized suspicion.

Today, it can fairly be said that fingerprints really are used to identify people—so well, in fact, that there would be no need for the expense of a separate, wholly redundant DNA confirmation of the same information. What DNA adds—what makes it a valuable weapon in the law-enforcement arsenal—is the ability to solve unsolved crimes, by matching old crime-scene evidence against the profiles of people whose identities are already known. That is what was going on when King's DNA was taken, and we should not disguise the fact. Solving unsolved crimes is a noble objective, but it occupies a lower place in the American pantheon of noble objectives than the protection of our people from suspicionless law-enforcement searches. The Fourth Amendment must prevail.

The Court disguises the vast (and scary) scope of its holding by promising a limitation it cannot deliver. The Court repeatedly says that DNA testing, and entry into a national DNA registry, will not befall thee and me, dear reader, but only those arrested for "serious offenses." I cannot imagine what principle could possibly justify this limitation, and the Court does not attempt to suggest any. If one believes that DNA will "identify" someone arrested for assault, he must believe that it will "identify" someone arrested for a traffic offense. This Court does not base its judgments on senseless distinctions. At the end of the day, *logic will out.* When there comes before us the taking of DNA from an arrestee for a traffic violation, the Court will predictably (and quite rightly) say, "We can find no significant difference between this case and *King.*" Make no mistake about it: As an entirely predictable consequence of today's decision, your DNA can be taken and entered into a national DNA database if you are ever arrested, rightly or wrongly, and for whatever reason.

The most regrettable aspect of the suspicionless search that occurred here is that it proved to be quite unnecessary. All parties concede that it would have been entirely permissible, as far as the Fourth Amendment is concerned, for Maryland to take a sample of King's DNA as a consequence of his conviction for second-degree assault. So the ironic result of the Court's error is this: The only arrestees to whom the outcome here will ever make a difference are those who *have been acquitted* of the crime of arrest (so that their DNA could not have been taken upon conviction). In other words, this Act manages to burden uniquely the sole group for whom the Fourth Amendment's protections ought to be most jealously guarded: people who are innocent of the State's accusations.

Today's judgment will, to be sure, have the beneficial effect of solving more crimes; then again, so would the taking of DNA samples from anyone who flies on an airplane (surely the Transportation Security Administration needs to know the "identity" of the flying public), applies for a driver's license, or attends a public school. Perhaps the construction of such a genetic panopticon is wise. But I doubt that the proud men who wrote the charter of our liberties would have been so eager to open their mouths for royal inspection.

Anonymous Tips—*Navarette v. California* (2014)

Dissent (joined by Justices Ginsburg, Sotomayor, and Kagan)

Police officers stopped a pickup truck occupied by two men because it matched the description of a vehicle that an anonymous 9-1-1 caller said had run her off the road. As they approached the car, they smelled marijuana. They searched the truck, found thirty pounds of marijuana, and arrested the two men. The men argued that the traffic stop violated their Fourth Amendment rights.

By a vote of 5 to 4, the Supreme Court ruled that the traffic stop was lawful. Disputing the conclusion that the anonymous call provided a reasonable suspicion of drunken driving, Justice Scalia declined to partake of the majority's "freedom-destroying cocktail."

Law enforcement agencies follow closely our judgments on matters such as this, and they will identify at once our new rule: So long as the caller identifies where the car is, anonymous claims of a single instance of possibly careless or reckless driving, called in to 911, will support a traffic stop. This is not my concept, and I am sure would not be the Framers', of a people secure from unreasonable searches and seizures.

The California Highway Patrol in this case knew nothing about the tipster on whose word—and that alone—they seized Lorenzo and José Prado Navarette. They did not know her name. They did not know her phone number or address. They did not even know where she called from (she may have dialed in from a neighboring county).

The tipster said the truck had "[run her] off the roadway," but the police had no reason to credit that charge and many reasons to doubt it, beginning with the peculiar fact that the accusation was anonymous. "Eliminating accountability is ordinarily the very purpose of anonymity."[1] The unnamed tipster "can lie with impunity."[2] Anonymity is especially suspicious with respect to the call that is the subject of the present case. When does a victim complain to the police about an arguably criminal act (running the victim off the road) without giving his identity, so that he can accuse and testify when the culprit is caught?

The anonymous caller said that the petitioners' truck "ran [me] off the roadway." That neither asserts that the driver was drunk nor even raises the *likelihood* that the driver was drunk. The most it conveys is that the truck did some apparently nontypical thing that forced the tipster off the roadway, whether partly or fully, temporarily or permanently. Who really knows what (if anything) happened? The truck might have swerved to avoid an animal, a pothole, or a jaywalking pedestrian.

But let us assume the worst of the many possibilities: that it was a careless, reckless, or even intentional maneuver that forced the tipster off the road. Lorenzo might have been distracted by his use of a hands-free cell phone or distracted by an intense sports argument with José. Or, indeed, he might have intentionally forced the tipster off the road because of some personal animus, or hostility to her "Make Love, Not War" bumper sticker. I fail to see how reasonable suspicion of a *discrete instance* of irregular or hazardous driving generates a reasonable suspicion of *ongoing intoxicated driving*. What proportion of the hundreds of thousands—perhaps millions—of careless, reckless, or intentional traffic violations committed each day is attributable to drunken drivers? I say 0.1 percent. I have no basis for that except my own guesswork. But unless the Court has some basis in reality to believe that the proportion is many orders of magnitude above that—say 1 in 10 or at least 1 in 20—it has no grounds for its unsupported assertion that the tipster's report in this case gave rise to a *reasonable suspicion* of drunken driving.

Bear in mind that that is the only basis for the stop that has been asserted in this litigation. The stop required suspicion of an ongoing crime, not merely suspicion of having run someone off the road earlier. And driving while being a careless or reckless person, unlike driving while being a drunk person, is not an ongoing crime. In other words, in order to stop the petitioners the officers here not only had to assume without basis the accuracy of the anonymous accusation but also had to posit an unlikely reason (drunkenness) for the accused behavior.

It gets worse. Not only, it turns out, did the police have no good reason *at first* to believe that Lorenzo was driving drunk, they had very good reason *at last* to know that he was not. The Court concludes that the tip, plus confirmation of the truck's location, produced reasonable suspicion that the truck not only had been *but still was* barreling dangerously and drunkenly down Highway 1. In fact, alas, it was not, and the officers knew it. They followed the truck for five minutes, presumably to see if it was being operated recklessly. And *that* was good police work. But the pesky little detail left out of the Court's reasonable-suspicion equation is that, for the five minutes that the truck was being followed (five minutes is a *long* time), Lorenzo's driving was irreproachable. And not only was the driving *irreproachable*, but the State offers no evidence to suggest that the petitioners even did anything *suspicious*, such as suddenly slowing down, pulling off to the side of the road, or turning somewhere to see whether they were being followed. Consequently, the tip's suggestion of ongoing drunken driving (if it could be deemed to suggest that) not only went uncorroborated; it was affirmatively undermined.

The Court's opinion serves up a freedom-destroying cocktail consisting of two parts patent falsity: (1) that anonymous 911 reports of traffic violations are reliable so long as they correctly identify a car and its location, and (2) that a single instance of careless or reckless driving necessarily supports a reasonable suspicion of drunkenness. All the malevolent 911 caller need do is assert a traffic violation, and the targeted car will be stopped, forcibly if necessary, by the police. If the driver turns out not to be drunk (which will almost always be the case), the caller need fear no consequences, even if 911 knows his identity. After all, he never alleged drunkenness, but merely called in a traffic violation—and on that point his word is as good as his victim's.

Drunken driving is a serious matter, but so is the loss of our freedom to come and go as we please without police interference. To prevent and detect murder we do not allow searches without probable cause or targeted *Terry* stops without reasonable suspicion. We should not do so for drunken driving either. After today's opinion all of us on the road, and not just drug dealers, are at risk of having our freedom of movement curtailed on suspicion of drunkenness, based upon a phone tip, true or false, of a single instance of careless driving. I respectfully dissent.

Limiting the Exclusionary Rule—
Hudson v. Michigan (2006)

Majority opinion (joined by Chief Justice Roberts and Justices Kennedy,* Thomas, and Alito)

The question whether a search violates the Fourth Amendment is distinct from the remedial question whether evidence obtained via an unconstitutional search should be suppressed. In this case, Justice Scalia wrote the majority opinion holding that violation of the "knock-and-announce" rule did not require suppression of the evidence found in the search.

We decide whether violation of the "knock-and-announce" rule requires the suppression of all evidence found in the search.

This case is before us only because of the method of entry into the house. When the police arrived to execute the warrant, they announced their presence, but waited only a short time—perhaps "three to five seconds"—before turning the knob of the unlocked front door and entering Hudson's home. Hudson moved to suppress all the inculpatory evidence, arguing that the premature entry violated his Fourth Amendment rights.

From the trial level onward, Michigan has conceded that the entry was a knock-and-announce violation. The issue here is remedy.

In *Weeks v. United States* (1914), we adopted the federal exclusionary rule for evidence that was unlawfully seized from a home without a warrant in violation of the Fourth Amendment. We began applying the same rule to the States, through the Fourteenth Amendment, in *Mapp v. Ohio* (1961).

Suppression of evidence, however, has always been our last resort, not our first impulse. The exclusionary rule generates substan-

---

* Justice Kennedy declined to join one part of Justice Scalia's opinion, but none of the passages here are from that part.

tial social costs, which sometimes include setting the guilty free and the dangerous at large. We have therefore been cautious against expanding it, and "have repeatedly emphasized that the rule's costly toll upon truth-seeking and law enforcement objectives presents a high obstacle for those urging its application."[1] We have rejected "indiscriminate application" of the rule,[2] and have held it to be applicable only "where its remedial objectives are thought most efficaciously served"—that is, "where its deterrence benefits outweigh its substantial social costs."[3]

The costs here are considerable. In addition to the grave adverse consequence that exclusion of relevant incriminating evidence always entails (viz., the risk of releasing dangerous criminals into society), imposing that massive remedy for a knock-and-announce violation would generate a constant flood of alleged failures to observe the rule. The cost of entering this lottery would be small, but the jackpot enormous: suppression of all evidence, amounting in many cases to a get-out-of-jail-free card. Courts would experience as never before the reality that "the exclusionary rule frequently requires extensive litigation to determine whether particular evidence must be excluded."[4]

Next to these substantial social costs we must consider the deterrence benefits, existence of which is a necessary condition for exclusion. To begin with, the value of deterrence depends upon the strength of the incentive to commit the forbidden act. Viewed from this perspective, deterrence of knock-and-announce violations is not worth a lot. Violation of the warrant requirement sometimes produces incriminating evidence that could not otherwise be obtained. But ignoring knock-and-announce can realistically be expected to achieve absolutely nothing except the prevention of destruction of evidence and the avoidance of life-threatening resistance by occupants of the premises—dangers which, if there is even "reasonable suspicion" of their existence, *suspend the knock-and-announce requirement anyway*. Massive deterrence is hardly required.

Hudson complains that "it would be very hard to find a lawyer to take a case such as this," but 42 U. S. C. § 1988(b) answers this objection. Since some civil-rights violations would yield damages too small to justify the expense of litigation, Congress has authorized attorney's fees for civil-rights plaintiffs. This remedy was unavailable in the heydays of our exclusionary-rule jurisprudence, because it is tied to the availability of a cause of action. For years after *Mapp*, "very few lawyers would even consider representation of persons who had civil rights claims against the police," but now "much has changed. Citizens and lawyers are much more willing to seek relief in the courts for police misconduct."[5] The number of public-interest law firms and lawyers who specialize in civil-rights grievances has greatly expanded.

Another development over the past half-century that deters civil-rights violations is the increasing professionalism of police forces, including a new emphasis on internal police discipline. Even as long ago as 1980 we felt it proper to "assume" that unlawful police behavior would "be dealt with appropriately" by the authorities,[6] but we now have increasing evidence that police forces across the United States take the constitutional rights of citizens seriously. There have been "wide-ranging reforms in the education, training, and supervision of police officers."[7] Numerous sources are now available to teach officers and their supervisors what is required of them under this Court's cases, how to respect constitutional guarantees in various situations, and how to craft an effective regime for internal discipline. Failure to teach and enforce constitutional requirements exposes municipalities to financial liability. Moreover, modern police forces are staffed with professionals; it is not credible to assert that internal discipline, which can limit successful careers, will not have a deterrent effect. There is also evidence that the increasing use of various forms of citizen review can enhance police accountability.

In sum, the social costs of applying the exclusionary rule to knock-and-announce violations are considerable; the incentive to such violations is minimal to begin with, and the extant deterrences against them are substantial—incomparably greater than the factors deterring warrantless entries when *Mapp* was decided. Resort to the massive remedy of suppressing evidence of guilt is unjustified.

COMPELLED TESTIMONY

Rejecting *Miranda*—*Dickerson v. United States* (2000)

Dissent (joined by Justice Thomas)

Among its many guarantees, the Fifth Amendment provides that no person "shall be compelled in any criminal case to be a witness against himself." In 1966, in Miranda v. Arizona, *the Supreme Court ruled that when a suspect is in police custody and is being interrogated, the suspect's statements will be deemed involuntary and inadmissible under the Fifth Amendment unless the police first provide what are now known as the* Miranda *warnings ("You have the right to remain silent," and so on). Two years later, in 1968, Congress tried to limit the effect of an officer's failure to provide the* Miranda *warnings. It enacted a law that directed federal judges to admit into evidence confessions they determined to have been voluntary, whether or not those confessions were preceded by the* Miranda *warnings.*

By the 1990s, the Court had come to re-conceive the Miranda *warnings as "prophylactic" in nature—providing an additional layer of protection against violation of the Fifth Amendment, but not actually required by that amendment. That led to the question whether the 1968 federal law could be enforced.*

By a 7–2 margin, the Supreme Court, in a majority opinion by Chief Justice Rehnquist, declined to enforce the 1968 law on the ground that it was inconsistent with Miranda, *and it declined to overrule* Miranda. *Justice Scalia responded with this dissent.*

Those to whom judicial decisions are an unconnected series of judgments that produce either favored or disfavored results will doubtless greet today's decision as a paragon of moderation, since it declines to overrule *Miranda v. Arizona* (1966). Those who understand the judicial process will appreciate that today's decision is not a reaffirmation of *Miranda,* but a radical revision of the most significant element of *Miranda* (as of all cases): the rationale that gives it a permanent place in our jurisprudence.

Marbury v. Madison (1803) held that an Act of Congress will not be enforced by the courts if what it prescribes violates the Constitution of the United States. That was the basis on which *Miranda* was decided. One will search today's opinion in vain, however, for a statement (surely simple enough to make) that what 18 U.S.C. § 3501 prescribes—the use at trial of a voluntary confession, even when a *Miranda* warning or its equivalent has failed to be given—violates the Constitution. The reason the statement does not appear is not only (and perhaps not so much) that it would be absurd, inasmuch as § 3501 excludes from trial precisely what the Constitution excludes from trial, viz., compelled confessions; but also that Justices whose votes are needed to compose today's majority are on record as believing that a violation of *Miranda* is *not* a violation of the Constitution. And so, to justify today's agreed-upon result, the Court must adopt a significant *new*, if not entirely comprehensible, principle of constitutional law. As the Court chooses to describe that principle, statutes of Congress can be disregarded, not only when what they prescribe violates the Constitution, but when what they prescribe contradicts a decision of this Court that "announced a constitutional rule." As I shall discuss in some detail, the only thing that can possibly mean in the context of this case is that this Court has the power, not merely to apply the Constitution but to expand it, imposing what it regards as useful "prophylactic" restrictions upon Congress and the States. That is an immense and frightening antidemocratic power, and it does not exist.

It takes only a small step to bring today's opinion out of the realm of power-judging and into the mainstream of legal reasoning: The Court need only go beyond its carefully couched iterations that "*Miranda* is a constitutional decision," that "*Miranda* is constitutionally based," that *Miranda* has "constitutional underpinnings," and come out and say quite clearly: "We reaffirm today that custodial interrogation that is not preceded by *Miranda* warnings or their equivalent violates the Constitution of the United States." It cannot say that, because a majority of the Court does not believe it. The Court therefore acts in plain violation of the Constitution when it denies effect to this Act of Congress.

Early in this Nation's history, this Court established the sound proposition that constitutional government in a system of separated powers requires judges to regard as inoperative any legislative act, even of Congress itself, that is "repugnant to the Constitution."

> So if a law be in opposition to the constitution; if both the law and the constitution apply to a particular case, so that the court must either decide that case conformably to the law, disregarding the constitution; or conformably to the constitution, disregarding the law; the court must determine which of these conflicting rules governs the case. [*Marbury v. Madison* (1803).]

The power we recognized in *Marbury* will thus permit us, indeed require us, to "disregard" § 3501, a duly enacted statute governing the admissibility of evidence in the federal courts, only if it "be in opposition to the constitution"—here, assertedly, the dictates of the Fifth Amendment.

It was once possible to characterize the so-called *Miranda* rule as resting (however implausibly) upon the proposition that what the statute here before us permits—the admission at trial of un-*Mirandized* confessions—violates the Constitution. That is the fairest reading of the *Miranda* case itself.

So understood, *Miranda* was objectionable for innumerable reasons, not least the fact that cases spanning more than 70 years had rejected its core premise that, absent the warnings and an effective waiver of the right to remain silent and of the (thitherto unknown) right to have an attorney present, a statement obtained pursuant to custodial interrogation was necessarily the product of compulsion. Moreover, history and precedent aside, the decision in *Miranda*, if read as an explication of what the Constitution *requires*, is preposterous. There is, for example, simply no basis in reason for concluding that a response to the very first question asked, by a suspect who already *knows* all of the rights described in the *Miranda* warning, is anything other than a volitional act. And even if one assumes that the elimination of compulsion absolutely requires informing even the most knowledgeable suspect of his right to remain silent, it cannot conceivably require the right to have *counsel* present. There is a world of difference, which the Court recognized under the traditional voluntariness test but ignored in *Miranda*, between compelling a suspect to incriminate himself and preventing him from foolishly doing so of his own accord. Only the latter (which is *not* required by the Constitution) could explain the Court's inclusion of a right to counsel and the requirement that it, too, be knowingly and intelligently waived. Counsel's presence is not required to tell the suspect that he *need* not speak; the interrogators can do that. The only good reason for having counsel there is that he can be counted on to advise the suspect that he *should* not speak.

Preventing foolish (rather than compelled) confessions is likewise the only conceivable basis for the rules (suggested in *Miranda*), that courts must exclude any confession elicited by questioning conducted, without interruption, after the suspect has indicated a desire to stand on his right to remain silent or initiated by police after the suspect has expressed a desire to have counsel present. Nonthreatening attempts to persuade the suspect to reconsider that initial decision are not, without more, enough to render a change of heart the product of anything other than the suspect's free will. Thus, what is most remarkable about the *Miranda* decision—and what made it unacceptable as a matter of straightforward constitutional interpretation in the *Marbury* tradition—is its palpable hostility toward the act of confession *per se*, rather than toward what the Constitution abhors, *compelled* confession. The Constitution is not, unlike the *Miranda* majority, offended by a criminal's commendable qualm of conscience or fortunate fit of stupidity.

For these reasons, and others more than adequately developed in the *Miranda* dissents and in the subsequent works of the decision's many critics, any conclusion that a violation of the *Miranda* rules *necessarily* amounts to a violation of the privilege against compelled self-incrimination can claim no support in history, precedent, or common sense, and as a result would at least presumptively be worth reconsidering even at this late date. But that is unnecessary, since the Court has (thankfully) long since abandoned the notion that failure to comply with *Miranda*'s rules is itself a violation of the Constitution.

As the Court today acknowledges, since *Miranda* we have explicitly, and repeatedly, interpreted that decision as having announced, not the circumstances in which custodial interrogation runs afoul of the Fifth or Fourteenth Amendment, but rather only "prophylactic" rules that go beyond the right against compelled self-incrimination. Of course the seeds of this "prophylactic" interpretation of *Miranda* were present in the decision itself. In subsequent cases, the seeds have sprouted and borne fruit: The Court has squarely concluded that it is possible—indeed not uncommon—for the police to violate *Miranda* without also violating the Constitution.

It is simply no longer possible for the Court to conclude, even if it wanted to, that a violation of *Miranda*'s rules is a violation of the Constitution. But as I explained at the outset, that is what is required before the Court may disregard a law of Congress governing the admissibility of evidence in federal court. The Court today insists that the *decision* in *Miranda* is a "constitutional" one; that it has "constitutional underpinnings," a "constitutional basis," and a "constitutional origin"; that it was "constitutionally based"; and that it announced a "constitutional rule." It is fine to play these word games; but what makes a decision "constitutional" in the only sense relevant here—in the sense that renders it impervious to supersession by congressional legislation such as § 3501—is the determination that the Constitution *requires* the result that the decision announces and the statute ignores. By disregarding congressional action that concededly does not violate the Constitution, the Court flagrantly offends fundamental principles of separation of powers, and arrogates to itself prerogatives reserved to the representatives of the people.

Today's judgment converts *Miranda* from a milestone of judicial overreaching into the very Cheops' Pyramid (or perhaps the Sphinx would be a better analogue) of judicial arrogance. In imposing its Court-made code upon the States, the original opinion at least *asserted* that it was demanded by the Constitution. Today's decision does not pretend that it is—and yet *still* asserts the right to impose it against the will of the people's representatives in Congress. Far from believing that *stare decisis* compels this result, I believe we cannot allow to remain on the books even a celebrated decision—*especially* a celebrated decision—that has come to stand for the proposition that the Supreme Court has power to impose extraconstitutional constraints upon Congress and the States. This is not the system that was established by the Framers, or that would be established by any sane supporter of government by the people.

CONFRONTING WITNESSES

Testimony by Video—*Maryland v. Craig* (1990)

Dissent (joined by Justices Brennan, Marshall, and Stevens)

The Confrontation Clause of the Sixth Amendment provides: "In all criminal prosecutions, the accused shall enjoy the right . . . to be confronted with the witnesses against him."

In 1987, Sandra Ann Craig was on trial for child abuse. In accordance with a Maryland statute, the trial judge allowed the victim to testify via one-way closed-circuit television. The prosecutor and defense counsel conducted the examination and cross-examination of the child in a separate room, while the judge, the jury, and Craig watched the live video of the testimony in the courtroom.

By a 5–4 vote, the Supreme Court ruled that allowing the child witness to testify, outside the defendant's physical presence, by one-way closed-circuit television did not violate the Confrontation Clause. Concluding that this procedure was "virtually" but not "actually" constitutional, Justice Scalia dissented.

Seldom has this Court failed so conspicuously to sustain a categorical guarantee of the Constitution against the tide of prevailing current opinion. The Sixth Amendment provides, with unmistakable clarity, that "[i]n all criminal prosecutions, the accused shall enjoy the right . . . to be confronted with the witnesses against him." The purpose of enshrining this protection in the Constitution was to assure that none of the many policy interests from time to time pursued by statutory law could overcome a defendant's right to face his or her accusers in court. The Court, however, says:

> We conclude today that a State's interest in the physical and psychological well-being of child abuse victims may be sufficiently important to outweigh, at least in some cases, a defendant's right

to face his or her accusers in court. That a significant majority of States has enacted statutes to protect child witnesses from the trauma of giving testimony in child abuse cases attests to the widespread belief in the importance of such a public policy.

Because of this subordination of explicit constitutional text to currently favored public policy, the following scene can be played out in an American courtroom for the first time in two centuries: A father whose young daughter has been given over to the exclusive custody of his estranged wife, or a mother whose young son has been taken into custody by the State's child welfare department, is sentenced to prison for sexual abuse on the basis of testimony by a child the parent has not seen or spoken to for many months; and the guilty verdict is rendered without giving the parent so much as the opportunity to sit in the presence of the child, and to ask, personally or through counsel, "it is really not true, is it, that I—your father (or mother) whom you see before you—did these terrible things?" Perhaps that is a procedure today's society desires; perhaps (though I doubt it) it is even a fair procedure; but it is assuredly not a procedure permitted by the Constitution.

Because the text of the Sixth Amendment is clear, and because the Constitution is meant to protect against, rather than conform to, current "widespread belief," I respectfully dissent.

According to the Court, "we cannot say that [face-to-face] confrontation [with witnesses appearing at trial] is an indispensable element of the Sixth Amendment's guarantee of the right to confront one's accusers." That is rather like saying "we cannot say that being tried before a jury is an indispensable element of the Sixth Amendment's guarantee of the right to jury trial." The Court makes the impossible plausible by recharacterizing the Confrontation Clause, so that confrontation (redesignated "face-to-face confrontation") becomes only one of many "elements of confrontation."

To say that a defendant loses his right to confront a witness when that would cause the witness not to testify is rather like saying that the defendant loses his right to counsel when counsel would save him, or his right to subpoena witnesses when they would exculpate him, or his right not to give testimony against himself when that would prove him guilty.

The State's interest here is in fact no more and no less than what the State's interest always is when it seeks to get a class of evidence admitted in criminal proceedings: more convictions of guilty defendants. That is not an unworthy interest, but it should not be dressed up as a humanitarian one.

In the last analysis, however, this debate is not an appropriate one. I have no need to defend the value of confrontation, because the Court has no authority to question it. It is not within our charge to speculate that, "where face-to-face confrontation causes significant emotional distress in a child witness," confrontation might "in fact *disserve* the Confrontation Clause's truth-seeking goal." If so, that is a defect in the Constitution—which should be amended by the procedures provided for such an eventuality, but cannot be corrected by judicial pronouncement that it is archaic, contrary to "widespread belief" and thus null and void. For good or bad, the Sixth Amendment requires confrontation, and we are not at liberty to ignore it. To quote the document one last time (for it plainly says all that need be said): "In *all* criminal prosecutions, the accused shall enjoy the right . . . to be confronted with the witnesses against him."

The Court today has applied interest-balancing analysis where the text of the Constitution simply does not permit it. We are not free to conduct a cost-benefit analysis of clear and explicit constitutional guarantees, and then to adjust their meaning to comport with our findings. The Court has convincingly proved that the Maryland procedure serves a valid interest, and gives the defendant virtually everything the Confrontation Clause guarantees (everything, that is, except confrontation). I am persuaded, therefore, that the Maryland procedure is virtually constitutional. Since it is not, however, actually constitutional, I would affirm the judgment of the Maryland Court of Appeals reversing the judgment of conviction.

Out-of-Court Statements—
Crawford v. Washington (2004)

Majority opinion (joined by Justices Stevens, Kennedy, Souter, Thomas, Ginsburg, and Breyer)

In 1980, the Supreme Court ruled in Ohio v. Roberts *that the Confrontation Clause allows an unavailable witness's out-of-court statement to be used as evidence against a criminal defendant if the statement bears "adequate indicia of reliability." Twenty-four years later, Justice Scalia's majority opinion for seven justices overruled that decision. (Two other justices—Chief Justice Rehnquist and Justice O'Connor—concurred in the judgment but declined to vote to overrule* Roberts.*)*

In cases like Crawford *where the constitutional text does not fully answer the question, history comes to the fore to shed light on the original public meaning of the text. Hence this opinion's references to the trial of Sir Walter Raleigh, common-law English decisions, and early decisions of the American state courts. Each source helps to reveal how the Americans who ratified the Bill of Rights would have understood the confrontation right. It is doubtful that any justice has done more for the cause of legal history—and the cause of understanding the meaning of the Constitution—than Justice Scalia.*

Petitioner Michael Crawford stabbed a man who allegedly tried to rape his wife, Sylvia. At his trial, the State played for the jury Sylvia's tape-recorded statement to the police describing the stabbing, even though he had no opportunity for cross-examination. The Washington Supreme Court upheld petitioner's conviction after determining that Sylvia's statement was reliable. The question presented is whether this procedure complied with the Sixth Amendment's guarantee that, "[i]n all criminal prosecutions, the accused shall enjoy the right . . . to be confronted with the witnesses against him."

The Constitution's text does not alone resolve this case. One could plausibly read "witnesses against" a defendant to mean those who actually testify at trial, those whose statements are offered at trial, or something in-between. We must therefore turn to the historical background of the Clause to understand its meaning.

The right to confront one's accusers is a concept that dates back to Roman times. The Founding generation's immediate source of the concept, however, was the common law. English common law has long differed from continental civil law in regard to the manner in which witnesses give testimony in criminal trials. The common-law tradition is one of live testimony in court subject to adversarial testing, while the civil law condones examination in private by judicial officers.

Nonetheless, England at times adopted elements of the civil-law practice. Justices of the peace or other officials examined suspects and witnesses before trial. These examinations were sometimes read in court in lieu of live testimony, a practice that "occasioned frequent demands by the prisoner to have his accusers, *i.e.* the witnesses against him, brought before him face to face."[1] In some cases, these demands were refused.

The most notorious instances of civil-law examination occurred in the great political trials of the 16th and 17th centuries. One such was the 1603 trial of Sir Walter Raleigh for treason. Lord Cobham, Raleigh's alleged accomplice, had implicated him in an examination before the Privy Council and in a letter. At Raleigh's trial, these were read to the jury. Raleigh argued that Cobham had lied to save himself: "Cobham is absolutely in the King's mercy; to excuse me cannot avail him; by accusing me he may hope for favour." Suspecting that Cobham would recant, Raleigh demanded that the judges call him to appear, arguing that "the Proof of the Common Law is by witness and jury: let Cobham be here, let him speak it. Call my accuser before my face." The judges refused, and, despite Raleigh's protestations that he was being tried "by the Spanish Inquisition," the jury convicted, and Raleigh was sentenced to death.

One of Raleigh's trial judges later lamented that "the justice of England has never been so degraded and injured as by the condemnation of Sir Walter Raleigh." Through a series of statutory and judicial reforms, English law developed a right of confrontation that limited these abuses. For example, treason statutes required witnesses to confront the accused "face to face" at his arraignment. Courts, meanwhile, developed relatively strict rules of unavailability, admitting examinations only if the witness was demonstrably unable to testify in person. Several authorities also stated that a suspect's confession could be admitted only against himself, and not against others he implicated.

Many declarations of rights adopted around the time of the Revolution guaranteed a right of confrontation. The proposed Federal Constitution, however, did not. At the Massachusetts ratifying convention, Abraham Holmes objected to this omission precisely on the ground that it would lead to civil-law practices: "The mode of trial is altogether indetermined; whether [the defendant] is to be allowed to confront the witnesses, and have the advantage of cross-examination, we are not yet told. We shall find Congress possessed of powers enabling them to institute judicatories little less inauspicious than a certain tribunal in Spain, the *Inquisition*." Similarly, a prominent Antifederalist writing under the pseudonym Federal Farmer criticized the use of "written evidence": "Nothing can be more essential than the cross examining [of] witnesses, and generally before the triers of the facts in question. Written evidence [is] almost useless; it must be frequently taken ex parte, and but very seldom leads to the proper discovery of truth." The First Congress responded by including the Confrontation Clause in the proposal that became the Sixth Amendment.

Early state decisions shed light upon the original understanding of the common-law right. *State v. Webb*, decided a mere three years after the adoption of the Sixth Amendment, held that depositions could be read against an accused only if they were taken in his presence. Rejecting a broader reading of the English authorities, the court held: "It is a rule of the common law, founded on natural justice, that no man shall be prejudiced by evidence which he had not the liberty to cross examine."

This history supports two inferences about the meaning of the Sixth Amendment.

First, the principal evil at which the Confrontation Clause was directed was the civil-law mode of criminal procedure, and particularly its use of *ex parte* examinations as evidence against the accused. It was these practices that the Crown deployed in notorious treason cases like Raleigh's; that the Marian statutes invited; that English law's assertion of a right to confrontation was meant to prohibit; and that the Founding-era rhetoric decried. The Sixth Amendment must be interpreted with this focus in mind.

The historical record also supports a second proposition: that the Framers would not have allowed admission of testimonial statements of a witness who did not appear at trial unless he was unavailable to testify, and the defendant had had a prior opportunity for cross-examination. The text of the Sixth Amendment does not suggest any open-ended exceptions from the confrontation requirement to be developed by the courts. Rather, the "right . . . to be confronted with the witnesses against him" is most naturally read as a reference to the right of confrontation at common law, admitting only those exceptions established at the time of the Founding. As the English authorities above reveal, the common law in 1791 conditioned admissibility of an absent witness's examination on unavailability and a prior opportunity to cross-examine. The Sixth Amendment therefore incorporates those limitations. The numerous early state decisions applying the same test confirm that these principles were received as part of the common law in this country.

Where testimonial statements are involved, we do not think the Framers meant to leave the Sixth Amendment's protection to the vagaries of the rules of evidence, much less to amorphous notions of "reliability." Certainly none of the authorities discussed above acknowledges any general reliability exception to the common-law rule. Admitting statements deemed reliable by a judge is fundamentally at odds with the right of confrontation. To be sure, the Clause's ultimate goal is to ensure reliability of evidence, but it is a procedural rather than a substantive guarantee. It commands, not that evidence be reliable, but that reliability be assessed in a particular manner: by testing in the crucible of cross-examination. The Clause thus reflects a judgment, not only about the desirability of reliable evidence (a point on which there could be little dissent), but about how reliability can best be determined.

Dispensing with confrontation because testimony is obviously reliable is akin to dispensing with jury trial because a defendant is obviously guilty. This is not what the Sixth Amendment prescribes.

That inculpating statements are given in a testimonial setting is not an antidote to the confrontation problem, but rather the trigger that makes the Clause's demands most urgent. It is not enough to point out that most of the usual safeguards of the adversary process attend the statement, when the single safeguard missing is the one the Confrontation Clause demands.

We have no doubt that the courts below were acting in utmost good faith when they found reliability. The Framers, however, would not have been content to indulge this assumption. They knew that judges, like other government officers, could not always be trusted to safeguard the rights of the people; the likes of the dread Lord Jeffreys were not yet too distant a memory. They were loath to leave too much discretion in judicial hands. By replacing categorical constitutional guarantees with open-ended balancing tests, we do violence to their design. Vague standards are manipulable, and, while that might be a small concern in run-of-the-mill assault prosecutions like this one, the Framers had an eye toward politically charged cases like Raleigh's—great state trials where the impartiality of even those at the highest levels of the judiciary might not be so clear.

JURY TRIAL

Facts at Sentencing—*Blakely v. Washington* (2004)

Majority opinion (joined by Justices Stevens, Souter, Thomas, and Ginsburg)

The Sixth Amendment guarantees to criminal defendants "the right to a speedy and public trial, by an impartial jury." How that right affects the factual determinations that a judge relies on in imposing a criminal sentence is a question that has divided the justices. In dissent in the 1990s, Justice Scalia had pointed out the risk that criminal sentences that turned on judicial fact-finding violated the jury guarantee. That minority position became a majority position in several later decisions, including this one.

Petitioner Ralph Howard Blakely, Jr., pleaded guilty to the kidnapping of his estranged wife. The facts admitted in his plea, standing alone, supported a maximum sentence of 53 months. Pursuant to state law, the court imposed an "exceptional" sentence of 90 months after making a judicial determination that he had acted with "deliberate cruelty." We consider whether this violated petitioner's Sixth Amendment right to trial by jury.

This case requires us to apply the rule we expressed in *Apprendi v. New Jersey* (2000): "Other than the fact of a prior conviction, any fact that increases the penalty for a crime beyond the prescribed statutory maximum must be submitted to a jury, and proved beyond a reasonable doubt." This rule reflects two longstanding tenets of common-law criminal jurisprudence: that the "truth of every accusation" against a defendant "should afterwards be confirmed by the unanimous suffrage of twelve of his equals and neighbours,"[1] and that "an accusation which lacks any particular fact which the law makes essential to the punishment is no accusation within the requirements of the common law, and it is no accusation in reason."[2]

Those who would reject *Apprendi* are resigned to one of two alternatives. The first is that the jury need only find whatever facts the legislature chooses to label elements of the crime, and that those it labels sentencing factors—no matter how much they may increase the punishment—may be found by the judge. This would mean, for example, that a judge could sentence a man for committing murder even if the jury convicted him only of illegally possessing the firearm used to commit it—or of making an illegal lane change while fleeing the death scene. Not even *Apprendi*'s critics would advocate this absurd result. The jury could not function as circuit breaker in the State's machinery of justice if it were relegated to making a determination that the defendant at some point did something wrong, a mere preliminary to a judicial inquisition into the facts of the crime the State *actually* seeks to punish.

The second alternative is that legislatures may establish legally essential sentencing factors *within limits*—limits crossed when, perhaps, the sentencing factor is a "tail which wags the dog of the substantive offense."[3] What this means in operation is that the law must not go *too far*—it must not exceed the judicial estimation of the proper role of the judge.

The subjectivity of this standard is obvious. Petitioner argued below that second-degree kidnapping with deliberate cruelty was essentially the same as first-degree kidnapping, the very charge he had avoided by pleading to a lesser offense. The court conceded this might be so but held it irrelevant. Petitioner's 90-month sentence exceeded the 53-month standard maximum by almost 70%; the Washington Supreme Court in other cases has upheld exceptional sentences 15 times the standard maximum. Did the court go *too far* in any of these cases? There is no answer that legal analysis can provide. With *too far* as the yardstick, it is always possible to disagree with such judgments and never to refute them.

Whether the Sixth Amendment incorporates this manipulable standard rather than *Apprendi*'s bright-line rule depends on the plausibility of the claim that the Framers would have left definition of the scope of jury power up to judges' intuitive sense of how far is *too far*. We think that claim not plausible at all, because the very reason the

Framers put a jury-trial guarantee in the Constitution is that they were unwilling to trust government to mark out the role of the jury.

Any evaluation of *Apprendi*'s "fairness" to criminal defendants must compare it with the regime it replaced, in which a defendant, with no warning in either his indictment or plea, would routinely see his maximum potential sentence balloon from as little as five years to as much as life imprisonment, based not on facts proved to his peers beyond a reasonable doubt, but on facts extracted after trial from a report compiled by a probation officer who the judge thinks more likely got it right than got it wrong.

Ultimately, our decision cannot turn on whether or to what degree trial by jury impairs the efficiency or fairness of criminal justice. One can certainly argue that both these values would be better served by leaving justice entirely in the hands of professionals; many nations of the world, particularly those following civil-law traditions, take just that course. There is not one shred of doubt, however, about the Framers' paradigm for criminal justice: not the civil-law ideal of administrative perfection, but the common-law ideal of limited state power accomplished by strict division of authority between judge and jury. As *Apprendi* held, every defendant has the *right* to insist that the prosecutor prove to a jury all facts legally essential to the punishment. Under the dissenters' alternative, he has no such right. That should be the end of the matter.

Petitioner was sentenced to prison for more than three years beyond what the law allowed for the crime to which he confessed, on the basis of a disputed finding that he had acted with "deliberate cruelty." The Framers would not have thought it too much to demand that, before depriving a man of three more years of his liberty, the State should suffer the modest inconvenience of submitting its accusation to "the unanimous suffrage of twelve of his equals and neighbours," rather than a lone employee of the State.

DEATH PENALTY

Adolescent Murderers—*Roper v. Simmons* (2005)

Dissent (joined by Chief Justice Rehnquist and Justice Thomas)*

In its 1958 decision in Trop v. Dulles, *the Supreme Court first asserted the authority to define the Eighth Amendment's ban on "cruel and unusual punishments" in accord with "the evolving standards of decency that mark the progress of a maturing society." After Justice Scalia joined the Court, he ardently disputed the idea that federal judges possessed any such authority, and he lambasted the manner in which the Court exercised that supposed authority, including by its selective resort to foreign law.*

When he was seventeen, Christopher Simmons planned a murder. He assured his friends they could "get away with it" because they were minors. In the middle of the night, Simmons and a friend broke into a woman's home, awakened her, covered her eyes and mouth with duct tape, bound her hands, put her in her minivan, drove to a state park, walked her to a railroad trestle spanning a river, tied her hands and feet together with electrical wire, wrapped her whole face in duct tape, and threw her from the bridge. His victim drowned in the waters below.

Simmons confessed to the murder. At the death-penalty phase of his trial, the judge instructed the jurors that they could consider Simmons's age as a mitigating factor, and the defense relied heavily on that factor. The jury nonetheless recommended, and the trial judge imposed, the death penalty.

By a 5–4 vote, the Court ruled that the Eighth Amendment forbids the execution of offenders who were seventeen at the time of their offense.

In urging approval of a constitution that gave life-tenured judges the power to nullify laws enacted by the people's representatives, Alexander Hamilton assured the citizens of New York that there was

---

* Justice O'Connor filed a separate dissent.

little risk in this, since "[t]he judiciary . . . ha[s] neither FORCE nor WILL but merely judgment." The Federalist No. 78. But Hamilton had in mind a traditional judiciary, "bound down by strict rules and precedents which serve to define and point out their duty in every particular case that comes before them." Bound down, indeed. What a mockery today's opinion makes of Hamilton's expectation, announcing the Court's conclusion that the meaning of our Constitution has changed over the past 15 years—not, mind you, that this Court's decision 15 years ago was *wrong*, but that the Constitution *has changed*. The Court reaches this implausible result by purporting to advert, not to the original meaning of the Eighth Amendment, but to "the evolving standards of decency" of our national society. It then finds, on the flimsiest of grounds, that a national consensus which could not be perceived in our people's laws barely 15 years ago now solidly exists. Worse still, the Court says in so many words that what our people's laws say about the issue does not, in the last analysis, matter: "In the end our own judgment will be brought to bear on the question of the acceptability of the death penalty under the Eighth Amendment." The Court thus proclaims itself sole arbiter of our Nation's moral standards—and in the course of discharging that awesome responsibility purports to take guidance from the views of foreign courts and legislatures. Because I do not believe that the meaning of our Eighth Amendment, any more than the meaning of other provisions of our Constitution, should be determined by the subjective views of five Members of this Court and like-minded foreigners, I dissent.

In determining that capital punishment of offenders who committed murder before age 18 is "cruel and unusual" under the Eighth Amendment, the Court first considers, in accordance with our modern (though in my view mistaken) jurisprudence, whether there is a "national consensus" that laws allowing such executions contravene our modern "standards of decency." We have held that this determination should be based on "objective indicia that reflect the public attitude toward a given sanction"—namely, "statutes passed by society's elected representatives."[1] The Court dutifully recites this test and claims halfheartedly that a national consensus has emerged since our decision in *Stanford v. Kentucky* (1989),* because 18 States—or 47% of States that permit capital punishment—now have legislation prohibiting the execution of offenders under 18, and because all of four States have adopted such legislation since *Stanford*.

Words have no meaning if the views of less than 50% of death penalty States can constitute a national consensus.

Of course, the real force driving today's decision is not the actions of four state legislatures, but the Court's "own judgment" that murderers younger than 18 can never be as morally culpable as older counterparts. If the Eighth Amendment set forth an ordinary rule of law, it would indeed be the role of this Court to say what the law is. But the Court having pronounced that the Eighth Amendment is an ever-changing reflection of "the evolving standards of decency" of our society, it makes no sense for the Justices then to *prescribe* those standards rather than discern them from the practices of our people. On the evolving-standards hypothesis, the only legitimate function of this Court is to identify a moral consensus of the American people. By what conceivable warrant can nine lawyers presume to be the authoritative conscience of the Nation?

Today's opinion provides a perfect example of why judges are ill equipped to make the type of legislative judgments the Court insists on making here. To support its opinion that States should be prohibited from imposing the death penalty on anyone who committed murder before age 18, the Court looks to scientific and sociological studies, picking and choosing those that support its position. It never explains why those particular studies are methodologically sound; none was ever entered into evidence or tested in an adversarial proceeding.

Even putting aside questions of methodology, the studies cited by the Court offer scant support for a categorical prohibition of the death penalty for murderers under 18. At most, these studies conclude that, *on average*, or *in most cases*, persons under 18 are unable to take moral responsibility for their actions. Not one of the cited

---

* In *Stanford*, the Court ruled by a vote of 5 to 4 that the Eighth Amendment did not prohibit the imposition of capital punishment on murderers who were sixteen or seventeen at the time of their offenses.

studies opines that all individuals under 18 are unable to appreciate the nature of their crimes.

Moreover, the cited studies describe only adolescents who engage in risky or antisocial behavior, as many young people do. Murder, however, is more than just risky or antisocial behavior. It is entirely consistent to believe that young people often act impetuously and lack judgment, but, at the same time, to believe that those who commit premeditated murder are—at least sometimes—just as culpable as adults. Christopher Simmons, who was only seven months shy of his 18th birthday when he murdered Shirley Crook, described to his friends *beforehand*—"in chilling, callous terms," as the Court puts it—the murder he planned to commit. He then broke into the home of an innocent woman, bound her with duct tape and electrical wire, and threw her off a bridge alive and conscious. The studies the Court cites in no way justify a constitutional imperative that prevents legislatures and juries from treating exceptional cases in an exceptional way—by determining that some murders are not just the acts of happy-go-lucky teenagers, but heinous crimes deserving of death.

That "almost every State prohibits those under 18 years of age from voting, serving on juries, or marrying without parental consent"[2] is patently irrelevant—and is yet another resurrection of an argument that this Court gave a decent burial in *Stanford*. (What kind of Equal Justice under Law is it that—without so much as a "Sorry about that"—gives as the basis for sparing one person from execution arguments *explicitly rejected* in refusing to spare another?) As we explained in *Stanford*, it is "absurd to think that one must be mature enough to drive carefully, to drink responsibly, or to vote intelligently, in order to be mature enough to understand that murdering another human being is profoundly wrong, and to conform one's conduct to that most minimal of all civilized standards." Serving on a jury and entering into marriage also involve decisions far more sophisticated than the simple decision not to take another's life.

Though the views of our own citizens are essentially irrelevant to the Court's decision today, the views of other countries and the so-called international community take center stage. The Court begins by noting that "Article 37 of the United Nations Convention on the

Rights of the Child, which every country in the world has ratified *save for the United States* and Somalia, contains an express prohibition on capital punishment for crimes committed by juveniles under 18."

Unless the Court has added to its arsenal the power to join and ratify treaties on behalf of the United States, I cannot see how this evidence favors, rather than refutes, its position. That the Senate and the President—those actors our Constitution empowers to enter into treaties, see Art. II, § 2—have declined to join and ratify treaties prohibiting execution of under-18 offenders can only suggest that *our country* has either not reached a national consensus on the question, or has reached a consensus contrary to what the Court announces.

More fundamentally, however, the basic premise of the Court's argument—that American law should conform to the laws of the rest of the world—ought to be rejected out of hand. In fact the Court itself does not believe it. In many significant respects the laws of most other countries differ from our law—including not only such explicit provisions of our Constitution as the right to jury trial and grand jury indictment, but even many interpretations of the Constitution prescribed by this Court itself. The Court-pronounced exclusionary rule, for example, is distinctively American. When we adopted that rule in *Mapp v. Ohio* (1961), it was "unique to American Jurisprudence."[3] Since then a categorical exclusionary rule has been "universally rejected" by other countries, including those with rules prohibiting illegal searches and police misconduct, despite the fact that none of these countries "appears to have any alternative form of discipline for police that is effective in preventing search violations."[4]

The Court has been oblivious to the views of other countries when deciding how to interpret our Constitution's requirement that "Congress shall make no law respecting an establishment of religion." Most other countries—including those committed to religious neutrality—do not insist on the degree of separation between church and state that this Court requires.

And let us not forget the Court's abortion jurisprudence, which makes us one of only six countries that allow abortion on demand until the point of viability. Though the Government and *amici* in cases following *Roe v. Wade* urged the Court to follow the international community's lead, these arguments fell on deaf ears.

The Court should either profess its willingness to reconsider all these matters in light of the views of foreigners, or else it should cease putting forth foreigners' views as part of the *reasoned basis* of its decisions. To invoke alien law when it agrees with one's own thinking, and ignore it otherwise, is not reasoned decision-making, but sophistry.

The Court responds that "it does not lessen our fidelity to the Constitution or our pride in its origins to acknowledge that the express affirmation of certain fundamental rights by other nations and peoples simply underscores the centrality of those same rights within our own heritage of freedom." To begin with, I do not believe that approval by "other nations and peoples" should buttress our commitment to American principles any more than (what should logically follow) disapproval by "other nations and peoples" should weaken that commitment. More importantly, however, the Court's statement flatly misdescribes what is going on here. Foreign sources are cited today, *not* to underscore our "fidelity" to the Constitution, our "pride in its origins," and "our own [American] heritage." To the contrary, they are cited *to set aside* the centuries-old American practice—a practice still engaged in by a large majority of the relevant States—of letting a jury of 12 citizens decide whether, in the particular case, youth should be the basis for withholding the death penalty. What these foreign sources "affirm," rather than repudiate, is the Justices' own notion of how the world ought to be, and their diktat that it shall be so henceforth in America. The Court's parting attempt to downplay the significance of its extensive discussion of foreign law is unconvincing. "Acknowledgment" of foreign approval has no place in the legal opinion of this Court *unless it is part of the basis for the Court's judgment*—which is surely what it parades as today.

Welcome to Groundhog Day—*Glossip v. Gross* (2015)

Concurrence (joined by Justice Thomas)

By a 5–4 vote, the Court ruled that Oklahoma's use of the sedative midazolam in carrying out capital punishment did not violate the Eighth Amendment. In his dissent, Justice Breyer, joined by Justice Ginsburg, expressed his view that it is "highly likely that the death penalty violates the Eighth Amendment." Justice Scalia's concurring opinion responds to Justice Breyer.

Welcome to Groundhog Day. The scene is familiar: Petitioners, sentenced to die for the crimes they committed (including, in the case of one petitioner since put to death, raping and murdering an 11-month-old baby), come before this Court asking us to nullify their sentences as "cruel and unusual" under the Eighth Amendment. They rely on this provision because it is the only provision they *can* rely on. They were charged by a sovereign State with murder. They were afforded counsel and tried before a jury of their peers—tried twice, once to determine whether they were guilty and once to determine whether death was the appropriate sentence. They were duly convicted and sentenced. They were granted the right to appeal and to seek postconviction relief, first in state and then in federal court. And now, acknowledging that their convictions are unassailable, they ask us for clemency, as though clemency were ours to give.

The response is also familiar: A vocal minority of the Court, waving over their heads a ream of the most recent abolitionist studies (a superabundant genre) as though they have discovered the lost folios of Shakespeare, insist that *now*, at long last, the death penalty must be abolished for good. Mind you, not once in the history of the American Republic has this Court ever suggested the death penalty is categorically impermissible. The reason is obvious: It is impossible to hold unconstitutional that which the Constitution explicitly *contemplates*. The Fifth Amendment provides that "[n]o person shall be held to answer for a capital . . . crime, unless on a presentment or indictment of a Grand Jury," and that no person shall be "deprived of life . . . without due process of law."

Justice Breyer says that the death penalty is cruel because it is arbitrary. To prove this point, he points to a study of 205 cases that "measured the egregiousness of the murderer's conduct" with "a system of metrics," and then "compared the egregiousness of the conduct of the 9 defendants sentenced to death with the egregiousness of the conduct of defendants in the remaining 196 cases [who were not sentenced to death]." If only Aristotle, Aquinas, and Hume knew that moral philosophy could be so neatly distilled into a pocket-sized, *vade mecum* "system of metrics." Of course it cannot: Egregiousness is a moral judgment susceptible of few hard-and-fast rules. More importantly, egregiousness of the crime is only one of several factors that render a punishment condign—culpability, rehabilitative potential, and the need for deterrence also are relevant. That is why this Court has required an individualized consideration of all mitigating circumstances, rather than formulaic application of some egregiousness test.

It is because these questions are contextual and admit of no easy answers that we rely on juries to make judgments about the people and crimes before them. The fact that these judgments may vary across cases is an inevitable consequence of the jury trial, that cornerstone of Anglo-American judicial procedure. But when a punishment is authorized by law—if you kill you are subject to death—the fact that some defendants receive mercy from their jury no more renders the underlying punishment "cruel" than does the fact that some guilty individuals are never apprehended, are never tried, are acquitted, or are pardoned.

Justice Breyer's next reason that the death penalty is cruel is that it entails delay, thereby (1) subjecting inmates to long periods on death row and (2) undermining the penological justifications of the death penalty. The first point is nonsense. Life without parole is an even lengthier period than the wait on death row; and if the objection is that death row is a more confining environment, the solution should be modifying the environment rather than abolishing the death penalty. As for the argument that delay undermines the penological rationales for the death penalty: In insisting that "the major alternative to capital punishment—namely, life in prison without possibility of parole—also incapacitates," Justice Breyer apparently forgets that one of the plaintiffs *in this very case* was already in prison when he committed the murder that landed him on death row. Justice Breyer further asserts that "whatever interest in retribution might be served by the death penalty as currently administered, that interest can be served almost as well by a sentence of life in prison without parole." My goodness. If he thinks the death penalty not much more harsh (and hence not much more retributive), why is he so keen to get rid of it? With all due respect, whether the death penalty and life imprisonment constitute more-or-less equivalent retribution is a question far above the judiciary's pay grade. Perhaps Justice Breyer is more forgiving—or more enlightened—than those who, like Kant, believe that death is the only just punishment for taking a life. I would not presume to tell parents whose life has been forever altered by the brutal murder of a child that life imprisonment is punishment enough.

And finally, Justice Breyer speculates that it does not "seem likely" that the death penalty has a "significant" deterrent effect. It seems very likely to me, and there are statistical studies that say so. But we federal judges live in a world apart from the vast majority of Americans. After work, we retire to homes in placid suburbia or to highrise co-ops with guards at the door. We are not confronted with the threat of violence that is ever present in many Americans' everyday lives. The suggestion that the incremental deterrent effect of capital punishment does not seem "significant" reflects, it seems to me, a let-them-eat-cake obliviousness to the needs of others. Let the People decide how much incremental deterrence is appropriate.

Of course, this delay is a problem of the Court's own making. As Justice Breyer concedes, for more than 160 years, capital sentences were carried out in an average of two years or less. But by 2014, he tells us, it took an average of 18 years to carry out a death sentence. What happened in the intervening years? Nothing other than the proliferation of labyrinthine restrictions on capital punishment, promulgated by this Court under an interpretation of the Eighth Amendment that empowered it to divine "the evolving standards of decency that mark the progress of a maturing society"[1]—a task for which we are eminently ill suited. Indeed, for the past two decades, Justice Breyer has been the Drum Major in this parade. His invocation of the resultant delay as grounds for abolishing the death penalty calls to mind the man sentenced to death for killing his parents, who pleads for mercy on the ground that he is an orphan. Amplifying the surrealism of his argument, Justice Breyer uses the fact that many States have abandoned capital punishment—have abandoned it *precisely because of* the costs those suspect decisions have imposed—to conclude that it is now "unusual."

If we were to travel down the path that Justice Breyer sets out for us and once again consider the constitutionality of the death penalty, I would ask that counsel also brief whether our cases that have abandoned the historical understanding of the Eighth Amendment, beginning with *Trop v. Dulles*, should be overruled. That case has caused more mischief to our jurisprudence, to our federal system, and to our society than any other that comes to mind. Justice Breyer's dissent is the living refutation of *Trop*'s assumption that this Court has the capacity to recognize "evolving standards of decency." Time and again, the People have voted to exact the death penalty as punishment for the most serious of crimes. Time and again, this Court has upheld that decision. And time and again, a vocal minority of this Court has insisted that things have "changed radically" and has sought to replace the judgments of the People with their own standards of decency.

Capital punishment presents moral questions that philosophers, theologians, and statesmen have grappled with for millennia. The Framers of our Constitution disagreed bitterly on the matter. For that reason, they handled it the same way they handled many other controversial issues: they left it to the People to decide. By arrogating to himself the power to overturn that decision, Justice Breyer does not just reject the death penalty, he rejects the Enlightenment.

DUE PROCESS

Vague Criminal Laws—*Johnson v. United States* (2015)

Majority opinion (joined by Chief Justice Roberts and Justices Ginsburg, Breyer, Sotomayor, and Kagan)

The Fifth Amendment guarantees that "[n]o person shall . . . be deprived of life, liberty, or property, without due process of law." Samuel Johnson pleaded guilty to the federal crime of being a felon in possession of a firearm. Under the Armed Career Criminal Act, he faced a minimum sentence of fifteen years if he had three earlier convictions for a "violent felony." In determining that Johnson had three convictions for a "violent felony," the sentencing judge included his conviction for the offense of unlawful possession of a short-barreled shotgun. That conviction counted, the judge determined, under a catch-all provision in the Act that defines a "violent felony" as any felony that "involves conduct that presents a serious risk of physical injury to another."

In a 6–3 decision issued during his last full term at the Court, Justice Scalia explained that a criminal law so vague that it "fails to give ordinary people fair notice of the conduct it punishes" violates the Due Process Clause. The decision places a capstone on his prior concurrences and dissents about the unconstitutional vagueness of the residual clause of the Armed Career Criminal Act. At the same time, the decision is consistent with his frequent invocation of the rule of lenity—the idea that ambiguous criminal laws should be construed in favor of the criminal defendant. No justice invoked the rule of lenity more than Justice Scalia did during his tenure on the Court.

Under the Armed Career Criminal Act of 1984, a defendant convicted of being a felon in possession of a firearm faces more severe punishment if he has three or more previous convictions for a "violent felony," a term defined to include any felony that "involves conduct that presents a serious potential risk of physical injury to another." We must decide whether this part of the definition of a violent felony survives the Constitution's prohibition of vague criminal laws.

The Fifth Amendment provides that "[n]o person shall . . . be deprived of life, liberty, or property, without due process of law." Our cases establish that the Government violates this guarantee by taking away someone's life, liberty, or property under a criminal law so vague that it fails to give ordinary people fair notice of the conduct it punishes, or so standardless that it invites arbitrary enforcement. The prohibition of vagueness in criminal statutes "is a well-recognized requirement, consonant alike with ordinary notions of fair play and the settled rules of law," and a statute that flouts it "violates the first essential of due process."[1] These principles apply not only to statutes defining elements of crimes, but also to statutes fixing sentences.

Two features of the residual clause conspire to make it unconstitutionally vague. In the first place, the residual clause leaves grave uncertainty about how to estimate the risk posed by a crime. It ties the judicial assessment of risk to a judicially imagined "ordinary case" of a crime, not to real-world facts or statutory elements. How does one go about deciding what kind of conduct the "ordinary case" of a crime involves? "A statistical analysis of the state reporter? A survey? Expert evidence? Google? Gut instinct?"[2] To take an example, does the ordinary instance of witness tampering involve offering a witness a bribe? Or threatening a witness with violence?

At the same time, the residual clause leaves uncertainty about how much risk it takes for a crime to qualify as a violent felony. It is one thing to apply an imprecise "serious potential risk" standard to real-world facts; it is quite another to apply it to a judge-imagined abstraction. By asking whether the crime "*otherwise* involves conduct that presents a serious potential risk," moreover, the residual clause forces courts to interpret "serious potential risk" in light of the four enumerated crimes—burglary, arson, extortion, and crimes involving the use of explosives. These offenses are "far from clear in respect to the degree of risk each poses." Does the ordinary burglar invade an occupied home by night or an unoccupied home by day? Does the typical extortionist threaten his victim in person with the use of force, or does he threaten his victim by mail with the revelation of embarrassing personal information? By combining indeterminacy about how to measure the risk posed by a crime with indeterminacy about how much risk it takes for the crime to qualify as a violent felony, the residual clause produces more unpredictability and arbitrariness than the Due Process Clause tolerates.

This Court has acknowledged that the failure of "persistent efforts . . . to establish a standard" can provide evidence of vagueness.[3] Here, this Court's repeated attempts and repeated failures to craft a principled and objective standard out of the residual clause confirm its hopeless indeterminacy.

It has been said that the life of the law is experience. Nine years' experience trying to derive meaning from the residual clause convinces us that we have embarked upon a failed enterprise. Each of the uncertainties in the residual clause may be tolerable in isolation, but "their sum makes a task for us which at best could be only guesswork."[4] Invoking so shapeless a provision to condemn someone to prison for 15 years to life does not comport with the Constitution's guarantee of due process.

ENEMY COMBATANTS

A Game of Bait and Switch—
Boumediene v. Bush (2008)

*Dissent (joined by Chief Justice Roberts and
Justices Thomas and Alito)*

*Lakhdar Boumediene and his fellow claimants were aliens detained at the U.S.
Naval Station at Guantánamo Bay, Cuba, after being captured abroad and
designated as enemy combatants. They each filed a petition for a writ of habeas
corpus to challenge their detention. In the Military Commissions Act of 2006,
Congress denied the federal courts jurisdiction over habeas actions filed by aliens
detained as enemy combatants. By a 5–4 vote, the Court ruled that the Act
amounted to an unconstitutional suspension of the writ of habeas corpus.*

Today, for the first time in our Nation's history, the Court confers
a constitutional right to habeas corpus on alien enemies detained
abroad by our military forces in the course of an ongoing war.

I shall devote most of what will be a lengthy opinion to the legal
errors contained in the opinion of the Court. Contrary to my usual
practice, however, I think it appropriate to begin with a description
of the disastrous consequences of what the Court has done today.

America is at war with radical Islamists. The enemy began by killing Americans and American allies abroad: 241 at the Marine bar-
racks in Lebanon, 19 at the Khobar Towers in Dhahran, 224 at our
embassies in Dar es Salaam and Nairobi, and 17 on the USS Cole in
Yemen. On September 11, 2001, the enemy brought the battle to
American soil, killing 2,749 at the Twin Towers in New York City,
184 at the Pentagon in Washington, D. C., and 40 in Pennsylvania. It
has threatened further attacks against our homeland; one need only
walk about buttressed and barricaded Washington, or board a plane
anywhere in the country, to know that the threat is a serious one.

Our Armed Forces are now in the field against the enemy, in Afghanistan and Iraq. Last week, 13 of our countrymen in arms were killed.

The game of bait-and-switch that today's opinion plays upon the Nation's Commander in Chief will make the war harder on us. It will almost certainly cause more Americans to be killed. That consequence would be tolerable if necessary to preserve a time-honored legal principle vital to our constitutional Republic. But it is this Court's blatant *abandonment* of such a principle that produces the decision today. The President relied on our settled precedent in *Johnson v. Eisentrager* (1950) when he established the prison at Guantanamo Bay for enemy aliens. Citing that case, the President's Office of Legal Counsel advised him "that the great weight of legal authority indicates that a federal district court could not properly exercise habeas jurisdiction over an alien detained at [Guantanamo Bay]." Had the law been otherwise, the military surely would not have transported prisoners there, but would have kept them in Afghanistan, transferred them to another of our foreign military bases, or turned them over to allies for detention. Those other facilities might well have been worse for the detainees themselves.

In the long term, then, the Court's decision today accomplishes little, except perhaps to reduce the well-being of enemy combatants that the Court ostensibly seeks to protect. In the short term, however, the decision is devastating. At least 30 of those prisoners hitherto released from Guantanamo Bay have returned to the battlefield. Some have been captured or killed. But others have succeeded in carrying on their atrocities against innocent civilians. In one case, a detainee released from Guantanamo Bay masterminded the kidnapping of two Chinese dam workers, one of whom was later shot to death when used as a human shield against Pakistani commandoes. Another former detainee promptly resumed his post as a senior Taliban commander and murdered a United Nations engineer and three Afghan soldiers. Still another murdered an Afghan judge. It was reported only last month that a released detainee carried out a suicide bombing against Iraqi soldiers in Mosul, Iraq.

These, mind you, were detainees whom *the military* had concluded were not enemy combatants. Their return to the kill illustrates the incredible difficulty of assessing who is and who is not an enemy combatant in a foreign theater of operations where the environment does not lend itself to rigorous evidence collection. Astoundingly, the Court today raises the bar, requiring military officials to appear before civilian courts and defend their decisions under procedural and evidentiary rules that go beyond what Congress has specified. As the Chief Justice's dissent makes clear, we have no idea what those procedural and evidentiary rules are, but they will be determined by civil courts and (in the Court's contemplation at least) will be more detainee-friendly than those now applied, since otherwise there would be no reason to hold the congressionally prescribed procedures unconstitutional. If they impose a higher standard of proof (from foreign battlefields) than the current procedures require, the number of the enemy returned to combat will obviously increase.

But even when the military has evidence that it can bring forward, it is often foolhardy to release that evidence to the attorneys representing our enemies. And one escalation of procedures that the Court *is* clear about is affording the detainees increased access to witnesses (perhaps troops serving in Afghanistan?) and to classified information. During the 1995 prosecution of Omar Abdel Rahman, federal prosecutors gave the names of 200 unindicted co-conspirators to the "Blind Sheik's" defense lawyers; that information was in the hands of Osama Bin Laden within two weeks. In another case, trial testimony revealed to the enemy that the United States had been monitoring their cellular network, whereupon they promptly stopped using it, enabling more of them to evade capture and continue their atrocities.

And today it is not just the military that the Court elbows aside. A mere two Terms ago in *Hamdan v. Rumsfeld*, when the Court held (quite amazingly) that the Detainee Treatment Act of 2005 had not stripped habeas jurisdiction over Guantanamo petitioners' claims, four Members of today's five-Justice majority joined an opinion saying the following:

Nothing prevents the President from returning to Congress to seek the authority [for trial by military commission] he believes necessary.

Where, as here, no emergency prevents consultation with Congress, judicial insistence upon that consultation does not weaken our Nation's ability to deal with danger. To the contrary, that insistence strengthens the Nation's ability to determine—through democratic means—how best to do so. The Constitution places its faith in those democratic means.

Turns out they were just kidding. For in response, Congress, at the President's request, quickly enacted the Military Commissions Act, emphatically reasserting that it did not want these prisoners filing habeas petitions. It is therefore clear that Congress and the Executive—*both* political branches—have determined that limiting the role of civilian courts in adjudicating whether prisoners captured abroad are properly detained is important to success in the war that some 190,000 of our men and women are now fighting.

But it does not matter. The Court today decrees that no good reason to accept the judgment of the other two branches is "apparent." "The Government," it declares, "presents no credible arguments that the military mission at Guantanamo would be compromised if habeas corpus courts had jurisdiction to hear the detainees' claims." What competence does the Court have to second-guess the judgment of Congress and the President on such a point? None whatever. But the Court blunders in nonetheless. Henceforth, as today's opinion makes unnervingly clear, how to handle enemy prisoners in this war will ultimately lie with the branch that knows least about the national security concerns that the subject entails.

American Citizens—*Hamdi v. Rumsfeld* (2004)

Dissent (joined by Justice Stevens)

Yaser Esam Hamdi was born in Louisiana as a citizen of the United States in 1980 and moved with his family to Saudi Arabia that same year. He was captured in Afghanistan in 2001 and detained by American forces as an illegal enemy combatant, first at Guantánamo Bay and then at military prisons in Norfolk, Virginia, and Charleston, South Carolina.

Justice O'Connor's plurality opinion concluded that Congress had authorized the detention of citizens as enemy combatants but that the Due Process Clause required that a citizen so detained in the United States be given a meaningful opportunity to contest the factual basis for his detention. Justice Scalia embraced a position that was more restrictive than Justice O'Connor's of the president's authority (and more restrictive than either of the other opinions rendered in the case): unless Congress exercises its constitutional authority to suspend the writ of habeas corpus, the federal government cannot detain an American citizen without charge but instead must prosecute him for a federal crime or release him.

Petitioner, a presumed American citizen, has been imprisoned without charge or hearing in the Norfolk and Charleston Naval Brigs for more than two years, on the allegation that he is an enemy combatant who bore arms against his country for the Taliban. His father claims to the contrary, that he is an inexperienced aid worker caught in the wrong place at the wrong time. This case brings into conflict the competing demands of national security and our citizens' constitutional right to personal liberty. Although I share the plurality's evident unease as it seeks to reconcile the two, I do not agree with its resolution.

Where the Government accuses a citizen of waging war against it, our constitutional tradition has been to prosecute him in federal court for treason or some other crime. Where the exigencies of war prevent that, the Constitution's Suspension Clause, Art. I, § 9, cl. 2, allows Congress to relax the usual protections temporarily. Absent suspension, however, the Executive's assertion of military exigency has not been thought sufficient to permit detention without charge. No one contends that the congressional Authorization for Use of Military Force, on which the Government relies to justify its actions here, is an implementation of the Suspension Clause. Accordingly, I would reverse the judgment below.

The very core of liberty secured by our Anglo-Saxon system of separated powers has been freedom from indefinite imprisonment at the will of the Executive. Blackstone stated this principle clearly:

> Of great importance to the public is the preservation of this personal liberty: for if once it were left in the power of any, the highest, magistrate to imprison arbitrarily whomever he or his officers thought proper . . . there would soon be an end of all other rights and immunities. . . . To bereave a man of life, or by violence to confiscate his estate, without accusation or trial, would be so gross and notorious an act of despotism, as must at once convey the alarm of tyranny throughout the whole kingdom. But confinement of the person, by secretly hurrying him to gaol, where his sufferings are unknown or forgotten; is a less public, a less striking, and therefore a more dangerous engine of arbitrary government.[1]

These words were well known to the Founders. Hamilton quoted from this very passage in The Federalist No. 84. The two ideas central to Blackstone's understanding—due process as the right secured, and habeas corpus as the instrument by which due process could be insisted upon by a citizen illegally imprisoned—found expression in the Constitution's Due Process and Suspension Clauses.

The gist of the Due Process Clause, as understood at the Founding and since, was to force the Government to follow those common-law procedures traditionally deemed necessary before depriving a person of life, liberty, or property. When a citizen was deprived of liberty because of alleged criminal conduct, those procedures typically required committal by a magistrate followed by indictment and trial. The Due Process Clause "in effect affirms the right of trial according to the process and proceedings of the common law."[2]

The writ of habeas corpus was preserved in the Constitution—the only common-law writ to be explicitly mentioned. Hamilton lauded "the establishment of the writ of *habeas corpus*" in his Federalist defense as a means to protect against "the practice of arbitrary imprisonments . . . in all ages, [one of] the favourite and most formidable instruments of tyranny." The Federalist No. 84. Indeed, availability of the writ under the new Constitution (along with the requirement of trial by jury in criminal cases, see Art. III, § 2, cl. 3) was his basis for arguing that additional, explicit procedural protections were unnecessary. See The Federalist No. 83.

The allegations here, of course, are no ordinary accusations of criminal activity. Yaser Esam Hamdi has been imprisoned because the Government believes he participated in the waging of war against the United States. The relevant question, then, is whether there is a different, special procedure for imprisonment of a citizen accused of wrongdoing *by aiding the enemy in wartime.*

Justice O'Connor, writing for a plurality of this Court, asserts that captured enemy combatants (other than those suspected of war crimes) have traditionally been detained until the cessation of hostilities and then released. That is probably an accurate description of wartime practice with respect to enemy *aliens.* The tradition with respect to American citizens, however, has been quite different. Citizens aiding the enemy have been treated as traitors subject to the criminal process.

There are times when military exigency renders resort to the traditional criminal process impracticable. English law accommodated such exigencies by allowing legislative suspension of the writ of habeas corpus for brief periods.

Our Federal Constitution contains a provision explicitly permitting suspension, but limiting the situations in which it may be invoked: "The privilege of the Writ of Habeas Corpus shall not be suspended, unless when in Cases of Rebellion or Invasion the public Safety may require it." Art. I, § 9, cl. 2. Although this provision does not state that suspension must be effected by, or authorized by, a legislative act, it has been so understood, consistent with English practice and the Clause's placement in Article I.

The Suspension Clause was by design a safety valve, the Constitution's only "express provision for exercise of extraordinary authority because of a crisis."[3] Very early in the Nation's history, President Jefferson unsuccessfully sought a suspension of habeas corpus to deal with Aaron Burr's conspiracy to overthrow the Government. During the Civil War, Congress passed its first Act authorizing Executive suspension of the writ of habeas corpus, to the relief of those many who thought President Lincoln's unauthorized proclamations of suspension unconstitutional. Later Presidential proclamations of suspension relied upon the congressional authorization.

The proposition that the Executive lacks indefinite wartime detention authority over citizens is consistent with the Founders' general mistrust of military power permanently at the Executive's disposal. In the Founders' view, the "blessings of liberty" were threatened by "those military establishments which must gradually poison its very fountain." The Federalist No. 45. No fewer than 10 issues of the Federalist were devoted in whole or part to allaying fears of oppression from the proposed Constitution's authorization of standing armies in peacetime. Many safeguards in the Constitution reflect these concerns. Congress's authority "[t]o raise and support Armies" was hedged with the proviso that "no Appropriation of Money to that Use shall be for a longer Term than two Years." Except for the actual command of military forces, all authorization for their maintenance and all explicit authorization for their use is placed in the control of Congress under Article I, rather than the President under Article II. A view of the Constitution that gives the Executive authority to use military force rather than the force of law against citizens on American soil flies in the face of the mistrust that engendered these provisions.

It follows from what I have said that Hamdi is entitled to a habeas decree requiring his release unless (1) criminal proceedings are promptly brought, or (2) Congress has suspended the writ of habeas corpus. A suspension of the writ could, of course, lay down conditions for continued detention, similar to those that today's opinion prescribes under the Due Process Clause. But there is a world of difference between the people's representatives' determining the need for that suspension (and prescribing the conditions for it), and this Court's doing so.

There is a certain harmony of approach in the plurality's making up for Congress's failure to invoke the Suspension Clause and its making up for the Executive's failure to apply what it says are needed procedures—an approach that reflects what might be called a Mr. Fix-it Mentality. The plurality seems to view it as its mission to Make Everything Come Out Right, rather than merely to decree the consequences, as far as individual rights are concerned, of the other two branches' actions and omissions. Has the Legislature failed to suspend the writ in the current dire emergency? Well, we will remedy that failure by prescribing the reasonable conditions that a suspension should have included. And has the Executive failed to live up to those reasonable conditions? Well, we will ourselves make that failure good, so that this dangerous fellow (if he is dangerous) need not be set free. The problem with this approach is not only that it steps out of the courts' modest and limited role in a democratic society; but that by repeatedly doing what it thinks the political branches ought to do it encourages their lassitude and saps the vitality of government by the people.

I frankly do not know whether these tools are sufficient to meet the Government's security needs, including the need to obtain intelligence through interrogation. It is far beyond my competence, or the Court's competence, to determine that. But it is not beyond Congress's. If the situation demands it, the Executive can ask Congress to authorize suspension of the writ—which can be made subject to whatever conditions Congress deems appropriate, including even the procedural novelties invented by the plurality today. To be sure, suspension is limited by the Constitution to cases of rebellion or invasion. But whether the attacks of September 11, 2001, constitute an "invasion," and whether those attacks still justify suspension several years later, are questions for Congress rather than this Court. If civil rights are to be curtailed during wartime, it must be done openly and democratically, as the Constitution requires, rather than by silent erosion through an opinion of this Court.

The Founders well understood the difficult tradeoff between safety and freedom. "Safety from external danger," Hamilton declared,

> is the most powerful director of national conduct. Even the ardent love of liberty will, after a time, give way to its dictates. The violent destruction of life and property incident to war; the continual effort and alarm attendant on a state of continual danger, will compel nations the most attached to liberty, to resort for repose and security to institutions which have a tendency to destroy their civil and political rights. To be more safe, they, at length, become willing to run the risk of being less free. [The Federalist No. 8.]

The Founders warned us about the risk, and equipped us with a Constitution designed to deal with it.

Many think it not only inevitable but entirely proper that liberty give way to security in times of national crisis—that, at the extremes of military exigency, *inter arma silent leges.** Whatever the general merits of the view that war silences law or modulates its voice, that view has no place in the interpretation and application of a Constitution designed precisely to confront war and, in a manner that accords with democratic principles, to accommodate it. Because the Court has proceeded to meet the current emergency in a manner the Constitution does not envision, I respectfully dissent.

---

* Commonly translated as "In times of war, the law falls silent."

3

Statutory Interpretation

Justice Scalia's mark on the law has perhaps been most clear in a renewed respect in the federal and state courts for textualism—the idea that, when interpreting a statute, judges should enforce the meaning of the words enacted by a legislature to implement its policies, not the intentions, hopes, or goals that various legislators might have had. Insistent that legal principles rather than policy preferences should govern judicial decision-making, Justice Scalia was vigilant in respecting the legal texts that our lawmakers enacted. In his view, courts should never re-write a discernible statutory text to conform to a law's unenacted legislative purposes. The Supreme Court came to embrace the principle, championed by Justice Scalia, that extrinsic clues of statutory intention, such as committee reports or floor statements by legislators, may not override a clear statutory text.

In Justice Kagan's words, first offered at the inaugural Scalia Lecture at Harvard Law School in 2015, "We are all textualists now." That proposition doesn't mean that the justices always agreed. Or, for that matter, that Justice Scalia and Justice Kagan always agreed. They didn't. But it does mean that they all committed to look for the same thing: a fair reading of the words that Congress enacted. That is no small accomplishment.

In the first chapter of this book, "General Principles of Interpretation," we set forth Justice Scalia's principles of textualism, drawn from his book *A Matter of Interpretation*. The materials in this chapter include another excerpt from that book arguing against the use of legislative history, along with some cases on the topic. The other case excerpts illustrate how Justice Scalia applied principles of textualism to other disputes—over the meaning of a federal health care law, the "meaning of golf," the proper use of dictionaries, and more.

Text and Context—*King v. Burwell* (2015)

Dissent (joined by Justices Thomas and Alito)

At issue in this case was the meaning of several provisions of the Patient Protection and Affordable Care Act. The Act provides that every state shall establish a health care "exchange"—a marketplace where people in that state can shop for health insurance plans. Under the Act, if a state does not set up a health care exchange, the federal government will "establish and operate such Exchange within the State."

In order to make health insurance more affordable, the Act grants tax credits to individuals who obtain their health insurance "through an Exchange established by the State." By 2015, however, only sixteen states and the District of Columbia had established exchanges for their residents. The IRS issued a regulation permitting the same tax credits to be awarded to individuals who bought their insurance from an exchange set up by the federal government. In a 6–3 decision, the Court construed the Act to authorize these tax credits for federal exchanges. Justice Scalia could not agree.

I wholeheartedly agree with the Court that sound interpretation requires paying attention to the whole law, not homing in on isolated words or even isolated sections. Context always matters. Let us not forget, however, *why* context matters: It is a tool for understanding the terms of the law, not an excuse for rewriting them.

Any effort to understand rather than to rewrite a law must accept and apply the presumption that lawmakers use words in "their natural and ordinary signification."[1] Ordinary connotation does not always prevail, but the more unnatural the proposed interpretation of a law, the more compelling the contextual evidence must be to show that it is correct. Today's interpretation is not merely unnatural; it is unheard of. Who would ever have dreamt that "Exchange established by the State" means "Exchange established by the State *or the Federal Government*"? Little short of an express statutory definition could justify adopting this singular reading. Yet the only pertinent definition here provides that "State" means "each of the 50 States and the District of Columbia." Because the Secretary is neither one of the 50 States nor the District of Columbia, that definition positively contradicts the eccentric theory that an Exchange established by the Secretary has been established by the State.

Statutory design and purpose matter only to the extent they help clarify an otherwise ambiguous provision. Could anyone maintain with a straight face that § 36B is unclear? To mention just the highlights, the Court's interpretation clashes with a statutory definition, renders words inoperative in at least seven separate provisions of the Act, overlooks the contrast between provisions that say "Exchange" and those that say "Exchange established by the State," gives the same phrase one meaning for purposes of tax credits but an entirely different meaning for other purposes, and (let us not forget) contradicts the ordinary meaning of the words Congress used. On the other side of the ledger, the Court has come up with nothing more than a general provision that turns out to be controlled by a specific one, a handful of clauses that are consistent with either understanding of establishment by the State, and a resemblance between the tax-credit provision and the rest of the Tax Code. If that is all it takes to make something ambiguous, everything is ambiguous.

Having gone wrong in consulting statutory purpose at all, the Court goes wrong again in analyzing it. The purposes of a law must be "collected chiefly from its words," not "from extrinsic circumstances."[2] Only by concentrating on the law's terms can a judge hope to uncover the scheme *of the statute*, rather than some other scheme that the judge thinks desirable.

Perhaps sensing the dismal failure of its efforts to show that "established by the State" means "established by the State or the Federal Government," the Court tries to palm off the pertinent statutory phrase as "inartful drafting." This Court, however, has no free-floating power "to rescue Congress from its drafting errors."[3] Only when it is patently obvious to a reasonable reader that a drafting mistake has occurred may a court correct the mistake. The occurrence of a misprint may be apparent from the face of the law, as it is where the

Affordable Care Act "creates three separate Section 1563s."[4] But the Court does not pretend that there is any such indication of a drafting error on the face of § 36B. The occurrence of a misprint may also be apparent because a provision decrees an absurd result—a consequence "so monstrous, that all mankind would, without hesitation, unite in rejecting the application."[5] But § 36B does not come remotely close to satisfying that demanding standard. It is entirely plausible that tax credits were restricted to state Exchanges deliberately—for example, in order to encourage States to establish their own Exchanges. We therefore have no authority to dismiss the terms of the law as a drafting fumble.

Let us not forget that the term "Exchange established by the State" appears twice in § 36B and five more times in other parts of the Act that mention tax credits. What are the odds, do you think, that the same slip of the pen occurred in seven separate places? No provision of the Act—none at all—contradicts the limitation of tax credits to state Exchanges. And as I have already explained, uses of the term "Exchange established by the State" beyond the context of tax credits look anything but accidental. If there was a mistake here, context suggests it was a substantive mistake in designing this part of the law, not a technical mistake in transcribing it.

The Court's decision reflects the philosophy that judges should endure whatever interpretive distortions it takes in order to correct a supposed flaw in the statutory machinery. That philosophy ignores the American people's decision to give *Congress* "[a]ll legislative Powers" enumerated in the Constitution. Art. I, § 1. They made Congress, not this Court, responsible for both making laws and mending them. This Court holds only the judicial power—the power to pronounce the law as Congress has enacted it. We lack the prerogative to repair laws that do not work out in practice, just as the people lack the ability to throw us out of office if they dislike the solutions we concoct. We must always remember, therefore, that "our task is to apply the text, not to improve upon it."[6]

Today's opinion changes the usual rules of statutory interpretation for the sake of the Affordable Care Act. That, alas, is not a novelty. In *NFIB v. Sebelius*, this Court revised major components of the statute in order to save them from unconstitutionality. The Act that Congress passed provides that every individual "shall" maintain insurance or else pay a "penalty." This Court, however, saw that the Commerce Clause does not authorize a federal mandate to buy health insurance. So it rewrote the mandate-cum-penalty as a tax. The Act that Congress passed also requires every State to accept an expansion of its Medicaid program, or else risk losing *all* Medicaid funding. This Court, however, saw that the Spending Clause does not authorize this coercive condition. So it rewrote the law to withhold only the *incremental* funds associated with the Medicaid expansion. Having transformed two major parts of the law, the Court today has turned its attention to a third. The Act that Congress passed makes tax credits available only on an "Exchange established by the State." This Court, however, concludes that this limitation would prevent the rest of the Act from working as well as hoped. So it rewrites the law to make tax credits available everywhere. We should start calling this law SCOTUScare.

Perhaps the Patient Protection and Affordable Care Act will attain the enduring status of the Social Security Act or the Taft-Hartley Act; perhaps not. But this Court's two decisions on the Act will surely be remembered through the years. The somersaults of statutory interpretation they have performed ("penalty" means tax, "further [Medicaid] payments to the State" means only incremental Medicaid payments to the State, "established by the State" means not established by the State) will be cited by litigants endlessly, to the confusion of honest jurisprudence. And the cases will publish forever the discouraging truth that the Supreme Court of the United States favors some laws over others, and is prepared to do whatever it takes to uphold and assist its favorites.

What Is Golf?—*PGA Tour v. Martin* (2001)

Dissent (joined by Justice Thomas)

Casey Martin was a professional golfer afflicted with a degenerative disease that prevented him from walking golf courses during tournaments. Under the rules of the Professional Golf Association, competitors could not use golf carts when competing in Tour-sponsored events. At stake in this case was whether the Americans with Disabilities Act required the PGA to accommodate Martin's disability by permitting him to use a cart during Tour events. A 7–2 majority of the Court ruled in Martin's favor. In his dissent, Justice Scalia dissects the relevant provisions of the Act and shows an impressive understanding of golf. The justice himself was not a golfer. . . .

In my view today's opinion exercises a benevolent compassion that the law does not place it within our power to impose. The judgment distorts the text of Title III of the Americans with Disabilities Act, the structure of the ADA, and common sense. I respectfully dissent.

The Court pronounces respondent to be a "customer" of the PGA Tour or of the golf courses on which it is played. That seems to me quite incredible. The PGA Tour is a professional sporting event, staged for the entertainment of a live and TV audience, the receipts from whom (the TV audience's admission price is paid by advertisers) pay the expenses of the tour, including the cash prizes for the winning golfers. The professional golfers on the tour are no more "enjoying" (the statutory term) the entertainment that the tour provides, or the facilities of the golf courses on which it is held, than professional baseball players "enjoy" the baseball games in which they play or the facilities of Yankee Stadium. To be sure, professional ballplayers *participate* in the games, and *use* the ballfields, but no one in his right mind would think that they are *customers* of the American League or of Yankee Stadium. They are themselves the entertainment that the customers pay to watch. And professional golfers are no different.

The ADA specifically identifies golf courses as one of the covered places of public accommodation, and the distinctive "good, service, facility, privilege, advantage, or accommodation" identified as distinctive to that category of place of public accommodation is "exercise or recreation." Respondent did not seek to "exercise" or "recreate" at the PGA Tour events; he sought to make money (which is why he is called a *professional* golfer). He was not a customer *buying* recreation or entertainment; he was a professional athlete *selling* it.

The Court relies heavily upon the Q-School.* It says that petitioner offers the golfing public the "privilege" of "competing in the Q-School and playing in the tours; indeed, the former is a privilege for which thousands of individuals from the general public pay, and the latter is one for which they vie." But the Q-School is no more a "privilege" offered for the general public's "enjoyment" than is the California Bar Exam. It is a competition for entry into the PGA Tour—an open tryout, no different in principle from open casting for a movie or stage production, or walk-on tryouts for other professional sports, such as baseball. It may well be that some amateur golfers enjoy trying to make the grade, just as some amateur actors may enjoy auditions, and amateur baseball players may enjoy open tryouts (I hesitate to say that amateur lawyers may enjoy taking the California Bar Exam). But the purpose of holding those tryouts is not to provide entertainment; it is to hire. At bottom, open tryouts for performances to be held at a place of public accommodation are no different from open bidding on contracts to cut the grass at a place of public accommodation, or open applications for any job at a place of public accommodation. Those bidding, those applying—and those trying out—are not converted into customers. By the Court's reasoning, a business exists not only to sell goods and services to the public, but to provide the "privilege" of employment to the public; wherefore it follows, like night the day, that everyone who seeks a job is a customer.

---

* A tryout competition for the PGA Tour.

Even if respondent here is a consumer of the "privilege" of the PGA Tour competition, I see no basis for considering whether the rules of that competition must be altered. It is as irrelevant to the PGA Tour's compliance with the statute whether walking is essential to the game of golf as it is to the shoe store's compliance whether "pairness" is essential to the nature of shoes. If a shoe store wishes to sell shoes only in pairs it may; and if a golf tour (or a golf course) wishes to provide only walk-around golf, it may. The PGA Tour cannot deny respondent *access* to that game because of his disability, but it need not provide him a game different (whether in its essentials or in its details) from that offered to everyone else.

Since it has held (or assumed) professional golfers to be customers "enjoying" the "privilege" that consists of PGA Tour golf; and since it inexplicably regards the rules of PGA Tour golf as merely "policies, practices, or procedures" by which access to PGA Tour golf is provided, the Court must then confront the question whether respondent's requested modification of the supposed policy, practice, or procedure of walking would "fundamentally alter the nature" of the PGA Tour game. The Court attacks this "fundamental alteration" analysis by asking two questions: first, whether the "essence" or an "essential aspect" of the sport of golf has been altered; and second, whether the change, even if not essential to the game, would give the disabled player an advantage over others and thereby "fundamentally alter the character of the competition." It answers no to both.

Before considering the Court's answer to the first question, it is worth pointing out that the assumption which underlies that question is false. Nowhere is it writ that PGA Tour golf must be classic "essential" golf. Why cannot the PGA Tour, if it wishes, promote a new game, with distinctive rules (much as the American League promotes a game of baseball in which the pitcher's turn at the plate can be taken by a "designated hitter")? If members of the public do not like the new rules—if they feel that these rules do not truly test the individual's skill at "real golf" (or the team's skill at "real baseball")—they can withdraw their patronage. But the rules are the rules. They are (as in all games) entirely arbitrary, and there is no basis on which anyone—not even the Supreme Court of the United States—can pronounce one or another of them to be "nonessential" if the rule-maker (here the PGA Tour) deems it to be essential.

If one assumes, however, that the PGA Tour has some legal obligation to play classic, Platonic golf—and if one assumes the correctness of all the other wrong turns the Court has made to get to this point—then we Justices must confront what is indeed an awesome responsibility. It has been rendered the solemn duty of the Supreme Court of the United States, laid upon it by Congress in pursuance of the Federal Government's power "[t]o regulate Commerce with foreign Nations, and among the several States," to decide What Is Golf. I am sure that the Framers of the Constitution, aware of the 1457 edict of King James II of Scotland prohibiting golf because it interfered with the practice of archery, fully expected that sooner or later the paths of golf and government, the law and the links, would once again cross, and that the judges of this august Court would some day have to wrestle with that age-old jurisprudential question, for which their years of study in the law have so well prepared them: Is someone riding around a golf course from shot to shot *really* a golfer? The answer, we learn, is yes. The Court ultimately concludes, and it will henceforth be the Law of the Land, that walking is not a "fundamental" aspect of golf.

Either out of humility or out of self-respect (one or the other) the Court should decline to answer this incredibly difficult and incredibly silly question. To say that something is "essential" is ordinarily to say that it is necessary to the achievement of a certain object. But since it is the very nature of a game to have no object except amusement (that is what distinguishes games from productive activity), it is quite impossible to say that any of a game's arbitrary rules is "essential." Eighteen-hole golf courses, 10-foot-high basketball hoops, 90-foot baselines, 100-yard football fields—all are arbitrary and none is essential. The only support for any of them is tradition and (in more modern times) insistence by what has come to be regarded as the ruling body of the sport—both of which factors support the PGA Tour's position in the present case. (Many, indeed, consider walking to be *the central feature* of the game of golf—hence Mark Twain's classic criticism of the sport: "a good walk spoiled.") I suppose there is some point at which the rules of a well-known game are changed to such a degree that no reasonable person would call it the same game. If the PGA Tour competitors were required to dribble a large, inflated ball and put it through a round hoop, the game could no longer reasonably be called golf. But this criterion—destroying recognizability as the same generic game—is surely not the test of "essentialness" or "fundamentalness" that the Court applies, since it apparently thinks that merely changing the diameter of the *cup* might "fundamentally alter" the game of golf.

Having concluded that dispensing with the walking rule would not violate federal-Platonic "golf," the Court moves on to the second part of its test: the competitive effects of waiving this nonessential rule. In this part of its analysis, the Court first finds that the effects of the change are "mitigated" by the fact that in the game of golf weather, a "lucky bounce," and "pure chance" provide different conditions for each competitor and individual ability may not "be the sole determinant of the outcome." I guess that is why those who follow professional golfing consider Jack Nicklaus the *luckiest* golfer of all time, only to be challenged of late by the phenomenal *luck* of Tiger Woods. The Court's empiricism is unpersuasive. "Pure chance" is randomly distributed among the players, but allowing respondent to use a cart gives him a "lucky" break every time he plays. Pure chance also only matters at the margin—a stroke here or there; the cart substantially improves this respondent's competitive prospects beyond a couple of strokes. But even granting that there are significant nonhuman variables affecting competition, that fact does not justify adding another variable that always favors one player.

In an apparent effort to make its opinion as narrow as possible, the Court relies upon the District Court's finding that even with a cart, respondent will be at least as fatigued as everyone else. This, the Court says, *proves* that competition will not be affected.

The statute, of course, provides no basis for this individualized analysis that is the Court's last step on a long and misguided journey. The statute seeks to assure that a disabled person's disability will not deny him *equal access* to (among other things) competitive sporting events—not that his disability will not deny him an *equal chance to win* competitive sporting events. The latter is quite impossible, since the very *nature* of competitive sport is the measurement, by uniform rules, of unevenly distributed excellence. This unequal distribution is precisely what determines the winners and losers—and artificially to even out that distribution, by giving one or another player exemption from a rule that emphasizes his particular weakness, is to destroy the game. That is why the "handicaps" that are customary in social games of golf—which, by adding strokes to the scores of the good players and subtracting them from scores of the bad ones, even out the varying abilities—are *not* used in professional golf. In the Court's world, there is one set of rules that is "fair with respect to the able-bodied" but "individualized" rules, mandated by the ADA, for "talented but disabled athletes." The ADA mandates no such ridiculous thing. Agility, strength, speed, balance, quickness of mind, steadiness of nerves, intensity of concentration—these talents are not evenly distributed. No wild-eyed dreamer has ever suggested that the managing bodies of the competitive sports that test precisely these qualities should try to take account of the uneven distribution of God-given gifts when writing and enforcing the rules of competition. And I have no doubt Congress did not authorize misty-eyed judicial supervision of such a revolution.

My belief that today's judgment is clearly in error should not be mistaken for a belief that the PGA Tour clearly *ought not* allow respondent to use a golf cart. *That* is a close question, on which even those who compete in the PGA Tour are apparently divided; but it is a *different* question from the one before the Court. Just as it is a different question whether the Little League *ought* to give disabled youngsters a fourth strike, or some other waiver from the rules that makes up for their disabilities. In both cases, whether they *ought* to do so depends upon (1) how central to the game that they have organized (and over whose rules they are the master) they deem the waived provision to be, and (2) how competitive—how strict a test of raw athletic ability in all aspects of the competition—they want their game to be. But whether Congress has said they *must* do so depends upon the answers to the legal questions I have discussed above.

Complaints about this case are not "properly directed to Congress."[1] They are properly directed to this Court's Kafkaesque determination that professional sports organizations, and the fields they rent for their exhibitions, are "places of public accommodation" to the competing athletes, and the athletes themselves "customers" of the organization that pays them; its Alice in Wonderland determination that there are such things as judicially determinable "essential" and "nonessential" rules of a made-up game; and its Animal Farm determination that fairness and the ADA mean that everyone gets to play by individualized rules which will assure that no one's lack of ability (or at least no one's lack of ability so pronounced that it amounts to a disability) will be a handicap. The year was 2001, and "everybody was finally equal."*

---

* Quoting Kurt Vonnegut's short story "Harrison Bergeron."

Text Versus Concerns of Legislators—
Oncale v. Sundowner Offshore Services (1998)

Majority opinion (unanimous)

*Title VII of the 1964 Civil Rights Act prohibits discrimination "because of"
sex. At issue in this case was whether the prohibition extended to male-on-
male harassment that satisfied the other statutory requirements. Writing for a
unanimous Court, Justice Scalia explained that it did. Even though the authors of Title VII may not have been thinking of same-sex harassment, Scalia
reasoned, "it is ultimately the provisions of our laws rather than the principal
concerns of our legislators by which we are governed."*

This case presents the question whether workplace harassment can
violate Title VII's prohibition against "discriminat[ion] . . . because of . . . sex" when the harasser and the harassed employee are of
the same sex.

Title VII's prohibition of discrimination "because of . . . sex"
protects men as well as women, and in the related context of racial
discrimination in the workplace we have rejected any conclusive presumption that an employer will not discriminate against members of
his own race. "Because of the many facets of human motivation, it
would be unwise to presume as a matter of law that human beings of
one definable group will not discriminate against other members of
their group."[1]

We see no justification in the statutory language or our precedents for a categorical rule excluding same-sex harassment claims
from the coverage of Title VII. As some courts have observed, male-
on-male sexual harassment in the workplace was assuredly not the
principal evil Congress was concerned with when it enacted Title
VII. But statutory prohibitions often go beyond the principal evil to
cover reasonably comparable evils, and it is ultimately the provisions
of our laws rather than the principal concerns of our legislators by

which we are governed. Title VII prohibits "discriminat[ion] . . . because of . . . sex" in the "terms" or "conditions" of employment. Our holding that this includes sexual harassment must extend to sexual harassment of any kind that meets the statutory requirements.

The critical issue, Title VII's text indicates, is whether members of one sex are exposed to disadvantageous terms or conditions of employment to which members of the other sex are not exposed.[2]

Courts and juries have found the inference of discrimination easy to draw in most male-female sexual harassment situations, because the challenged conduct typically involves explicit or implicit proposals of sexual activity; it is reasonable to assume those proposals would not have been made to someone of the same sex. The same chain of inference would be available to a plaintiff alleging same-sex harassment, if there were credible evidence that the harasser was homosexual. But harassing conduct need not be motivated by sexual desire to support an inference of discrimination on the basis of sex. A trier of fact might reasonably find such discrimination, for example, if a female victim is harassed in such sex-specific and derogatory terms by another woman as to make it clear that the harasser is motivated by general hostility to the presence of women in the workplace. A same-sex harassment plaintiff may also, of course, offer direct comparative evidence about how the alleged harasser treated members of both sexes in a mixed-sex workplace. Whatever evidentiary route the plaintiff chooses to follow, he or she must always prove that the conduct at issue was not merely tinged with offensive sexual connotations, but actually constituted "*discrimina[tion]* . . . because of . . . sex."

And there is another requirement that prevents Title VII from expanding into a general civility code: The statute does not reach genuine but innocuous differences in the ways men and women routinely interact with members of the same sex and of the opposite sex. The prohibition of harassment on the basis of sex requires neither asexuality nor androgyny in the workplace; it forbids only behavior so objectively offensive as to alter the "conditions" of the victim's employment. "Conduct that is not severe or pervasive enough to create an objectively hostile or abusive work environment—an environment that a reasonable person would find hostile or abusive—is beyond Title VII's purview."[3] We have always regarded that requirement as crucial, and as sufficient to ensure that courts and juries do not mistake ordinary socializing in the workplace—such as male-on-male horseplay or intersexual flirtation—for discriminatory "conditions of employment."

We have emphasized, moreover, that the objective severity of harassment should be judged from the perspective of a reasonable person in the plaintiff's position, considering "all the circumstances."[4] In same-sex (as in all) harassment cases, that inquiry requires careful consideration of the social context in which particular behavior occurs and is experienced by its target. A professional football player's working environment is not severely or pervasively abusive, for example, if the coach smacks him on the buttocks as he heads onto the field—even if the same behavior would reasonably be experienced as abusive by the coach's secretary (male or female) back at the office. The real social impact of workplace behavior often depends on a constellation of surrounding circumstances, expectations, and relationships which are not fully captured by a simple recitation of the words used or the physical acts performed. Common sense, and an appropriate sensitivity to social context, will enable courts and juries to distinguish between simple teasing or roughhousing among members of the same sex, and conduct which a reasonable person in the plaintiff's position would find severely hostile or abusive.

Implied Rights of Action—*Alexander v. Sandoval* (2001)

Majority opinion (joined by Chief Justice Rehnquist and Justices O'Connor, Kennedy, and Thomas)

Recipients of federal aid must comply with Title VI of the Civil Rights Act of 1964. Section 601 of the law bans discrimination based on race, color, or national origin. Section 602 of the law authorizes federal agencies to issue regulations designed to implement these provisions. The question in this case was whether individuals could sue to enforce the regulations, as opposed to the statute itself. In a 5–4 decision, the Court ruled that they could not.

Writing for the Court, Justice Scalia critiqued prior decisions of the Court that had casually implied private rights of action to enforce statutes and regulations. Because the Act nowhere permitted individuals to sue to enforce such regulations, he explained, the federal courts had no warrant to permit such actions. In his words: "Agencies may play the sorcerer's apprentice but not the sorcerer himself."

This case presents the question whether private individuals may sue to enforce disparate-impact regulations promulgated under Title VI of the Civil Rights Act of 1964.

Like substantive federal law itself, private rights of action to enforce federal law must be created by Congress. The judicial task is to interpret the statute Congress has passed to determine whether it displays an intent to create not just a private right but also a private remedy. Statutory intent on this latter point is determinative. Without it, a cause of action does not exist and courts may not create one, no matter how desirable that might be as a policy matter, or how compatible with the statute. "Raising up causes of action where a statute has not created them may be a proper function for common-law courts, but not for federal tribunals."[1]

Respondents would have us revert in this case to the understanding of private causes of action that held sway 40 years ago when Title

VI was enacted. That understanding is captured by the Court's statement in *J. I. Case Co. v. Borak* (1964), that "it is the duty of the courts to be alert to provide such remedies as are necessary to make effective the congressional purpose" expressed by a statute. We abandoned that understanding in *Cort v. Ash* (1975)—which itself interpreted a statute enacted under the *ancien regime*—and have not returned to it since. Not even when interpreting the same Securities Exchange Act of 1934 that was at issue in *Borak* have we applied *Borak*'s method for discerning and defining causes of action. Having sworn off the habit of venturing beyond Congress's intent, we will not accept respondents' invitation to have one last drink.

We therefore begin (and find that we can end) our search for Congress's intent with the text and structure of Title VI. Far from displaying congressional intent to create new rights, § 602 limits agencies to "effectuat[ing]" rights already created by § 601. Section 602 is "phrased as a directive to federal agencies engaged in the distribution of public funds." So far as we can tell, this authorizing portion of § 602 reveals no congressional intent to create a private right of action.

Both the Government and respondents argue that the *regulations* contain rights-creating language and so must be privately enforceable, but that argument skips an analytical step. Language in a regulation may invoke a private right of action that Congress through statutory text created, but it may not create a right that Congress has not. Thus, when a statute has provided a general authorization for private enforcement of regulations, it may perhaps be correct that the intent displayed in each regulation can determine whether or not it is privately enforceable. But it is most certainly incorrect to say that language in a regulation can conjure up a private cause of action that has not been authorized by Congress. Agencies may play the sorcerer's apprentice but not the sorcerer himself.

Dictionary Definitions—*MCI v. AT&T* (1994)

Majority opinion (joined by Chief Justice Rehnquist and Justices Kennedy, Thomas, and Ginsburg)

Textualists take words seriously. Dictionaries are one important resource for discerning the meaning of words, but they must be used with care. These excerpts from Justice Scalia's majority opinion exemplify these points and along the way explain why he was critical of Webster's Third New International Dictionary *and much preferred the first two editions of the dictionary. The legal question in the case was whether the Federal Communications Commission's authority to "modify" provisions in the relevant law permitted a substantial revision of a significant part of the Act: the tariff-filing requirement.*

The dispute between the parties turns on the meaning of the phrase "modify any requirement" in § 203(b)(2). Petitioners argue that it gives the Commission authority to make even basic and fundamental changes in the scheme created by that section. We disagree. The word "modify"—like a number of other English words employing the root "mod" (deriving from the Latin word for "measure"), such as "moderate," "modulate," "modest," and "modicum"—has a connotation of increment or limitation. Virtually every dictionary we are aware of says that "to modify" means to change moderately or in minor fashion.

In support of their position, petitioners cite dictionary definitions contained in or derived from a single source, Webster's Third New International Dictionary (1976), which includes among the meanings of "modify," "to make a basic or important change in." Petitioners contend that this establishes sufficient ambiguity to entitle the Commission to deference in its acceptance of the broader meaning, which in turn requires approval of its permissive detariffing policy. In short, they contend that the courts must defer to the agency's choice among available dictionary definitions.

Most cases of verbal ambiguity in statutes involve a selection between accepted alternative meanings shown as such by many dictionaries. One can envision (though a court case does not immediately come to mind) having to choose between accepted alternative meanings, one of which is so newly accepted that it has only been recorded by a single lexicographer. But what petitioners demand that we accept as creating an ambiguity here is a rarity even rarer than that: a meaning set forth in a single dictionary (and, as we say, its progeny) which not only *supplements* the meaning contained in all other dictionaries, but *contradicts* one of the meanings contained in virtually all other dictionaries. Indeed, contradicts one of the alternative meanings contained in the out-of-step dictionary itself—for as we have observed, Webster's Third itself defines "modify" to connote *both* (specifically) major change *and* (specifically) minor change. It is hard to see how that can be. When the word "modify" has come to mean *both* "to change in some respects" *and* "to change fundamentally" it will in fact mean *neither* of those things. It will simply mean "to change," and some adverb will have to be called into service to indicate the great or small degree of the change.

If that is what the peculiar Webster's Third definition means to suggest has happened—and what petitioners suggest by appealing to Webster's Third—we simply disagree. "Modify," in our view, connotes moderate change. It might be good English to say that the French Revolution "modified" the status of the French nobility—but only because there is a figure of speech called understatement and a literary device known as sarcasm. And it might be unsurprising to discover a 1972 White House press release saying that "the Administration is modifying its position with regard to prosecution of the war in Vietnam"—but only because press agents tend to impart what is nowadays called "spin." Such intentional distortions, or simply careless or ignorant misuse, must have formed the basis for the usage that Webster's Third, and Webster's Third alone, reported. It is perhaps gilding the lily to add this: In 1934, when the Communications Act became law—the most relevant time for determining a statutory term's meaning—Webster's Third was not yet even contemplated. To our knowledge *all* English dictionaries provided the narrow definition of "modify." We have not the slightest doubt that is the meaning the statute intended.

For the body of a law, as for the body of a person, whether a change is minor or major depends to some extent upon the importance of the item changed to the whole. Loss of an entire toenail is insignificant; loss of an entire arm tragic. The tariff-filing requirement is, to pursue this analogy, the heart of the common-carrier section of the Communications Act.

What we have here, in reality, is a fundamental revision of the statute, changing it from a scheme of rate regulation in long-distance common-carrier communications to a scheme of rate regulation only where effective competition does not exist. That may be a good idea, but it was not the idea Congress enacted into law in 1934.

LEGISLATIVE HISTORY

A Failed Experiment

This excerpt is from Justice Scalia's A Matter of Interpretation.[1]

Let me turn now to an interpretative device whose widespread use is relatively new: legislative history, by which I mean the statements made in the floor debates, committee reports, and even committee testimony, leading up to the enactment of the legislation. My view that the objective indication of the words, rather than the intent of the legislature, is what constitutes the law leads me, of course, to the conclusion that legislative history should not be used as an authoritative indication of a statute's meaning. This was the traditional English, and the traditional American, practice.

Extensive use of legislative history in this country dates only from about the 1940s. It was still being criticized by such respected justices as Frankfurter and Jackson as recently as the 1950s. Jackson, for example, wrote in one concurrence:

> I should concur in this result more readily if the Court could reach it by analysis of the statute instead of by psychoanalysis of Congress. When we decide from legislative history, including statements of witnesses at hearings, what Congress probably had in mind, we must put ourselves in the place of a majority of Congressmen and act according to the impression we think this history should have made on them. Never having been a Congressman, I am handicapped in that weird endeavor. That process seems to me not interpretation of a statute but creation of a statute.

In the past few decades, however, we have developed a legal culture in which lawyers routinely—and I do mean routinely—make no distinction between words in the text of a statute and words in its legislative history. My Court is frequently told, in briefs and in oral argument, that "Congress said thus-and-so"—when in fact what is being quoted is not the law promulgated by Congress, nor even any text endorsed by a single house of Congress, but rather the statement of a single committee of a single house, set forth in a committee report. Resort to legislative history has become so common that lawyerly wags have popularized a humorous quip inverting the oft-recited (and oft-ignored) rule as to when its use is appropriate: "One should consult the text of the statute," as the joke goes, "only when the legislative history is ambiguous." Alas, that is no longer funny. Reality has overtaken parody. A few terms ago, I read a brief that *began* the legal argument with a discussion of legislative history and then continued (I am quoting it verbatim): "Unfortunately, the legislative debates are not helpful. Thus, we turn to the other guidepost in this difficult area, statutory language."

As I have said, I object to the use of legislative history on principle, since I reject intent of the legislature as the proper criterion of the law. What is most exasperating about the use of legislative history, however, is that it does not even make sense for those who *accept* legislative intent as the criterion. It is much more likely to produce a false or contrived legislative intent than a genuine one. The first and most obvious reason for this is that, with respect to 99.99 percent of the issues of construction reaching the courts, there *is* no legislative intent, so that any clues provided by the legislative history are bound to be false. Those issues almost invariably involve points of relative detail, compared with the major sweep of the statute in question. That a majority of both houses of Congress (never mind the president, if he signed rather than vetoed the bill) entertained *any* view with regard to such issues is utterly beyond belief. For a virtual certainty, the majority was blissfully unaware of the *existence* of the issue, much less had any preference as to how it should be resolved.

But assuming, contrary to all reality, that the search for "legislative intent" is a search for something that exists, that something is not likely to be found in the archives of legislative history. In earlier days, when Congress had a smaller staff and enacted less legislation, it might have been possible to believe that a significant number of senators or representatives were present for the floor debate, or read the committee reports, and actually voted on the basis of what they heard or read. Those days, if they ever existed, are long gone. The floor is rarely crowded for a debate, the members generally being occupied with committee business and reporting to the floor only when a quorum call is demanded or a vote is to be taken. And as for committee reports, it is not even certain that the members of the issuing *committees* have found time to read them, as demonstrated by the following Senate floor debate on a tax bill, which I had occasion to quote in an opinion written when I was on the Court of Appeals:

> MR. ARMSTRONG: My question, which may take the chairman of the Committee on Finance by surprise, is this: Is it the intention of the chairman that the Internal Revenue Service and the Tax Court and other courts take guidance as to the intention of Congress from the committee report which accompanies this bill?
>
> MR. DOLE: I would certainly hope so.
>
> MR. ARMSTRONG: Mr. President, will the senator tell me whether or not he wrote the committee report?
>
> MR. DOLE: Did I write the committee report?
>
> MR. ARMSTRONG: Yes.
>
> MR. DOLE: No; the senator from Kansas did not write the committee report.
>
> MR. ARMSTRONG: Did any senator write the committee report?
>
> MR. DOLE: I have to check.
>
> MR. ARMSTRONG: Does the senator know of any senator who wrote the committee report?
>
> MR. DOLE: I might be able to identify one, but I would have to search. I was here all during the time it was written, I might say, and worked carefully with the staff as they worked.
>
> MR. ARMSTRONG: Mr. President, has the senator from Kansas, the chairman of the Finance Committee, read the committee report in its entirety?

MR. DOLE: I am working on it. It is not a bestseller, but I am working on it.

MR. ARMSTRONG: Mr. President, did members of the Finance Committee vote on the committee report?

MR. DOLE: No.

MR. ARMSTRONG: Mr. President, the reason I raise the issue is not perhaps apparent on the surface, and let me just state it. The report itself is not considered by the Committee on Finance. It was not subject to amendment by the Committee on Finance. It is not subject to amendment now by the Senate.

If there were matter within this report which was disagreed to by the senator from Colorado or even by a majority of all senators, there would be no way for us to change the report. I could not offer an amendment tonight to amend the committee report.

For any jurist, administrator, bureaucrat, tax practitioner, or others who might chance upon the written record of this proceeding, let me just make the point that this is not the law, it was not voted on, it is not subject to amendment, and we should discipline ourselves to the task of expressing congressional intent in the statute.

Ironically, but quite understandably, the more courts have relied upon legislative history, the less worthy of reliance it has become. In earlier days, it was at least genuine and not contrived—a real part of the legislation's *history*, in the sense that it was part of the *development* of the bill, part of the attempt to inform those who voted. Nowadays, however, when it is universally known and expected that judges will resort to floor debates and (especially) committee reports as authoritative expressions of "legislative intent," affecting the courts rather than informing the Congress has become the primary purpose of the exercise. It is less that the courts refer to legislative history because it exists than that legislative history exists because the courts refer to it. One of the routine tasks of the Washington lawyer-lobbyist is to draft language that sympathetic legislators can recite in a pre-written "floor debate"—or, even better, insert into a committee report.

There are several common responses to these criticisms. One is "So what if most members of Congress do not themselves know what is in the committee report? Most of them do not know the details of the legislation itself, either—but that is valid nonetheless. In fact, they are probably more likely to read and understand the committee reports than to read and understand the text." That ignores the central point that genuine knowledge is a pre-condition for the supposed authoritativeness of a statute. The committee report has no claim to our attention except on the assumption that it was the *basis* for the house's vote and thus represents the house's "intent," which we (presumably) are searching for. A statute, however, has a claim to our attention simply because Article I, section 7 of the Constitution provides that since it has been passed by the prescribed majority (*with or without adequate understanding*), it is a law.

Another response simply challenges head-on the proposition that legislative history must reflect congressional thinking: "Committee reports are *not* authoritative because the full house presumably knows and agrees with them, but rather because the full house *wants* them to be authoritative—that is, leaves to the committees the details of its legislation." It may or may not be true that the houses entertain such a desire; the sentiments of Senator Armstrong quoted earlier suggest that it is not. But if it is true, it is unconstitutional. "All legislative Powers herein granted," the Constitution says, "shall be vested in a Congress of the United States, which shall consist of a Senate and House of Representatives." The legislative power is the power to make laws, not the power to make legislators. It is non-delegable. Congress can no more authorize one committee to "fill in the details" of a particular law in a binding fashion than it can authorize a committee to enact minor laws. Whatever Congress has not *itself* prescribed is left to be resolved by the executive or (ultimately) the judicial branch. That is the very essence of the separation of powers. The only conceivable basis for considering committee reports authoritative, therefore, is that they are a genuine indication of the will of the entire house—which, as I have been at pains to explain, they assuredly are not.

On balance, legislative history has facilitated rather than deterred decisions that are based upon the courts' policy preferences, rather than neutral principles of law. Since there are no rules as to how much weight an element of legislative history is entitled to, it can usually be either relied upon or dismissed with equal plausibility. If the willful judge does not like the committee report, he will not follow it; he will call the statute not ambiguous enough, the committee report too ambiguous, or the legislative history (this is a favorite phrase) "as a whole, inconclusive." It is ordinarily very hard to demonstrate that this is false so convincingly as to produce embarrassment. To be sure, there are ambiguities involved, and hence opportunities for judicial willfulness, in other techniques of interpretation as well—the canons of construction, for example. But the manipulability of legislative history has not *replaced* the manipulabilities of these other techniques; it has *augmented* them. There are still the canons of construction to play with, *and in addition* legislative history. Legislative history provides, moreover, a uniquely broad playing field. In any major piece of legislation, the legislative history is extensive, and there is something for everybody. As Judge Harold Leventhal used to say, the trick is to look over the heads of the crowd and pick out your friends. The variety and specificity of result that legislative history can achieve is unparalleled.

I think it is time to call an end to a brief and failed experiment, if not for reasons of principle then for reasons of practicality. I have not used legislative history to decide a case for, I believe, the past nine terms. Frankly, that has made very little difference (since legislative history is ordinarily so inconclusive). In the only case I recall in which, had I followed legislative history, I *would* have come out the other way, the rest of my colleagues (who *did* use legislative history) did not come out the other way either. The most immediate and tangible change the abandonment of legislative history would effect is this: judges, lawyers, and clients will be saved an enormous amount of time and expense.

Conroy v. Aniskoff (1993)

Concurrence in the judgment

Justice Scalia agreed with the majority that a member of the military qualified for a statutory benefit. He wrote separately to explain why the majority's exegesis of the legislative history was a wasted frolic and a distracting detour—an examination he refused to conduct himself and one he would inflict only on "a hapless law clerk."

The Court begins its analysis with the observation: "The statutory command in § 525 is unambiguous, unequivocal, and unlimited." In my view, discussion of that point is where the remainder of the analysis should have ended. Instead, however, the Court feels compelled to demonstrate that its holding is consonant with legislative history, including some dating back to 1917—*a full quarter century* before the provision at issue was enacted. That is not merely a waste of research time and ink; it is a false and disruptive lesson in the law. It says to the bar that even an unambiguous and unequivocal statute can never be dispositive; that, presumably under penalty of malpractice liability, the oracles of legislative history, far into the dimmy past, must always be consulted.

This undermines the clarity of law, and condemns litigants (who, unlike us, must pay for it out of their own pockets) to subsidizing historical research by lawyers.

The greatest defect of legislative history is its illegitimacy. We are governed by laws, not by the intentions of legislators. As the Court said in 1844: "The law as it passed is the will of the majority of both houses, *and the only mode in which that will is spoken is in the act itself.*"[1] But not the least of the defects of legislative history is its indeterminacy. If one were to search for an interpretive technique that, *on the whole*, was more likely to confuse than to clarify, one could hardly find a more promising candidate than legislative history. And the present case nicely proves that point.

Judge Harold Leventhal used to describe the use of legislative history as the equivalent of entering a crowded cocktail party and looking over the heads of the guests for one's friends. If I may pursue that metaphor: The legislative history of § 525 contains a variety of diverse personages, a selected few of whom—its "friends"—the Court has introduced to us in support of its result. But there are many other faces in the crowd, most of which, I think, are set against today's result.*

After reading the legislative history, one might well conclude that the result reached by the Court today, though faithful to law, betrays the congressional intent. Many have done so. Indeed, as far as I am aware, *every court* that has chosen to interpret § 525 in light of its legislative history rather than on the basis of its plain text has found that Congress did not intend § 525 to apply to career members of the military who cannot show prejudice or hardship. The only scholarly commentary I am aware of addressing this issue concludes: "An examination of the legislative history of the Act shows that the prevailing interpretation of section 525 [i.e., the Court's interpretation] is not consistent with congressional intent."[2] Finally, even the Government itself, which successfully urged in this case the position we have adopted, until recently believed, on the basis of legislative history, the contrary.

I confess that I have not personally investigated the entire legislative history. The excerpts I have examined and quoted were unearthed by a hapless law clerk to whom I assigned the task. The other Justices have, in the aggregate, many more law clerks than I, and it is quite possible that if they all were unleashed upon this enterprise they would discover, in the legislative materials dating back to 1917 *or earlier*, many faces friendly to the Court's holding. Whether they would or not makes no difference to me—and evidently makes no difference to the Court, which gives lip service to legislative history

---

* At this point, Justice Scalia discussed several passages of legislative history.

but does not trouble to set forth and discuss the foregoing material that others found so persuasive. In my view, that is as it should be, except for the lip service. The language of the statute is entirely clear, and if that is not what Congress meant then Congress has made a mistake and Congress will have to correct it. We should not pretend to care about legislative intent (as opposed to the meaning of the law), lest we impose upon the practicing bar and their clients obligations that we do not ourselves take seriously.

United States v. R.L.C. (1992)

*Concurrence in the judgment (joined by
Justices Kennedy and Thomas)*

*If legislative history is problematic when used to interpret run-of-the-mill stat-
utes, it is particularly troubling when used to send people to jail or to increase
their sentences. What the justice once referred to as "that last hope of lost interpretive causes, that St. Jude of the hagiology of statutory construction, legislative history,"[1] has especially severe consequences in criminal law. In this
excerpt, Justice Scalia shows why the unexamined premises of using legislative
history ought to be examined more carefully and why that is especially so when
interpreting criminal laws.*

In my view it is not consistent with the rule of lenity to construe a
textually ambiguous penal statute against a criminal defendant on
the basis of legislative history.

Armed with its warrant of textual ambiguity, the plurality con-
ducts a search of 18 U.S.C. § 5037's legislative history to determine
whether that clarifies the statute. Happily for *this* defendant, the plurality's extratextual inquiry is benign: It uncovers evidence that the
"better understood" reading of § 5037 is the more lenient one. But
this methodology contemplates as well a different ending, one in
which something said in a Committee Report causes the criminal law
to be stricter than the text of the law displays.

"The rule of lenity ensures that criminal statutes will provide fair
warning concerning conduct rendered illegal."[2] It may well be true
that in most cases the proposition that the words of the United States
Code or the Statutes at Large give adequate notice to the citizen is
something of a fiction; but necessary fiction descends to needless
farce when the public is charged even with knowledge of Committee
Reports.

A mode of analysis that requires consideration of legislative history also disserves the rule of lenity's other purpose: assuring that the society, through its representatives, has genuinely called for the punishment to be meted out. "Because of the seriousness of criminal penalties, and because criminal punishment usually represents the moral condemnation of the community, legislatures and not courts should define criminal activity."[3] The rule reflects "the instinctive distaste against men languishing in prison unless the lawmaker has clearly said they should."[4] But legislative history can never provide assurance against that unacceptable result. After all, "a statute is a statute,"[5] and no matter how "authoritative" the history may be— even if it is that veritable Rosetta Stone of legislative archaeology, a crystal clear Committee Report—one can never be sure that the legislators who voted for the text of the bill were aware of it. The only thing that was authoritatively adopted *for sure* was the text of the enactment; the rest is necessarily speculation. Where it is doubtful whether the text includes the penalty, the penalty ought not be imposed. "The moral condemnation of the community" is no more reflected in the views of a majority of a single committee of congressmen (assuming, of course, they have genuinely considered what their staff has produced) than it is reflected in the views of a majority of an appellate court; we should feel no less concerned about "men languishing in prison" at the direction of the one than of the other.

Koons Buick Pontiac GMC v. Nigh (2004)

Dissent

Here Justice Scalia takes on a different problem with legislative history. His concern is not with the Court's reliance on what members of Congress said in speeches and reports but with its reliance on what they did not say.

The Court finds "scant indication that Congress meant to alter the meaning of clause (i)" in 1995 and compares this to "Sir Arthur Conan Doyle's dog that didn't bark." I hardly think it "scant indication" of intent to alter that Congress *amended the text of the statute* by moving the exception from the end of the list to the middle, making it impossible, without doing violence to the text, to read the exception as applying to the entire list. Needless to say, I also disagree with the Court's reliance on things that the sponsors and floor managers of the 1995 amendment *failed* to say. I have often criticized the Court's use of legislative history because it lends itself to a kind of ventriloquism. The Congressional Record or committee reports are used to make words appear to come from Congress's mouth which were spoken or written by others (individual Members of Congress, congressional aides, or even enterprising lobbyists). The Canon of Canine Silence that the Court invokes today introduces a reverse—and at least equally dangerous—phenomenon, under which courts may refuse to believe Congress's *own* words unless they can see the lips of others moving in unison.

4

Review of Agency Action

Complicated and sometimes arcane, "administrative law is not for sissies," Justice Scalia warned audiences on many occasions. But the authority of federal agencies, whether the Internal Revenue Service, the Environmental Protection Agency, or countless others, over the lives of Americans is central to understanding power in American government—and thus central to understanding who governs us. The topic pulls together two ever-present questions in American law: Who decides? And how? The first question implicates the Constitution's allocation of power among the three branches of the national government. The second question takes us back to principles of statutory interpretation—and the proper reading of federal statutes that govern the activities of federal agencies. As the administrative state has continued to grow over the last century, the stakes in how both questions are answered have continued to increase.

This was a familiar topic for Justice Scalia. Before becoming Justice Scalia, Professor Scalia taught administrative law at the University of Virginia and the University of Chicago, and his academic scholarship focused on the subject. His key government posts before becoming a Supreme Court justice also involved a heavy dose of administrative law. From 1972 to 1974, he chaired the Administrative Conference of the United States, an agency that oversaw the decision-making processes of other federal agencies. From 1974 to 1976, he was the assistant attorney general for the Office of Legal Counsel. And from 1982 to 1986, he was a judge on the United States Court of Appeals for the District of Columbia Circuit, which handles many administrative-law disputes. Justice Scalia's views on administrative law were informed and invigorated by his decades of thought and experience.

This chapter contains excerpts from two speeches and two opinions. The speeches, delivered roughly twenty years apart, convey Justice Scalia's developing views about the pros and cons of a landmark case in administrative law decided by the Supreme Court in 1984, two years before he joined the Court: *Chevron U.S.A. v. Natural Resources Defense Council*. The basic idea of the *Chevron* decision is that courts must defer to reasonable interpretations of federal statutes that Congress directs a federal agency to administer. The two case excerpts address appropriate limits on administrative deference.

On *Chevron* Deference in 1989

This speech, delivered at Duke University Law School in 1989, addresses the strengths and weaknesses of Chevron deference. In the speech, Justice Scalia largely defends the decision, which requires courts to defer to reasonable agency interpretations of the statutes they administer. What makes Chevron deference controversial is that it appears to cede legislative authority to executive-branch agencies (to fill policy gaps in statutes) and to cede judicial authority to agencies (to fill interpretive gaps in statutes). What makes Chevron deference complicated is that, long before 1984, courts had been applying on-again, off-again theories of deference to administrative agencies. Justice Scalia defends Chevron deference as the best option among a host of difficult options and the best way forward for establishing a clear rule that was easy for litigants to predict and for courts to follow in a principled and neutral way.

Administrative law is not for sissies—so you should lean back, clutch the sides of your chairs, and steel yourselves.

Five terms ago, the Supreme Court issued its opinion in the case of *Chevron, U.S.A. v. Natural Resources Defense Council*, which announced the principle that the courts will accept an agency's reasonable interpretation of the ambiguous terms of a statute that the agency administers. Justice Stevens for a unanimous Court adopted an analytical approach that deals with the problem of judicial deference to agency interpretations of law in two steps:

> First, always, is the question whether Congress has directly spoken to the precise question at issue. If the intent of Congress is clear, that is the end of the matter; for the court, as well as the agency, must give effect to the unambiguously expressed intent of Congress.

Failing an affirmative response to the first inquiry, the *Chevron* analysis moves to step two:

If, however, the court determines that Congress has not directly addressed the precise question at issue, the court does not simply impose its own construction on the statute, as would be necessary in the absence of an administrative interpretation. Rather, if the statute is silent or ambiguous with respect to the specific issue, the question for the court is whether the agency's answer is based on a permissible construction of the statute.

It should not be thought that the *Chevron* doctrine—except in the clarity and the seemingly categorical nature of its expression—is entirely new law. To the contrary, courts have been content to accept "reasonable" executive interpretations of law for some time. Consider the following description of judicial review of administrative action, written almost fifty years ago by the Attorney General's Committee on Administrative Procedure, whose Report formed the basis for enactment of our basic charter of administrative law, the Administrative Procedure Act:

> Even on questions of law, [independent judicial] judgment seems not to be compelled. The question of statutory interpretation might be approached by the court *de novo* and given the answer which the court thinks to be the "right interpretation." Or the court might approach it, somewhat as a question of fact, to ascertain, not the "right interpretation," but only whether the administrative interpretation has substantial support. Certain standards of interpretation guide in that direction. Thus, where the statute is reasonably susceptible of more than one interpretation, the court may accept that of the administrative body. Again, the administrative interpretation is to be given weight—not merely as the opinion of some men or even of a lower tribunal, but as the opinion of the body especially familiar with the problems dealt with by the statute and burdened with the duty of enforcing it.

That was written, as I say, almost half a century ago, and was an accurate description of the caselaw. Judge Henry Friendly observed the same landscape thirty years later, when he wrote:

We think it is time to recognize that there are two lines of Supreme Court decisions on this subject which are analytically in conflict, with the result that a court of appeals must choose the one it deems more appropriate for the case at hand. Leading cases support the view that great deference must be given to the decisions of an administrative agency applying a statute to the facts and that such decisions can be reversed only if without rational basis. However, there is an impressive body of law sanctioning free substitution of judicial for administrative judgment when the question involves the meaning of a statutory term.

Chevron, if its categorical language is to be believed, and if the Court intends to stand by it, essentially chose between these two conflicting lines of decision.

It is not immediately apparent why a court should ever accept the judgment of an executive agency on a question of law. Indeed, on its face the suggestion seems quite incompatible with Marshall's aphorism that "[i]t is emphatically the province and duty of the judicial department to say what the law is." *Marbury v. Madison* (1803). Surely the law, that immutable product of Congress, is what it is, and its content—ultimately to be decided by the courts—cannot be altered or affected by what the executive thinks about it. I suppose it is harmless enough to speak about "giving deference to the views of the executive" concerning the meaning of a statute, just as we speak of "giving deference to the views of the Congress" concerning the constitutionality of particular legislation—the mealy-mouthed word "deference" not necessarily meaning anything more than considering those views with attentiveness and profound respect, before we reject them. But to say that those views, if at least reasonable, will ever be *binding*—that is, seemingly, a striking abdication of judicial responsibility.

What, then, is the theoretical justification for allowing reasonable administrative interpretations to govern? The cases, old and new, that accept administrative interpretations, often refer to the "expertise" of the agencies in question, their intense familiarity with the history and purposes of the legislation at issue, their practical knowledge of what will best effectuate those purposes. In other words, they are more likely than the courts to reach the correct result. That is, if true, a good practical reason for accepting the agency's views, but hardly a valid theoretical justification for doing so. If I had been sitting on the Supreme Court when Learned Hand was still alive, it would similarly have been, as a practical matter, desirable for me to accept his views in all of his cases under review, on the basis that he is a lot wiser than I, and more likely to get it right. But that would hardly have been theoretically valid. Even if Hand would have been *de facto* superior, I would have been *ex officio* so. So also with judicial acceptance of the agencies' views. If it is, as we have always believed, the constitutional duty of the *courts* to say what the law is, we must search for something beyond relative competence as a basis for ignoring that principle when agency action is at issue.

One possible validating rationale that has been suggested in some recent articles—and that can perhaps even be derived from some of the language of *Chevron* itself—is that the constitutional principle of separation of powers requires *Chevron*. The argument goes something like this: When, in a statute to be implemented by an executive agency, Congress leaves an ambiguity that cannot be resolved by text or legislative history, the "traditional tools of statutory construction," the resolution of that ambiguity necessarily involves policy judgment. Under our democratic system, policy judgments are not for the courts but for the political branches; Congress having left the policy question open, it must be answered by the executive.

Now there is no one more fond of our system of separation of powers than I am, but even I cannot agree with this approach. To begin with, it seems to me that the "traditional tools of statutory construction" include not merely text and legislative history but also, quite specifically, the consideration of policy consequences. Indeed, that tool is so traditional that it has been enshrined in Latin: *"Ratio est legis anima; mutata legis ratione mutatur et lex."* ("Reason is the soul of the law; when the reason for the law changes, the law changes as well.") Surely one of the most frequent justifications courts give for choosing a particular construction is that the alternative interpretation would produce "absurd" results, or results less compatible with the reason or purpose of the statute. This, it seems to me, un-questionably involves judicial consideration and evaluation of com-peting policies, and for precisely the same purpose for which (in the context we are discussing here) *agencies* consider and evaluate them—to determine which one will best effectuate the statutory purpose.* Policy evaluation is, in other words, part of the traditional judicial tool kit that is used in applying the first step of *Chevron*—the step that determines, *before* deferring to agency judgment, whether the law is indeed ambiguous. Only when the court concludes that the policy furthered by *neither* textually possible interpretation will be clearly "better" (in the sense of achieving what Congress apparently wished to achieve) will it, pursuant to *Chevron*, yield to the agency's choice. But the reason it yields is assuredly *not* that it has no constitu-tional competence to consider and evaluate policy.

The separation-of-powers justification can be rejected even more painlessly by asking one simple question: if, in the statute at issue in *Chevron*, Congress had specified that in all suits involving interpreta-tion or application of the Clean Air Act the courts were to give no deference to the agency's views, but were to determine the issue *de novo*, would the Supreme Court nonetheless have acquiesced in the agency's views? I think the answer is clearly no, which means that it is not any constitutional impediment to "policy making" that ex-plains *Chevron*.

In my view, the theoretical justification for *Chevron* is no differ-ent from the theoretical justification for those pre-*Chevron* cases that sometimes deferred to agency legal determinations. As the D.C. Cir-cuit, quoting the First Circuit, expressed it: "The extent to which courts should defer to agency interpretations of law is ultimately a function of Congress's intent on the subject as revealed in the par-

---

* To similar effect, Justice Scalia states in *Reading Law: The Interpretation of Legal Texts* (co-authored with Bryan A. Garner) that the "term *purposivism* suggests, wrongly, that its supposed antonym—namely *textualism*—precludes consideration of a text's purpose." But in fact "the textualist routinely takes purpose into account." What distinguishes the textualist from the purposivist is that the textualist looks to purpose "in its concrete manifestations as deduced from close reading of the text," whereas the purposivist allows "abstract purpose . . . to super-sede text," thus resulting in "what Justice Felix Frankfurter cautioned against: 'interpretations by judicial libertines' who 'draw prodigally upon unformulated purposes or directions.'"

ticular statutory scheme at issue." An ambiguity in a statute committed to agency implementation can be attributed to either of two congressional desires: (1) Congress intended a particular result, but was not clear about it; or (2) Congress had no particular intent on the subject, but meant to leave its resolution to the agency. When the former is the case, what we have is genuinely a question of law, properly to be resolved by the courts. When the latter is the case, what we have is the conferral of discretion upon the agency, and the only question of law presented to the courts is whether the agency has acted within the scope of its discretion—i.e., whether its resolution of the ambiguity is reasonable. As I read the history of developments in this field, the pre-*Chevron* decisions sought to choose between (1) and (2) on a statute-by-statute basis. Hence the relevance of such frequently mentioned factors as the degree of the agency's expertise, the complexity of the question at issue, and the existence of rule-making authority within the agency. All these factors make an intent to confer discretion upon the agency more likely. *Chevron*, however, if it is to be believed, replaced this statute-by-statute evaluation (which was assuredly a font of uncertainty and litigation) with an across-the-board presumption that, in the case of ambiguity, agency discretion is meant.

It is beyond the scope of these remarks to defend that presumption (I was not on the Court, after all, when *Chevron* was decided). Surely, however, it is a more rational presumption today than it would have been thirty years ago—which explains the change in the law. Broad delegation to the executive is the hallmark of the modern administrative state; agency rule-making powers are the rule rather than, as they once were, the exception; and as the sheer number of modern departments and agencies suggests, we are awash in agency "expertise." If the *Chevron* rule is not a 100 percent accurate estimation of modern congressional intent, the prior case-by-case evaluation was not so either—and was becoming less and less so, as the sheer volume of modern dockets made it less and less possible for the Supreme Court to police diverse application of an ineffable rule. And to tell the truth, the quest for the "genuine" legislative intent is probably a wild-goose chase anyway. In the vast majority of cases I expect that Congress *neither* (1) intended a single result *nor* (2) meant to confer discretion upon the agency, but rather (3) didn't think about the matter at all. If I am correct in that, then any rule adopted in this field represents merely a fictional, presumed intent, and operates principally as a background rule of law against which Congress can legislate.

If that is the principal function to be served, *Chevron* is unquestionably better than what preceded it. Congress now knows that the ambiguities it creates, whether intentionally or unintentionally, will be resolved, within the bounds of permissible interpretation, not by the courts but by a particular agency, whose policy biases will ordinarily be known. The legislative process becomes less of a sporting event when those supporting and opposing a particular disposition do not have to gamble upon whether, if they say nothing about it in the statute, the ultimate answer will be provided by the courts or rather by the Department of Labor.

The theory that judicial acquiescence in reasonable agency determinations of law rests upon real or presumed legislative intent to confer discretion has certain consequences which the courts do not yet seem to have grasped. For one thing, there is no longer any justification for giving "special" deference to "long-standing and consistent" agency interpretations of law. That venerable principle made a lot of sense when we assumed that both court and agency were searching for the one, permanent, "correct" meaning of the statute; it makes no sense when we acknowledge that the agency is free to give the statute whichever of several possible meanings it thinks most conducive to accomplishment of the statutory purpose. Under the latter regime, there is no apparent justification for holding the agency to its first answer, or penalizing it for a change of mind.

Indeed, it seems to me that such an approach would deprive *Chevron* of one of its major advantages from the standpoint of governmental theory, which is to permit needed flexibility, and appropriate political participation, in the administrative process. One of the major disadvantages of having the courts resolve ambiguities is that they resolve them for ever and ever; only statutory amendment can produce a change. If the term *stationary source* in the Clean Air Act did not permit the "bubble concept" today, it would not permit the "bubble concept" four years from now either, no matter how much the perception of whether that concept impairs or furthers the objectives of the Act may change. Under *Chevron*, however, "stationary source" can mean a range of things, and it is up to the agency, in light of its advancing knowledge (and also, to be realistic about it, in light of the changing political pressures that it feels from Congress and from its various constituencies) to specify the correct meaning. If Congress is to delegate broadly, as modern times are thought to demand, it seems to me desirable that the delegee be able to suit its actions to the times, and that continuing political accountability be assured, through direct political pressures upon the executive and through the indirect political pressure of congressional oversight. All this is lost if "new" or "changing" agency interpretations are somehow suspect. There are, of course, well-established restrictions upon sudden and irrational changes of interpretation through adjudication, and statutorily prescribed procedures (including a requirement of reasoned justification) for changes of interpretation through rule making. And at some point, I suppose, repeated changes back and forth may rise (or descend) to the level of "arbitrary and capricious," and thus unlawful, agency action. But so long as these limitations are complied with, there seems to me no reason to value a new interpretation less than an old one.

Let me digress for a moment here, to note that the capacity of the *Chevron* approach to accept changes in agency interpretation *ungrudgingly* seems to me one of the strongest indications that the *Chevron* approach is correct. It has always seemed to me utterly unrealistic to believe that when an agency revises one of its interpretative regulations, or one of the legal rules that it applies in its adjudications—when the NLRB, for example, decides that employer action previously held to be an "unfair labor practice" is no longer so, or when the Federal Trade Commission amends one of its regulations to declare action previously permitted to be an "unfair or deceptive trade practice"—the agency was admitting that it had "got the law wrong." And it has thus seemed to me inappropriate to look askance at such changes, as though we were dealing with a judge who cannot make up his mind whether the Rule in Shelley's Case applies or not. Rather, the agency was simply "changing the law," in light of new information or even new social attitudes impressed upon it through the political process—all within the limited range of discretion to "change the law" conferred by the governing statute. *Chevron*, as I say, permits recognition of this reality.

There is one final point I wish to discuss: what does it take to satisfy the first step of *Chevron*—that is, when is a statute ambiguous? *Chevron* becomes virtually meaningless, it seems to me, if ambiguity exists only when the arguments for and against the various possible interpretations are in absolute equipoise. If nature knows of such equipoise in legal arguments, the courts at least do not. The judicial task, every day, consists of finding the *right* answer, no matter how closely balanced the question may *seem* to be. In appellate opinions, there is no such thing as a tie. If the judicial mentality that is developed by such a system were set to answering the question "When are the arguments for and against a particular statutory interpretation in equipoise?," I am certain that the response would be "almost never." If *Chevron* is to have any meaning, then, congressional intent must be regarded as "ambiguous" not just when no interpretation is even marginally better than any other, but rather when two or more reasonable, though not necessarily equally valid, interpretations exist. This is indeed intimated by the opinion in *Chevron*—which suggests that the opposite of *ambiguity* is not *resolvability* but rather *clarity*. Here, of course, is the chink in *Chevron*'s armor—the ambiguity that prevents it from being an absolutely clear guide to future judicial decisions (though still a better one than what it supplanted). How clear is clear? It is here, if *Chevron* is not abandoned, that the future battles over acceptance of agency interpretations of law will be fought. Some indications of that can already be found in Supreme Court opinions.

I cannot resist the temptation to tie this lecture into an impenetrable whole, by observing that where one stands on this last point—how clear is clear—may have much to do with where one stands on the earlier points of what *Chevron* means and whether *Chevron* is desirable. In my experience, there is a fairly close correlation between the degree to which a person is (for want of a better term) a "strict constructionist" of statutes, and the degree to which that person favors *Chevron* and is willing to give it broad scope. The reason is obvious. One who finds *more* often (as I do) that the meaning of a statute is apparent from its text and from its relationship with other laws, thereby finds *less* often that the triggering requirement for *Chevron* deference exists. It is thus relatively rare that *Chevron* will require me to accept an interpretation which, though reasonable, I would not personally adopt. Contrariwise, one who abhors a "plain meaning" rule, and is willing to permit the apparent meaning of a statute to be impeached by the legislative history, will more frequently find agency-liberating ambiguity, and will discern a much broader range of "reasonable" interpretation that the agency may adopt and to which the courts must pay deference. The frequency with which *Chevron* will require *that* judge to accept an interpretation he thinks wrong is infinitely greater.

The law does not move in a straight line, and I will be surprised if the implications of *Chevron* that I have discussed—and others that I have not mentioned—are immediately grasped and applied by the federal courts. The opinions we federal judges read, and the cases we cite, are full of references to the old criteria of "agency expertise," "the technical and complex nature of the question presented," "the consistent and long-standing agency position"—and it will take some time to understand that those concepts are no longer relevant, or no longer relevant in the same way. Indeed, it may be that, for a time at least, fidelity to the old formulations will unnaturally constrict *Chevron*, or even produce a retreat from its basic perception. I tend to think, however, that in the long run *Chevron* will endure and be given its full scope—not so much because it represents a rule that is easier to follow and thus easier to predict (though that is true enough), but because it more accurately reflects the reality of government, and thus more adequately serves its needs.

On *Chevron* Deference Twenty Years Later

In this second speech, delivered two decades later at the American University Washington College of Law,[1] Justice Scalia reflects on whether his assessment of Chevron *was correct and accounts for a decision in the intervening years—* United States v. Mead Corp. *(2001)—from which he strongly dissented. As he saw it,* Mead *muddied the clarity of the* Chevron *rule, returned the courts to the back-and-forth theories of deference that predated* Chevron, *and left us in the end with the worst of all options: no improvement on the separation-of-powers problems that underlie* Chevron *and no compensating benefits of an easy-to-administer rule. Taken together, the two speeches cover a topic that the justice encountered firsthand in a variety of capacities and exemplify his default position that the rule of law works best when it is a law of rules.*

Twenty years ago, I was invited to give a talk similar to this at an-other law school on the occasion of *Chevron*'s fifth anniversary. At the time, it was already clear that *Chevron* was a watershed deci-sion. Still in its infancy, the Court's opinion had already been cited hundreds of times by the lower courts. With the passage of time that number has grown into the thousands. Of course, *Chevron* did not break entirely new ground. Courts had long deferred to agency de-terminations, including determinations concerning the law, and in my view the same theory underlies both the pre- and the post-*Chevron* regimes, namely the theory that courts had to defer to agency decisions because and to the extent that Congress has dele-gated lawmaking authority to administrative agencies.

Chevron's innovation, as I saw it two decades ago, was the adop-tion of a blanket default rule, which presumed that statutory ambi-guity constituted a conferral of delegation from the Congress. Pre-*Chevron*, the question whether there was agency discretion was answered on a statute-by-statute basis, or indeed on a case-by-case basis, resting on various factors that courts deemed relevant as evi-dence of congressional conferral of authority. *Chevron*, as I said at the time, "replaced this statute-by-statute evaluation with an across-the-board presumption that in the case of ambiguity, agency discretion is meant."

This presumption was, I conceded, like all presumptions, imperfect, but it was no worse than the proxies courts had long used as evidence of congressional so-called delegation, and in any event the existence of genuine congressional intent regarding delegation is largely a fiction. And so I believed it best to adopt a straightforward default rule that courts could easily administer and that Congress, if it wished, could legislate against. I concluded my remarks with the following prediction, which I tempered with the standard caveats that go with predicting the future: "I tend to think, however, that in the long run *Chevron* will endure and be given its full scope—not so much because it represents a rule that is easier to follow and thus easier to predict (though that is true enough), but because it more accurately reflects the reality of government and thus more adequately serves [government's] needs."

Eight years ago my Court proved that prediction wrong, when in its decision in *United States v. Mead Corporation* the Court returned in large part to the case-by-case, statute-by-statute mode of analysis that preceded the decision in *Chevron*, with all the harmful side effects that generally attend that mode of analysis. I made a series of predictions at the time the Court took this wrong turn—in my dissent in the case—and now, with some water having gone under the bridge, it may be time to reflect on those predictions. While my prediction about *Chevron*'s endurance may have been optimistic, I believe I can safely say that my predictions about the harmful effects of *Mead* were if anything not pessimistic enough.

In *Mead*, the Court considered whether certain tariff classification decisions made by the United States Customs Service were entitled to *Chevron* deference. The Court answered no, holding that *Chevron* deference is only warranted "when it appears that Congress delegated authority to the agency generally to make rules carrying the force of law, and that the agency interpretation claiming deference was promulgated in the exercise of that authority." How would we know when Congress had so delegated? The formality of the administrative procedure used was one such way, the Court said; but formality, the Court also said, was not a necessary condition. The predictions I made in my dissent have, to the extent they can be tested, either come to pass or been averted only by further wrong turns, or further elaborations at least, in our administrative law jurisprudence.

I first predicted that the Court's decision would create a perverse incentive for agencies to adopt bare-bones regulations, because acting by regulation showed that you were acting pursuant to congressional delegation. The agency could, with the benefit of substantial judicial deference, later interpret or clarify those regulations, by adjudication or even by simply agency pronouncement, without any bothersome procedural formality. The initial regulation having been adopted via notice and comment would earn *Chevron* deference, and the subsequent agency clarification would earn the so-called *Auer* deference, which we accord to an agency's interpretation of its own regulations. Thus would an agency receive deference through evasion of the very procedural formalities that *Mead* sought to impose.

Well, it's hard to confirm or to refute this particular prediction. I really don't know if agency rules have in fact become less detailed and more ambiguous since the Court's decision in *Mead*. I'm not even sure how one would measure that or how one would control for the various other factors that undoubtedly bear upon a regulation's clarity. But that may not matter, because in any event the Court has in at least one instance refused to defer to an agency interpretation of its own regulation because the regulation did not "give specificity to a statutory scheme," but rather "did little more than restate the terms of the statute itself." A new administrative law doctrine, the so-called anti-parroting principle—first discovered in the Court's 2006 decision in *Gonzales v. Oregon*—limits agencies' ability to take advantage of *Mead*'s loophole. To that extent I suppose the doctrine is useful, but I had never heard of it before and you are now going to have to decide case by case whether an agency is parroting or not. But the perverse incentive for ambiguous agency rule making remains, and time may tell whether agencies get wise to this gimmick.

I next predicted in *Mead* that the Court's decision would lead to the ossification of our statutory law. With *Chevron*'s scope more limited, more statutory ambiguities would be resolved by the courts, and agency discretion would be similarly constrained or simply preempted, as in the case where the Court just happened to reach the question before the agency did. Well, that problem was also "fixed," when four years later in *National Cable & Telecommunications Association v. Brand X Internet Services* the Court held that—and this was a staggering revelation to me—even when the court resolved the statutory ambiguity and thereby determined the meaning of the statute, an agency could still decide to the contrary, so long as the court's decision did not rest on the determination that the statute was unambiguous to begin with. As I stated at the time, that decision cured one of *Mead*'s infirmities only by inventing yet another breathtaking novelty, judicial decision subject to reversal by executive officials. In my view, the cure is worse than the disease, but it has at the very least rendered one of my *Mead* predictions moot.

My third *Mead* prediction was an easy one. I anticipated that the lower courts and the agencies and litigants who appear before them would not know what to make of the Court's new approach. The Court had given virtually no guidance as to which types of agency actions would henceforth merit *Chevron* deference. Notice-and-comment rule making and formal adjudication appeared to be safe harbors, but outside of those rather narrow confines deference would depend on a host of factors. And since the whole *Chevron* game is (now) about divining congressional intent, the field was potentially cast wide open.

Well, you can take that prediction to the bank. Lower courts are indeed utterly confused as to what triggers *Chevron* deference. We know some formality is needed, but we don't know how much. Some expertise, but how much? Some public participation, but how much? So some courts look at a policy statement and see a document that the agency treats as a rule or regulation that is published in the *Federal Register* and that is promulgated by an expert agency. Other courts see in the same thing a document that was produced without public involvement, without the formality of notice-and-comment rule making, and without sufficient explanation to invoke the agency's expertise. Since under *Mead* the universe of relevant factors is wide open, and the quantum of each factor needed to trigger *Chevron* deference is unknown, it would be hard to say which of these decisions is right and which is wrong. Surely a decision that cannot give guidance to lower courts is not very helpful.

Given the emerging mess in the courts of appeals, one might have hoped that the Court in subsequent decisions would have clarified matters, but it seems headed in just the other direction. In *Barnhart v. Walton*, just one year after *Mead*, the Court added to the grab bag of factors that trigger *Chevron* deference "the interstitial nature of the legal question, the related expertise of the Agency, the importance of the question to administration of the statute, the complexity of that administration, and the careful consideration the Agency has given the question over a long period of time." All of those factors were identified as relevant in the *Chevron* inquiry. Throw those in with the factors discussed in *Mead* and we are left with what I have described as "th'ol' totality of the circumstances test." Which is of course no test at all.

Perhaps the best evidence of the mess left by *Mead* is the sheer reluctance of courts to engage the question altogether. The phenomenon is so pervasive that it has earned its own name—in a law-review article it is called "*Chevron* avoidance." Lower courts have repeatedly noted their preference for avoiding the muck of *Mead*.

Perhaps this suggests that the whole exercise is not worth the candle. If there is little practical difference between *Skidmore* and *Chevron* deference, then why fret over whether and when *Chevron* applies? Of course this argument cuts both ways. If the question is easily ducked, perhaps it is not as much of a burden on the lower courts as I suppose. Conversely, if there is little practical difference—and this is the course I would propose—why create a complex totality-of-the-circumstances standard for determining when deference is triggered? If it matters so little, let's just have an easily administrable rule and be done with it.

And of course, even if courts can dodge the bullet, litigants cannot. They must go through the effort of explaining why *Chevron* deference is or is not merited. They cannot take the chance that the level of deference will not matter. And so they are forced to expend resources arguing a preliminary question whose answer cannot be predicted and whose impact may be slight.

There is a further reason why the Court's case-by-case approach in *Mead* is not worth the candle. *Mead*, of course, implicates the age-old debate between rules and standards. It is assumed that flexible standards are more accurate but less administrable, whereas rules are more administrable but less precise, less accurate. And our choice is simply one of two imperfect approaches. But I'm not certain that is the case here. As I've argued previously, judicial deference to agency decision making is a function of congressional delegation of authority to an agency. I have also argued previously that, generally speaking, statutory ambiguity is a product not of consensus on the part of Congress, but rather of congressional omission. That is, usually it is the case that where there is a statutory ambiguity or a silence, Congress simply failed to consider the matter altogether. You don't really think that where it's ambiguous Congress said, "Let's leave it ambiguous and leave it up to the agency." That may happen sometimes, but surely not as a general rule.

The inference of congressional delegation is thus a legal fiction. If that is true, then it makes no sense to ask which approach, *Chevron*'s or *Mead*'s, more closely or accurately predicts a congressional intent that probably does not exist. There simply is no congressional intent to discern; there is only a legal fiction to construct. If courts are inventing congressional intent rather than discerning it, then there is no right answer, and if there is no right answer, we might as well have a clear answer. Put somewhat differently, *Mead* produces all the costs and none of the benefits of a flexible standard, while a clear, consistent rule would achieve the opposite. And since our deference regime rests upon a default assumption that is subject to legislative alteration, it's no big deal. If Congress does not like the default rule, it can act to override it. This is thus not simply another battlefield in the ongoing debate between rules versus standards. It is an area where a flexible standard simply serves no purpose and makes no sense.

Agency Interpretation of Agency Rules— *Decker v. Northwest Environmental Defense Center* (2013)

Concurrence in part and dissent in part

In this case, Justice Scalia wrote separately to take on a misstep in administrative law. In 1945, in Bowles v. Seminole Rock & Sand Co., *the Supreme Court held that an agency's interpretation of its own rules received near-absolute deference. And in 1997, the Supreme Court stood by that decision in* Auer v. Robbins, *a decision written by Justice Scalia. In his concurrence in* Decker, *Justice Scalia, re-considering the matter, explained the separation-of-powers problems that arise from deferring to an agency's interpretations of its own rules or interpretive guidance, and he called for the overruling of both* Seminole Rock *and his own decision in* Auer.

Three years after Justice Scalia's death, in Kisor v. Wilkie *(2019), the Court took many of these criticisms to heart, opting to cut back on* Auer *and* Seminole Rock *deference without overruling those decisions.*

For decades, and for no good reason, we have been giving agencies the authority to say what their rules mean, under the harmless-sounding banner of "deferring to an agency's interpretation of its own regulations." This is generally called *Seminole Rock* or *Auer* deference.

Our cases have not put forward a persuasive justification for *Auer* deference. The first case to apply it, *Seminole Rock*, offered no justification whatever—just the *ipse dixit* that "the administrative interpretation becomes of controlling weight unless it is plainly erroneous or inconsistent with the regulation." Our later cases provide two principal explanations, neither of which has much to be said for it. First, some cases say that the agency, as the drafter of the rule, will have some special insight into its intent when enacting it. The implied premise of this argument—that what we are looking for is the agency's *intent* in adopting the rule—is false. There is true of regulations what is true of statutes. As Justice Holmes put it: "we do not inquire what the legislature meant; we ask only what the statute means."[1] Whether governing rules are made by the national legislature or an administrative agency, we are bound *by what they say,* not by the unexpressed intention of those who made them.

The other rationale our cases provide is that the agency possesses special expertise in administering its "complex and highly technical regulatory program." That is true enough, and it leads to the conclusion that agencies and not courts should make regulations. But it has nothing to do with who should interpret regulations—unless one believes that the purpose of interpretation is to make the regulatory program work in a fashion that the current leadership of the agency deems effective. Making regulatory programs effective is the purpose of *rulemaking,* in which the agency uses its "special expertise" to formulate the best rule. But the purpose of interpretation is to determine the fair meaning of the rule—to "say what the law is." *Marbury v. Madison* (1803). Not to make policy, but to determine what policy has been made and promulgated by the agency, to which the public owes obedience. Indeed, since the leadership of agencies (and hence the policy preferences of agencies) changes with Presidential administrations, an agency head can only be sure that the application of his "special expertise" to the issue addressed by a regulation *will be given effect* if we adhere to predictable principles of textual interpretation rather than defer to the "special expertise" of his successors. If we take agency enactments as written, the Executive has a stable background against which to write its rules and achieve the policy ends it thinks best.

Another conceivable justification for *Auer* deference, though not one that is to be found in our cases, is this: If it is reasonable to defer to agencies regarding the meaning of statutes that *Congress* enacted, as we do per *Chevron,* it is *a fortiori* reasonable to defer to them regarding the meaning of regulations *that they themselves crafted.* To give an agency less control over the meaning of its own regulations than it has over the meaning of a congressionally enacted statute seems quite odd.

But it is not odd at all. The theory of *Chevron* (take it or leave it) is that when Congress gives an agency authority to administer a statute, including authority to issue interpretive regulations, it implicitly accords the agency a degree of discretion, which the courts must respect, regarding the meaning of the statute. While the implication of an agency power to clarify the statute is reasonable enough, there is surely no congressional implication that the agency can resolve ambiguities in its own regulations. For that would violate a fundamental principle of separation of powers—that the power to write a law and the power to interpret it cannot rest in the same hands. "When the legislative and executive powers are united in the same person, there can be no liberty; because apprehensions may arise, lest the same monarch or senate should enact tyrannical laws, to execute them in a tyrannical manner." Montesquieu, *Spirit of the Laws*. Congress cannot enlarge its *own* power through *Chevron*—whatever it leaves vague in the statute will be worked out *by someone else*. *Chevron* represents a presumption about who, as between the Executive and the Judiciary, that someone else will be. So Congress's incentive is to speak as clearly as possible on the matters it regards as important.

But when an agency interprets its *own* rules—that is something else. Then the power to prescribe is augmented by the power to interpret; and the incentive is to speak vaguely and broadly, so as to retain a "flexibility" that will enable "clarification" with retroactive effect. "It is perfectly understandable" for an agency to "issue vague regulations" if doing so will "maximize agency power."[2] Combining the power to prescribe with the power to interpret is not a new evil: Blackstone condemned the practice of resolving doubts about "the construction of the Roman laws" by "stat[ing] the case to the emperor in writing, and tak[ing] his opinion upon it."[3] And our Constitution did not mirror the British practice of using the House of Lords as a court of last resort, due in part to the fear that he who has "agency in passing bad laws" might operate in the "same spirit" in their interpretation. The Federalist No. 81. *Auer* deference encourages agencies to be "vague in framing regulations, with the plan of issuing 'interpretations' to create the intended new law without observance of notice and comment procedures."[4] *Auer* is not a logical corollary to *Chevron* but a dangerous permission slip for the arrogation of power.

Agency Interpretation of Criminal Laws—
Whitman v. United States (2014)

Statement respecting the denial of certiorari
(joined by Justice Thomas)

A certiorari petition* presented the question whether the Court should revisit a prior decision of the Court, Babbitt v. Sweet Home Chapter of Communities for a Great Oregon *(1995), which held that* Chevron *deference applied to agency interpretations of statutes that have civil and criminal applications. Because the same kind of ambiguity that triggers* Chevron *deference also implicates the rule of lenity,† Justice Scalia thought the rule of lenity must control.*

Justice Scalia's statement features two of his jurisprudential concerns—that the Court should not lightly interpret federal statutes to expand the coverage of a criminal law and that it should not lightly allow federal agencies to take on authority to define crimes.

A court owes no deference to the prosecution's interpretation of a criminal law. Criminal statutes "are for the courts, not for the Government, to construe."[1] This case, a criminal prosecution under § 10(b) of the Securities Exchange Act of 1934, raises a related question: Does a court owe deference to an executive agency's interpretation of a law that contemplates both criminal and administrative enforcement?

The Second Circuit thought it does. It deferred to the Securities and Exchange Commission's interpretation of § 10(b), and on that basis affirmed petitioner Douglas Whitman's criminal conviction. Its decision tilled no new ground. Other Courts of Appeals have de-

---

* A petition for certiorari is the usual means by which a party asks the Supreme Court to review a decision of a lower court.

† Under the rule of lenity, an ambiguity in a criminal law is to be construed in favor of the criminal defendant.

ferred to executive interpretations of a variety of laws that have both criminal and administrative applications.

I doubt the Government's pretensions to deference. They collide with the norm that legislatures, not executive officers, define crimes. When King James I tried to create new crimes by royal command, the judges responded that "the King cannot create any offence by his prohibition or proclamation, which was not an offence before." James I, however, did not have the benefit of *Chevron* deference. With deference to agency interpretations of statutory provisions to which criminal prohibitions are attached, federal administrators can in effect create (and uncreate) new crimes at will, so long as they do not roam beyond ambiguities that the laws contain. Undoubtedly Congress may make it a crime to violate a regulation, but it is quite a different matter for Congress to give agencies—let alone for us to *presume* that Congress gave agencies—power to resolve ambiguities in criminal legislation.

The Government's theory that was accepted here would, in addition, upend ordinary principles of interpretation. The rule of lenity requires interpreters to resolve ambiguity in criminal laws in favor of defendants. Deferring to the prosecuting branch's expansive views of these statutes "would turn their normal construction upside-down, replacing the doctrine of lenity with a doctrine of severity."[2]

Acknowledgments

We formed an enduring friendship when we clerked together for Justice Scalia nearly three decades ago. It was a real pleasure to work with each other again on this monument to Justice Scalia's legacy. In the process, Jeff developed a new appreciation for how accommodating his judicial colleagues are, and Ed learned what it must be like to be one of Jeff's law clerks.

We thank Mrs. Scalia for entrusting us with this undertaking, Eugene Scalia for his supervision of the project, Mary Reynics of Crown Forum for her valuable guidance throughout, and Justice Elena Kagan for her beautiful foreword.

We also thank Rishabh Bhandari, Nicholas Cordova, Ryan Kearney, Michael Lemanski, James McGlone, R. J. McVeigh, Branton Nestor, Nathaniel Sutton, and Kees Thompson for their assistance in selecting the materials for this volume and for reviewing the manuscript; and Natalie Robertson and Mark Shanoudy of the Ethics and Public Policy Center for their logistical support.

We also thank our wives for their love throughout the process and always.

Notes

INTRODUCTION

1. *Kyles v. Whitley* (1995).
2. *Community Nutrition Institute v. Block* (D.C. Cir. 1984).
3. *Mistretta v. United States* (1989) (dissent).
4. *Bendix Autolite v. Midwesco Enterprises* (1988) (concurrence in judgment).
5. *Whitman v. American Trucking Associations* (2001).
6. *PGA Tour v. Martin* (2001) (dissent).

1: GENERAL PRINCIPLES OF INTERPRETATION
The Rule of Law

1. The speech was published in the fall 1989 issue of the *University of Chicago Law Review*.
2. Aristotle's *Politics*.

Originalism

1. The speeches are under the headings "Interpreting the Constitution" and "The Freedom of Speech" in *Scalia Speaks: Reflections on Law, Faith, and Life Well Lived* (Crown Forum, 2017).

Textualism

1. Excerpted from *A Matter of Interpretation: Federal Courts and the Law*, an essay by Antonin Scalia, with commentary by Amy Gutmann, Gordon S. Wood, Laurence H. Tribe, Mary Ann Glendon, Ronald Dworkin, with a new introduction by Akhil Reed Amar and a new afterword by Steven G. Calabresi. Copyright © 1997 by Princeton University Press. Reprinted by permission.

2: CONSTITUTIONAL INTERPRETATION

Constitutional Structure

THE IMPORTANCE OF STRUCTURE

In Praise of the Humdrum

1. From "The Idea of the Constitution" in *Scalia Speaks*.

LEGISLATIVE POWER

The Commerce Clause Is Not *Carte Blanche*—*NFIB v. Sebelius*

1. Quoting early dictionaries.

EXECUTIVE POWER

This Wolf Comes as a Wolf—*Morrison v. Olson*

1. Quoting then-existing federal statute 28 U.S.C. § 594(a).

JUDICIAL POWER

Against Novel Theories of Standing—*Lujan v. Defenders of Wildlife*

1. *Whitmore v. Arkansas* (1990).
2. *United States v. SCRAP* (1973).
3. *Frothingham v. Mellon* (1923).
4. *Laird v. Tatum* (1972).

Final Judgments Are Really Final—*Plaut v. Spendthrift Farm*

1. *Robertson v. Seattle Audubon Society* (1992).
2. Quoting a law-review article by Judge Frank Easterbrook.
3. *United States v. Schooner Peggy* (1801).

Political Gerrymandering—*Vieth v. Jubelirer*

1. Quoting a history of the gerrymander.

FEDERALISM

The Two Faces of Federalism

1. The speech was published under the title "The Two Faces of Federalism" in the *Harvard Journal of Law & Public Policy*, Vol. 6 (1982).

Our System of Dual Sovereignty—*Printz v. United States*

1. *Helvering v. Gerhardt* (1938).
2. Quoting *Records of the Federal Convention of 1787* (M. Farrand, ed., 1911).
3. *New York v. United States* (1992).
4. *U.S. Term Limits v. Thornton* (1995) (Kennedy concurrence).
5. *Gregory v. Ashcroft* (1991).

There Is No Dormant Commerce Clause—
Comptroller of Treasury of Maryland v. Wynne

1. Quoting a book by Felix Frankfurter.

Civil Liberties

1. Excerpted from *A Matter of Interpretation: Federal Courts and the Law*, an essay by Antonin Scalia, with commentary by Amy Gutmann, Gordon S. Wood, Laurence H. Tribe, Mary Ann Glendon, Ronald Dworkin, with a new introduction by Akhil Reed Amar and a new afterword by Steven G. Calabresi. Copyright © 1997 by Princeton University Press. Reprinted by permission.

FREE SPEECH
Peaceful Speech Outside Abortion Clinics—*Hill v. Colorado*

1. Quoting from his dissent in *Madsen v. Women's Health Center* (1994).
2. Quoting from his dissent in *Madsen*.

The Right to Criticize the Government—
McConnell v. Federal Election Commission

1. Quoting a treatise on corporations.

Violent Video Games—*Brown v. Entertainment Merchants Association*

1. *Winters v. New York* (1948).
2. *United States v. Playboy Entertainment Group* (2000).
3. *Joseph Burstyn, Inc. v. Wilson* (1952).
4. *Ashcroft v. ACLU* (2002).
5. *United States v. Stevens* (2010).
6. *Chaplinsky v. New Hampshire* (1942).
7. Quoting a *New York Times* article from 1909.
8. *Mutual Film Corp. v. Industrial Commission of Ohio* (1915).
9. Quoting a *Harvard Law Review* article from 1955.
10. *American Amusement Machine Association v. Kendrick* (7th Cir. 2001).
11. *Chaplinsky v. New Hampshire* (1942).

Hate Speech—*R.A.V. v. City of St. Paul*

1. *Chaplinsky v. New Hampshire* (1942).
2. *Niemotko v. Maryland* (1951) (opinion concurring in the result).

RELIGIOUS LIBERTY
Prayer at Public Ceremonies—*Lee v. Weisman*

1. *Lynch v. Donnelly* (1984).
2. *School District of Abington v. Schempp* (1963) (Brennan concurrence).

3. *Marsh v. Chambers* (1983).
4. *Walz v. Tax Commission of the City of New York* (1970) (Brennan concurrence).
5. *Lynch v. Donnelly* (1984).
6. Quoting an article.
7. Quoting a book on school commencements.
8. *American Jewish Congress v. Chicago* (7th Cir. 1987) (Easterbrook dissent).
9. Quoting L. Levy, *The Establishment Clause* (1986).
10. *American Jewish Congress v. Chicago* (7th Cir. 1987) (Easterbrook dissent).

The Establishment Clause Ghoul—*Lamb's Chapel v. Center Moriches Union Free School District*

1. *Lee v. Weisman* (1992) (dissent).

Ten Commandments Displays—*McCreary County v. ACLU*

1. *School District of Abington v. Schempp* (1963).
2. *Zorach v. Clauson* (1952).

Neutral and General Laws—*Employment Division v. Smith*

1. *Sherbert v. Verner* (1963).
2. *Lyng v. Northwest Indian Cemetery Protective Association* (1988).
3. *Reynolds v. United States* (1879).
4. *United States v. Lee* (1982) (Stevens concurrence in the judgment).
5. *Hernandez v. Commissioner* (1989).
6. *Braunfeld v. Brown* (1961) (plurality).

RIGHT TO BEAR ARMS

Individual Right to Possess a Handgun—*District of Columbia v. Heller*

1. *United States v. Sprague* (1931).
2. Quoting an English court ruling from 1802.
3. Quoting the 1773 edition of Samuel Johnson's *Dictionary of the English Language*.
4. Quoting Noah Webster's *American Dictionary of the English Language* (1828).
5. Quoting *Collected Works of James Wilson*.
6. *United States v. Miller* (1939).
7. Citing Blackstone and other treatises.
8. Quoting the D.C. Circuit opinion under review.
9. Quoting the dissent of Justice Breyer.

SUBSTANTIVE DUE PROCESS

Abortion—*Planned Parenthood v. Casey*

1. Quoting the joint opinion of Justices O'Connor, Kennedy, and Souter.
2. *Lee v. Weisman* (1992).

Marriage—*Obergefell v. Hodges*

1. *United States v. Windsor* (2013).

Punitive Damages—*BMW of North America v. Gore*

1. *Pacific Mutual Life Insurance Co. v. Haslip* (1991).

EQUAL PROTECTION
The Disease as Cure

1. 1979 *Wash U. L. Q.* 147.

Racial Preferences in Government Contracting—
City of Richmond v. J. A. Croson Co.

1. Bickel, *The Morality of Consent* (1975).
2. Bickel, *The Morality of Consent* (1975).
3. Bickel, *The Morality of Consent* (1975).

All-Male Military Institutions—*United States v. Virginia*

1. Quoting from his dissent in *Rutan v. Republican Party of Illinois* (1990).
2. *Mississippi University for Women v. Hogan* (1982) (Powell, dissenting).

ECONOMIC LIBERTIES
Economic Affairs as Human Affairs

1. These excerpts are published with the permission of the Cato Institute.

Regulatory Takings—*Lucas v. South Carolina Coastal Council*

1. *Penn Central Transportation Co. v. New York City* (1978).
2. *Agins v. Tiburon* (1980).
3. *Pennsylvania Coal Co. v. Mahon* (1922).

Criminal Protections

UNREASONABLE SEARCHES AND SEIZURES
Thermal Imaging—*Kyllo v. United States*

1. *Silverman v. United States* (1961).
2. *Boyd v. United States* (1886) (quoting an English case).

Anonymous Tips—*Navarette v. California*

1. Quoting his own dissent in *McIntyre v. Ohio Elections Commission* (1995).
2. *Florida v. J.L.* (2000).

Limiting the Exclusionary Rule—*Hudson v. Michigan*

1. *Pennsylvania Board of Probation and Parole v. Scott* (1998).
2. *United States v. Leon* (1984).
3. *Pennsylvania Board of Probation and Parole v. Scott* (1998).
4. *Pennsylvania Board of Probation and Parole v. Scott* (1998).
5. Quoting a treatise on police misconduct.
6. *United States v. Payner* (1980).
7. Quoting a treatise on criminal justice.

CONFRONTING WITNESSES
Out-of-Court Statements—*Crawford v. Washington*

1. Quoting a treatise on the history of English criminal law.

JURY TRIAL
Facts at Sentencing—*Blakely v. Washington*

1. Quoting Blackstone's *Commentaries on the Laws of England* (1769).
2. Quoting a nineteenth-century treatise on criminal procedure.
3. *McMillan v. Pennsylvania* (1986).

DEATH PENALTY
Adolescent Murderers—*Roper v. Simmons*

1. *Stanford v. Kentucky* (1989).
2. Quoting the majority opinion.
3. *Bivens v. Six Unknown Federal Narcotics Agents* (1971) (Burger dissent).
4. Quoting a 2001 law-review article.

Welcome to Groundhog Day—*Glossip v. Gross*

1. *Trop v. Dulles* (1958) (plurality opinion).

DUE PROCESS
Vague Criminal Laws—*Johnson v. United States*

1. *Connally v. General Construction Co.* (1926).
2. *United States v. Mayer* (9th Cir. 2009) (Kozinski dissent from denial of re-hearing en banc).
3. *United States v. L. Cohen Grocery Co.* (1921).
4. *United States v. Evans* (1948).

ENEMY COMBATANTS
American Citizens—*Hamdi v. Rumsfeld*

1. Quoting *Commentaries on the Laws of England* (1765).
2. Quoting Joseph Story's *Commentaries on the Constitution of the United States* (1833).
3. *Youngstown Sheet & Tube Co. v. Sawyer* (1952) (Jackson concurrence).

3: STATUTORY INTERPRETATION
Text and Context—*King v. Burwell*

1. *Pensacola Telegraph Co. v. Western Union Telegraph Co.* (1878).
2. *Sturges v. Crowninshield* (1819).
3. *Lamie v. United States Trustee* (2004).
4. Quoting the majority opinion.
5. *Sturges v. Crowninshield* (1819).
6. *Pavelic & LeFlore v. Marvel Entertainment Group* (1989).

What Is Golf?—*PGA Tour v. Martin*

1. Quoting the majority opinion.

Text Versus Concerns of Legislators— *Oncale v. Sundowner Offshore Services*

1. *Castaneda v. Partida* (1977).
2. This sentence (which is in quotes in the opinion) is from the concurring opinion of Justice Ginsburg in *Harris v. Forklift Systems* (1993).
3. *Harris v. Forklift Systems* (1993).
4. *Harris v. Forklift Systems* (1993).

Implied Rights of Action—*Alexander v. Sandoval*

1. Quoting his own concurring opinion in *Lampf, Pleva, Lipkind, Prupis & Petigrow v. Gilbertson* (1991).

LEGISLATIVE HISTORY
A Failed Experiment

1. Excerpted from *A Matter of Interpretation: Federal Courts and the Law*, an essay by Antonin Scalia, with commentary by Amy Gutmann, Gordon S. Wood, Laurence H. Tribe, Mary Ann Glendon, Ronald Dworkin, with a new introduction by Akhil Reed Amar and a new afterword by Steven G. Calabresi. Copyright © 1997 by Princeton University Press. Reprinted by permission.

Conroy v. Aniskoff

1. *Aldridge v. Williams* (1844).
2. Quoting a 1983 law-review article.

United States v. R.L.C.

1. *United States v. Thompson/Center Arms Co.* (1992) (concurring opinion).
2. *Liparota v. United States* (1985).
3. *United States v. Bass* (1971).
4. Henry J. Friendly, *Benchmarks*.
5. Quoting the majority opinion.

4: REVIEW OF AGENCY ACTION

On *Chevron* Deference Twenty Years Later

1. Published in the *Administrative Law Review*, Vol. 66, No. 2 (Spring 2014). The excerpts here are reprinted with the permission of the American Bar Association.

Agency Interpretation of Agency Rules— *Decker v. Northwest Environmental Defense Center*

1. Quoting an 1899 law-review article, "The Theory of Legal Interpretation," by Holmes.
2. Quoting Justice Thomas's dissent in *Thomas Jefferson University v. Shalala* (1994).
3. Blackstone, *Commentaries on the Laws of England*.
4. Quoting a 1996 law-review article.

Agency Interpretation of Criminal Laws— *Whitman v. United States*

1. *Abramski v. United States* (2014).
2. Quoting his own opinion in *Crandon v. United States* (1990).

Index

ABOUT THE AUTHORS

ANTONIN GREGORY SCALIA was born on March 11, 1936, in Trenton, New Jersey, the only child of Eugene and Catherine Scalia. His father, who had emigrated from Sicily as a young man, was a professor of Romance languages at Brooklyn College. His mother, a schoolteacher, was one of eleven children of Italian immigrants. He grew up in Queens, where he played stickball, rooted for the Yankees, and joined the Boy Scouts. He was valedictorian of the Xavier High School class of 1953 and valedictorian of the Georgetown University class of 1957. He attended Harvard Law School, where he earned high honors and was a notes editor for the law review.

While at Harvard, Scalia went on a blind date with a Radcliffe student named Maureen McCarthy. They wed in 1960. Scalia then studied in Europe for a year as Sheldon Fellow of Harvard University before working at the law firm Jones Day in Cleveland from 1961 to 1967. He left private practice to become a professor of law at the University of Virginia from 1967 to 1971 and then served in a number of government positions: general counsel of the Office of Telecommunications Policy from 1971 to 1972, chairman of the Administrative Conference of the United States from 1972 to 1974, and assistant attorney general for the Office of Legal Counsel in the U.S. Department of Justice from 1974 to 1977.

He returned to academic life in 1977, joining the faculty at the University of Chicago. He was also visiting professor of law at both Georgetown and Stanford and was chairman of the American Bar Association's Section of Administrative Law from 1981 to 1982 and its Conference of Section chairman from 1982 to 1983.

In 1982, President Reagan nominated Scalia to join the U.S. Court of Appeals for the District of Columbia Circuit. Four years later, Reagan nominated him to the Supreme Court of the United States, to which he was confirmed by the Senate, 98–0. Justice Scalia took his seat on the bench on September 26, 1986.

As a Supreme Court justice, Scalia articulated and exercised the interpretive methods of originalism and textualism. He established himself as a forceful presence on the bench, a vivid and compelling writer, and a gregarious public presence. One of the most significant justices in the history of the Court, he served for nearly thirty years before his death on February 13, 2016.

Antonin Scalia was married to Maureen for fifty-five years. Together they had nine children and dozens of grandchildren. He was a loving husband, a devoted father, a devout Catholic, and a proud American.

THE HONORABLE JEFFREY S. SUTTON is a judge on the United States Court of Appeals for the Sixth Circuit, where he has served since 2003. A graduate of Williams College and The Ohio State University's Moritz College of Law, he clerked for Justice Scalia and for retired Justice Lewis F. Powell Jr. during the Supreme Court's October 1991 term. After that, he was a partner with the law firm of Jones Day and was the state solicitor of Ohio. He is the author of *51 Imperfect Solutions: States and the Making of American Constitutional Law* (Oxford University Press, 2018), and teaches classes on federal and state constitutional law at the Moritz College of Law and Harvard Law School.

EDWARD WHELAN was a law clerk for Justice Scalia during the Supreme Court's October 1991 term. A graduate of Harvard College and Harvard Law School, he has also served as general counsel to the U.S. Senate Committee on the Judiciary and as principal deputy assistant attorney general in the Office of Legal Counsel at the U.S. Department of Justice. Since 2004, he has been president of the Ethics and Public Policy Center. Mr. Whelan is co-editor (with Christopher J. Scalia) of two other collections of Justice Scalia's works, the *New York Times* bestseller *Scalia Speaks: Reflections on Law, Faith, and Life Well Lived* (Crown Forum, 2017) and *On Faith: Lessons from an American Believer* (Crown Forum, 2019).

ABOUT THE TYPE

This book was set in Bembo, a typeface based on an old-style Roman face that was used for Cardinal Pietro Bembo's tract *De Aetna* in 1495. Bembo was cut by Francesco Griffo (1450–1518) in the early sixteenth century for Italian Renaissance printer and publisher Aldus Manutius (1449–1515). The Lanston Monotype Company of Philadelphia brought the well-proportioned letterforms of Bembo to the United States in the 1930s.